AF443272

# The Chameleon State

# The Chameleon State

*Global Culture and Policy Shifts in Britain and Germany, 1914-1933*

Tien-Lung Liu

*Berghahn Books*
NEW YORK • OXFORD

First published in 1999 by
**Berghahn Books**






**Library of Congress Cataloging-in-Publication Data**

Liu, Tien-lung.
  The chameleon state: global culture and policy shifts in Britain
and Germany, 1914-1933 / Tien-Lung Liu.
      p.     cm. --
  Includes bibliographical references and index.
  ISBN 1-57181-174-5 (alk. paper).
  1. Labor policy--Great Britain--History--20th century.   2.
Arbitration, Industrial--Great Britain--History--20th century.
3. Arbitration, Industrial--Germany--History--20th century.   4.
Labor policy--Germany--History--20th century.   I. Title.
HD8390.L49   1999
331'.0941'09041--dc21                                 98-16240
                                                         CIP

**British Library Cataloguing in Publication Data**

A catalogue record for this book is available from the British Library.


Printed in the United States on acid-free paper.

# Contents

# Abbreviations

| | |
|---|---|
| ADGB | Allgemeiner Deutscher Gewerkschaftsbund/ The General Federation of German Trade Union |
| BOT | Board of Trade |
| DMV | Deutscher Metallarbeiter-Verband/The German Unions of Metal Workers |
| FBI | Federation of British Industries |
| MFGB | The Miners' Federation of Great Britain |
| NCEO | National Confederation of Employers' Organizations |
| NIC | National Industrial Conference |
| RAA | Reichsarbeitsamt/Office of Labor |
| RDI | Reichsverband der Deutschen Industrie/The National Association of German Industry |
| SPD | Sozialdemokratische Partei Deutschlands/The German Social Democratic Party |
| STC | Supply and Transport Committee |
| STO | Supply and Transport Organization |
| TUC | Trades Union Congress |
| VDA | Vereinigung der Deutschen Arbeitgeberverbände/The Federation of German Employers' Associations |
| ZAG | Zentralarbeitsgemeinschaft der industriellen und gewerblichen Arbeitgeber und Arbeitnehmer Deutschlands /The Central Industrial Working Group of Employers and Workers |

# List of Tables

# List of Figures

# Preface

The state in capitalist societies has been a bone of considerable contention among scholars. The two founding fathers of sociology, Karl Marx and Max Weber, held radically different views of the executive, legislative, judicial, and military entities that form the core of political power. Marx was adamant that regardless of its relationship to ruling classes, the state in capitalist societies serves the interests of those who own the means of production. In contrast, Weber argued that the bureaucratic state enjoys a high degree of independence and uses its own logic to manage public affairs. Since their time, the clashes between Marxian and Weberian perspectives have shaped the controversies and spawned various competing schools. However, despite a growing literature over several decades and numerous lively debates, the perennial question is yet to be answered: On whose side is the state?

This book attempts to build an alternative theoretical framework in order to explain the complex and contradictory behavior of the state as an agent of social and industrial policies in the twentieth century. I develop a contingency theory of state intervention and use archival sources to examine how and why, from the First World War to the Depression of the 1930s, the British and German centralized, cabinet-ranking Labor Ministries simultaneously or alternately sided with business, supported organized labor, pursued geopolitical goals, or made compromises under such particular conditions as the First World War, crises of institutional reconstruction, crises of industrial relations, challenges in international economic relations, and threats to capitalist property relations. This comparative study of the British and German Labor Ministries shows that neither national political culture nor powerful-group theories capture the veering and tacking of industrial relations policies in Britain and Germany, and advances an explanation that focuses on the interactions among historical contingencies, the global cultural context, and political processes.

To formulate such a contingency theory of state intervention, I draw on the insights of organizational research on economic firms and apply them to state agencies. Of particular importance are the ideas of adaptation, resource dependence, policy paradigms, and cultural norms. I also rely on the literature of international regime and social construction of the state to explain the uniformity of policy shifts in culturally different states. In a nutshell, my comparative study tries to elicit the historical conditions under which state agencies become open or closed to influences from state and societal actors in capitalist countries.

In this endeavor, I had been motivated by the challenge to confront complexity head-on. When I was an undergraduate at Brandeis University, the late Ralph Miliband introduced me to the web of affiliation networks in which state managers are embedded and showed how the state is inherently tied to the capitalist elite. His seminar opened my eyes to the fascinating research in political sociology. Then, as a graduate student at the University of Chicago, I was exposed to the teaching of Theda Skocpol, who emphasizes the autonomy of state managers from capitalist classes and their capacity to influence politics and policies. My exposure to these two opposite views whetted my appetite to find the truth on my own, that is, to test the prevailing competing theories of the state.

This book also came about as a result of my desire to conduct original research based on archival sources. In my previous work on the Iranian and Polish states, I came to realize that much information about the state cannot be extricated from secondary sources. Theory-testing and the examination of the multiple facets of the state have to rely on historical, primary, and archival research to some extent. I found that the British and German archives served my purpose very well. The abundance of memos, correspondence, and policy papers drafted by politicians and bureaucrats in these archives is crucial in conveying the complexity of policy-making and providing the necessary information to explain the shifting behaviors of state managers under certain historical circumstances.

I pursue my line of argument in several phases. Chapter 1 discusses the competing theories of the state – national political culture, pluralist, social democratic, neo-Marxist, corporatist, and statist. I try to show that each one of them is limited in explanatory power. I then present my contingency theory of state intervention. I conceive state agencies as chameleonic in nature, explain the organizational mechanisms of the veering and tacking of the two Labor Ministries' policies, define the inclusionary, exclusionary, and autonomous processes, and advance four propositions regarding the connections between contingencies, the global cultural context, and political processes.

Chapter 2 presents the similarities between the British and German cases and describes their differences in industrial relations policies, administrative capacity, and historical contexts. I emphasize the differences between the two Labor Ministries in order to show that the contingency theory of state intervention is applicable across cases.

Chapter 3 traces changes in industrial relations policies in Britain and Germany during the period preceding the First World War and the immediate postwar years. In both countries, the idea of a centralized, cabinet-ranking labor ministry languished for decades before the war due to the opposition of the state. The First World War broke the stalemate and led to the creation of the British and German Labor Ministries. The two Ministries became vehicles of working-class interests after the war because of the state's reliance on their cooperation for economic reconstruction.

Chapter 4 identifies the contingencies that compelled the British Labor Ministry to veer and tack among inclusionary, exclusionary, and autonomous processes during the interwar period. In brief, while pluralist in ideology and in regard to most industrial disputes, the interwar British Ministry became capitalist in major crises and subject to state managers' geopolitical goals. I identify crises of institutional reconstruction, crises of industrial relations, challenges in international economic relations, and threats to capitalist property relations and related social order during the interwar period as the major causes of policy shifts.

Chapter 5 focuses on the German arbitration policy that was shot through with class and pluralist forces. The German Labor Ministry unilaterally implemented the state arbitration decree in most conflicts, sometimes in favor of employers and other times in favor of labor, but it acted pluralistically in large-scale industrial disputes between 1924 and 1930 while protecting employers in major economic crises throughout the period. These shifts can only be understood in terms of the state's responses to domestic and geopolitical factors.

Chapter 6 develops the findings of the previous chapters into more general propositions that can be used to predict the connections between contingencies, the transnational cultural context, and the orientations of state policies.

My labor could not have borne fruit without the critical inputs of two sets of scholars. The first of these scholars guided my dissertation while I was at the University of California at Berkeley. I am thankful to Victoria E. Bonnell, my adviser and chair, who inculcated in me the importance of archival research in historical comparative sociology and encouraged me to refine my arguments and writing all along. To my delight, historian Gerald D. Feldman was extremely supportive of my project. He guided me through the historical literature, acquainted me with the German archives, and always quickly provided comments on the earlier drafts.

A second set of macrosociologists played a crucial role in shaping and refining the theoretical foundation and empirical analysis of this book when I moved to the Department of Sociology at Emory University. I am indebted to Alex Hicks for tirelessly making extensive comments on numerous drafts, pushing me to strengthen my contingency argument, and rearranging Table 7. I am also grateful to my next-door colleague, John Boli, who generously commented on every aspect of my work and offered plenty of advice. Though retired, Al Boskoff patiently provided helpful substantive comments and editorial suggestions. Jeff Haydu kindly read the entire manuscript and offered valuable suggestions on preemptive writing. Bernard Phillips prodded me to make the book speak to a wider range of sociologists in different areas and communicate with a larger audience. I doubt that my work could have come to fruition without the kind assistance of these colleagues.

I thank the staff of the libraries and archives I visited. These are the Bundesarchiv, Koblenz; the Zentrales Staatsarchiv, Potsdam; the Staats-Bibliothek Preussischer Kulturbesitz, Berlin; the Public Record Office, Richmond; the House of Lords Record Office, London; and the School of Economics Library, London. All translations are the author's unless otherwise noted.

The University of California at Berkeley provided generous financial support, which includes a 1989-1990 Simpson Fellowship from the Institute of International Studies; a 1990 Phi Beta Kappa Scholarship; a 1990 Dissertation Research Grant from the Center for German and European Studies, and a 1991-1992 Chancellor's Dissertation-Year Fellowship. The research trip to Britain and Germany was partially funded by a 1990-1991 Sociology Dissertation Improvement Award, # SES-8918003, from the National Science Foundation. The rewriting of the book was facilitated by a 1996 summer Faculty Development Award from Emory.

Of course, it goes without saying that I drew most of my strength from those closest to me. My parents were a source of constant encouragement during my two years of semi-employment and my years at Emory. My late father volunteered to edit my writing on several occasions, even when ailing from metastasized lung cancer. My wife, Rae-Chuan, helped through my few ups and numerous downs. I am thankful for her patience with the slowness of my work. Fortunately, while laboring over this book, I had been blessed with taking my turn to care for and playing with my daughter Hailin, whose joy is nothing but contagious.

# Chapter One

# Theorizing the State
## Contingencies, Global Culture, and Policy Shifts

This book deals with a central issue in the current research on the states and state agencies in capitalist democracies: Under what conditions do state policies simultaneously or alternately favor important groups such as capitalists, organized labor, and public officials?

The hallmark of the states in capitalist democracies is their ability to veer back and forth among different forces; they side with employers and keep workers in line in some instances, promote the causes of organized labor in other reversals, make compromises to solve conflicts at other times, or, even more dramatically, subordinate private interests to the pursuit of national objectives in the name of the common good. Policies are, at best, inconsistent in formulation, volatile in implementation, and contradictory in outcomes. State managers and societal actors benefit unevenly from these apparently chaotic fluctuations and about-faces.

This complex seesawing behavior of states has remained a puzzle in the study of political power. Policy evolution has "often been neglected," as Peter Hall points out in a seminal article, "relative to static, one-shot comparisons of policy across nations."[1] Despite their contributions, the existing approaches have not adequately captured how, why, and under what conditions the states and state agencies change from their apparent character, and have not accounted for the circumstances under which they can pursue a course that seems to be anti-democratic.

Notes for this chapter begin on page 31.

Furthermore, the issue of whether state agencies are embedded within broader class relations and economic processes or are autonomous from society, and the question of who the most powerful actors are in relation to the state, are yet to be answered satisfactorily.[2] Culture proponents argue that national political culture molds policy-making and that cultural legacies are the best predictors of policy orientations. Liberals insist that the democratic government is responsive to various societal interests, electoral votes, and public opinion. Neo-Marxists vociferously attack the pluralist view and characterize the capitalist state as a perpetual prisoner of dominant classes and long-term capital accumulation. Social democratic theorists emphasize the power of the working class and socialist political parties in shaping social policies. Somewhat in the middle ground, corporatists depict the state in Europe since the end of the First World War as a broker that selectively integrates the elites of both capital and organized labor at the highest level of the decision-making process. In contrast, statists insist that the state is an actor in its own right and pursues its own political and economic objectives independently of social classes. What all these debates reveal is that each theory is limited in its explanatory power.

In recent years, the debates have centered on who made and benefited from the policies of the welfare state.[3] For instance, one area of disagreement is the interpretation of the state agencies involved in the U.S. New Deal. Statists such as Theda Skocpol argue that the Department of Agriculture was "an island of strength in a sea of weakness,"[4] whereas in their emphatic stress on "structural bias" neo-Marxists such as Gilbert and Howe show that the New Deal agricultural state agencies were penetrated by dominant agricultural classes.[5] Statists and neo-Marxists draw radically different conclusions from the same objects of analysis such as the U.S. New Deal in the 1930s and the origins and functions of the welfare state in industrialized countries.

As a historical comparative sociologist, I am primarily interested in explaining *the shifting nature of the state over time.* In my view, the important question in the study of political power is "Why and how does the state change its nature?" rather than the question "What is the nature of the state?" The crux of the matter is that the state is a complex entity that undergoes changes over time, while the relationships among the state, employers, and organized labor vary as the three actors make alliances or fight one another. We need a theory that is able to explain the ways in which state agencies respond to and deal with the demands of employers, organized labor, and other state actors. Who wins a political contest is less a function of the power of the groups involved than a function of the context of the contest.

This book has its origins in my preoccupation with reconciling historical complexity and theoretical generalizations. I became interested in a comparative study of the changing nature of the British and German Labor Ministries from the First World War to the Depression of the early 1930s because their industrial relations policies went through major shifts at the level of formulation and implementation. At different times, these two state agencies favored employers, organized labor, and national interests. They veered back and forth among different forces, and their strengths waxed and waned over the nineteen years examined here. Moreover, adding to this layer of complexity, the two Labor Ministries pursued radically different industrial relations policies. With its minimally interventionist policy, the British Labor Ministry seems to be a textbook case of a weak agency dominated by either organized labor or capitalist interests. With its maximally interventionist policy, the German Labor Ministry seems, for eight to ten years during the Weimar period, to transcend the interests of both employers and organized labor. My research and reflections in the last six years have convinced me that it is possible to build a plausible, middle-range theory of the state that combines the historians' quest for a faithful rendition of historical details and the sociologists' pursuit of causal generalizations.

The British and German Labor Ministries' seesawing behavior is puzzling in light of the existing theories of the state. The more I dug into the abundant archival sources collected in Britain and Germany and consulted the relevant secondary works, the more skeptical I became of the fit between the two cases and abstract theories. Many important aspects of the two Labor Ministries are lost in the attempts to squeeze the two cases into general theoretical frameworks.

The British and German Labor Ministries are ideal cases to address the issue of the shifting nature of the state, on three counts. First, labor departments and the development of state institutions during the interwar period have received little attention in comparative analysis. During the war and the interwar period, the labor question dominated politics and had a major impact on the political order in both countries. As historian Gerald D. Feldman, an authority on the Weimar Republic, emphatically states in his comparative discussion of the British and German industrial conflicts, Germany "did not possess a monopoly of social conflicts."[6] Furthermore, the political, economic, and social crises (postwar adaptation, deep economic depression, runaway inflation, and extremist social movements) during the nineteen years under study are magnified to such a great extent that they allow researchers to focus on *vacillations and their effects on the power structure*. In this respect, both Britain and Germany are ideal social laboratories for an in-depth examination of policy changes over time and for the formulation of a robust, historically and contextually nuanced comparative narrative about the shifting policies of the Labor Ministries in those turbulent societies at an uncertain time.

Second, labor departments were the loci of struggles *par excellence* among state managers, employers, and organized labor because of their symbolic significance in a capitalist economy and their pivotal role in industrial relations and the labor market, which together constitute the single most important issue in capitalist societies. Instead of focusing on the labor movement, its variable strengths, and its relationships with the state and employers, topics that are the subject of a great amount of scholarship,[7] I contend that theorizing the complex behaviors of state agencies is needed to increase our understanding of the processes and outcomes of conflicts in industrial societies. Like most studies in the field, this one uses state agencies – the bones of considerable contention – as the units of analysis in order to throw light on the validity of general theories of the state. It is necessary to deconstruct the state, that is, to examine its component parts and their relationships with each other, in order to explain public policy. Different state agencies may behave differently with respect to societal interest groups. Some may be captured or subject to undue influence. Others may be autonomous. This book attempts to carefully examine the internal structure of the capitalist state.

Third, current state theories have neglected the contributions of the literature on the social construction of the state. Most studies on the states implicitly or explicitly rely on distinctive national political culture as a major explanatory factor that accounts for differences among countries and play down the impacts of the global cultural context on state behaviors. My research shows that while different in national political cultures, the British and German Labor Ministries shifted their industrial relations policies in a strikingly similar way. I argue that this unexpected uniformity in the cultural practices of the states can be explained at the transnational level, rather than at the national level.

Existing research portrays labor departments as exclusively subservient to private interests in many respects. Scholars agree that labor departments are closely related to the interests of employers and trade unions because of their origins and their involvement in class relations, and their impacts on the general and long-term interests (private property, capital accumulation, and the market economy) of the business community. The dominant view is that labor departments are created as a result of pressures from organized labor. Once established, they are seen as externally controlled agencies, the quintessential examples of "weak" public bureaucracies locked into the system of group competition and class struggles. Their roles in mediating, arbitrating, and suppressing industrial conflicts invariably reflect various group demands or reproduce capitalist domination. The assumption is that unlike, for instance, the U.S. State Department and the Pentagon, which deal with matters that concern foreign and defense policies and are thus relatively more insulated from societal influence,[8] labor departments are not only less insulated from societal forces but also closely tied to dominant classes. They are less likely to launch policies that transcend class interests. In this respect, the British and German Labor Ministries are what most theorists of the state would consider to be hard cases that favor dominant perspectives.

The various theoretical arguments and their biases are reproduced in historical monographs that include limited discussions of the role of labor ministries. As discussed below, Rodney Lowe contends that the British Labor Ministry was open to a variety of interests, while Robert Middlemas argues that it was a vehicle of corporatism. In a landmark comparative study of bourgeois restoration, Charles Maier puts the German Labor Ministry squarely within his corporatist framework. Johannes Bähr characterizes it as a corporatist agency firmly anchored in the prewar authoritarian tradition. David Abraham's controversial book shows the applicability of structuralist neo-Marxism to the Weimar regime.[9] Each approach claims that it alone provides a superior causal explanation and better predictions than its rivals. Each identifies a fixed set of actors that made and benefited from state policies. Yet, as I shall argue below, none of these theoretical frameworks is able to account single-handedly for major policy shifts in industrial relations in both Britain and Germany or to encompass a broad range of causally relevant factors.

## Culture and Policy-Making

A major line of thought argues that national culture is a potent explanatory variable that accounts for change or variation in political behaviors and conceptions of labor and industrial relations. In an impressive study, Richard Biernacki demonstrates the independent impact of distinctive culture on British and German labor practices in the textile industry.[10] In his study of railway policy in three countries, Frank Dobbin argues that the state in the U.S., Britain, and France used their distinctive political traditions to shape economic policies. National political culture, "comprising practices and their meanings," guided each government to "perceive and respond to problems"[11] in their own way. Thus, French state centralism gave government engineers control over railroad development; British belief in individual sovereignty empowered entrepreneurs; and U.S. federalism delegated the authority to municipalities. Dobbin further contends that this cultural theory has predictive power: "One need only grasp the logic underlying current policies to be able to guess what future policies will look like, because policies in different countries follow fundamentally different logics."[12]

It is undeniable that national political culture played a major role in shaping British self-determination and German state arbitration policies in industrial relations. The strong tradition of the interventionist Beamtenstaat in Germany and liberal tendencies in Britain were in large measure based upon centuries of political development, i.e., a specific path of state-building. According to the cultural logic, Britain was the quintessential liberal state with great tolerance for freedoms of organization, competition, and pressure politics in the political realm.[13] Drawing on its cultural repertoire, the British government fashioned the paradigm of minimal state intervention in industrial relations. The policy of "self-determination," as it is known in Britain, reflected the desires of both employers and unions to settle industrial disputes through free collective bargaining. The notion of fair play in industrial relations assumed a mythic proportion with a life of its own. The Labor Ministry remained on the sidelines in industrial relations, even though Britain, which had relatively fewer industrial disputes than Germany, had its fair share of workers involved and days lost in industrial disputes. It is no wonder that Rodney Lowe, the authority on the British Labor Ministry, came to the conclusion that the Labor Ministry was "a graveyard of social reform" and "a failure" in the formulation of social policy.[14]

Germany's Prusso-centered tradition of authoritarianism, which is hailed as the archetype of strong state, was transposed to the area of industrial relations. Faced with political and socioeconomic crises, Weimar Germany fell back on familiar methods. The German Labor Ministry unilaterally imposed coercive state arbitration (Zwangsschlichtung) on both employers and unions. In many instances, the labor minister and his state arbitrators resolved disputes on wages and working hours by declaring awards compulsorily binding (Verbindlichkeitserklärung) and therefore making subsequent strikes and lockouts illegal. The authoritarian legacy persisted in spite of great uncertainty marked by military defeat, the Communist revolution of November 1918, and political democratization. Critics quickly pointed out that the arbitration system in Weimar Germany bore strong resemblance to that of Mussolinian Italy.

Scholars agree that the tradition of strong state left indelible imprints on the Labor Ministry's industrial relations policy. Ludwig Preller, a Labor Ministry official between 1926 and 1928, criticizes its authoritarian tendencies and considers the state arbitration decree as alien to the democratic order.[15] He assails Labor Minister Heinrich Brauns for being "the single official" to influence decisively the policy of the government and faults the state bureaucracy for transgressing its assigned duties, abusing the emergency decrees, escaping from parliamentary control, and causing the breakdown of the Weimar democracy.[16] Joining the chorus against authoritarianism, Frieda Wunderlich characterizes state compulsory arbitration as "a drift from liberal democracy toward a new political institution" and "a means of enforcing state policy in a mild dictatorship"[17] that went against the democratic ideal of self-determination. Johannes Bähr describes the Weimar state as one with a strong authoritarian state tradition.[18]

This view of German authoritarianism is left unchallenged by the recent revisions of the German Sonderweg. Geoff Eley and his associates criticize the West German historians for describing the prewar German state as a means to protect traditional elites, a cultural vehicle for their preindustrial mentalities, and a precursor of Nazism.[19] The crucial issue in this debate is whether authoritarianism was in the service of the preindustrial elites or bourgeois interests.[20] Significantly, the historical revision does not dispute the fact that authoritarianism was part and parcel of German politics and society.

The pluralist-liberal stance of the British Labor Ministry and the authoritarian disposition of the German Labor Ministry were implemented regardless of ideological stands. All interwar British government – one coalition led by a Liberal, three Conservative, and two Labour – conformed to these practices. The hands-off policy was further stengthened by Conservatives' rule for most of the period, except for coalition and brief socialist interludes. In Weimar Germany, various sorts of coalition governments involving the Social Democratic party, the bourgeois parties, and the Catholic Center party allowed the Labor Ministry to pursue state arbitration. As Chancellor Luther once declared, Labor Minister "Brauns was an independent politician. For eight years, he reigned absolutely sovereign as the labor minister in the domain of Sozialpolitik."[21]

Yet, the emphasis on cultural legacy as a time-immemorial template brushes aside the diversity of prewar policy-making. In spite of the pluralist-liberal tradition, the British Board of Trade (BOT) was a major center of policy innovations under the Liberal-Labour coalition governments of 1906-1914. The Labour Department of the BOT innovated "in all areas of social policy,"[22] such as trade union recognition, collective bargaining, and settlement of industrial disputes. As presidents of the BOT, Lloyd George and Winston Churchill actively and personally intervened in industrial disputes. Lloyd George (1905-1908) warded off a national rail strike in 1907, and his subsequent interventions "helped to consolidate acceptance of government interventions in industrial disputes."[23] He was far from being a champion of the working class, though. His reform policy and concessions were meant to appease workers and to maintain the status quo. Churchill (1908-1910) sought to increase state capacity in industrial interventions, but his proposal was rebuffed by both capital and organized labor. Under their presidency, sixty-seven new Trade Boards were established. Despite their eagerness to bring the two sides together, both "believed in efficient, competitive, capitalist enterprise and felt that the bulk of trade unionists could be won to their point of view."[24] Between 1906 and 1914, the Labour Department settled ten percent of the industrial stoppages,[25] handling, for instance, ninety-nine cases in 1913, as opposed to twelve in 1898 and eleven in 1899.[26] Thus, one cannot assert that British culture was devoid of state intervention in the form of conciliation and arbitration. The interventionist posture by Liberal politicians was short-lived because Conservatives took over political power.[27]

Recent research uncovers a far more complex German legacy than the image of inflexible authoritarian rulers conveys. Social policy was far from being unified in Imperial Germany. George Steinmetz clearly demonstrates that a "proto-corporatist policy" was pursued at the local state level, incorporating the socialist labor movement as a junior partner in decision-making before 1914.[28] The socialist Trade Unions became the conveyor belts between the rank and file and municipal governments, and carried out the new social policies such as public subsidies of unions' unemployment insurance funds. German authoritarianism only prevailed at the central state level. The monarchy excluded the working class and the Social Democratic party from policy-making until the First World War and pursued the Bismarckian worker policy designed to neutralize labor power.[29]

Most importantly, national political culture theory is unable to account for changes in the practices and meanings it is supposed to explain and the similar behaviors of culturally divergent states. In many instances, the line between liberal and illiberal, especially at the stage of policy implementation and outcome, can itself be contingent. Interwar Britain's liberal practices were punctuated with political, administrative, and repressive measures to buttress the capitalist class and to further political goals. Political disorders and economic chaos compelled the apparently more liberal British governments to crack down on workers in major conflicts in a quite brutal way. Political leaders ruled out conciliation and opted for a fight by mobilizing the repressive system – i.e., police, army, and strike-breaking organs.[30] In reference to the railway strike in 1920, Thomas Jones, Prime Minister Lloyd George's right-hand man, put it aptly: "What Churchill and Co. forget is that there are other ways of averting discontent than with civil guards and the military."[31] The government eventually settled the railway dispute, but this event set the tone of the political elite toward other strikes. The British government found an easy solution in repression.

The German Labor Ministry turned out to be a paper tiger; its iron-fisted state arbitration policy floundered in the face of major crises. Germany's dictatorial style in industrial relations was shot through with compromises to employers and unions or categorical support of the aims of capitalists. Resistance from employers and organized labor led the allegedly authoritarian German state to be conciliatory in many of its actions, seeking compromises and doling out concessions to employers and trade unions alike. Unlike its British counterpart, the German Labor Ministry opposed the use of repressive and strike-breaking forces against the labor movement.

Crackdown on workers was out of the question even when bourgeois governments were in power. As the German Labor Minister Rudolf Wissell emphatically stated, "on the basis of the arbitration decree and thanks to the arbitration system, a thousand, yes, ten thousand cases of difficult industrial conflicts were solved *peacefully*."[32] Labor Minister Brauns, the architect of strong intervention, ruled out police intervention in labor conflicts and declared that "the inclusion of other authorities may be contrary to law and undermines the position of the arbitration authorities and prevents them from carrying out their duties."[33] Carl Severing, then a state arbitrator under Brauns and later interior minister, once observed that in his arbitration proceedings, there were many times that "the Prussian Ministry of Police looked like a subsidiary agency adjunct to the Ministry of Labor."[34]

Although accounting for overall divergent historical trajectories, enduring political culture is unable to come to terms with a similar, predictable pattern of shifts in state intervention in both Britain and Germany. The jarring fact is that contingencies twisted British liberalism and German authoritarianism beyond recognition on crucial occasions and compelled the British and German Labor Ministries to respond in a similar way.

## Powerful Actors and State Agencies

In this book, I argue that the most challenging task is to account for the similar policy shifts that took place in both Britain and Germany, rather than to explain the differences between two radically different policies. To be persuasive, a theory of the state needs to be valid across cases. The powerful-group theories of the state – pluralist, social democratic, neo-Marxist, corporatist, and statist – provide insights into the British and German Labor Ministries, but their predilection for a fixed set of actors does not coherently capture the multiple facets of state agencies. The fit is imperfect, at best.

### Labor Departments as Pluralist Mirrors

Pluralists posit a weak state with little autonomy from interest groups, which are the multiple centers of power with limited popular sovereignty.[35] In this framework, the state is a neutral arena for interest-group politics, i.e., a "Swiss-cheese" organization riddled with multiple points of formal and informal access through which groups compete for influence on the executive offices and legislative bodies. Interest groups, rather than state officials, exercise political power. They define public interests, shape the policy agenda, and pressure the government to convert their demands into policies.[36] To satisfy the interested parties, public officials take into account interest-group demands and public opinion,[37] balance out competing interests, and incorporate them into policies,[38] but, sometimes, they fall under the sway of the stronger groups.[39] Governance becomes an exercise in merely mirroring group pressures and conforming to public opinion.

Accordingly, the labor department reflects various interests in a liberal-democratic setting dominated by interest groups. The British Labor Ministry is a case in point, according to Rodney Lowe. He argues that the advent of mass universal suffrage required the government to proceed pragmatically. From 1916 to 1939, the Labor Ministry favored neither employers nor organized labor. Instead, it responded to a combination of sundry factors such as leadership, economic fluctuations, the strengths of employers and trade unions, and Treasury intervention.[40] Policy is, he further declares, "a pragmatic and often erratic response by government to the immediate problems with which it is faced – 'organized chaos rather than carefully-planned conspiracy'."[41] There is no "far-reaching, rational blueprint," but only "small adjustments, often governed by expediency and limited objectives" with unpredictable effects.[42] Lowe's analysis rebukes the neo-Marxist "simplistic and naïve" view of a capitalist-controlled labor department acting on a "carefully-planned conspiracy."[43]

Theodore Lowi, a proponent of a neo-pluralist view of American politics, holds that the labor department is captured by organized labor to block state intervention. He describes the U.S. Federal Department of Labor as a small clientèle agency run and privatized by former union officials, who advocated laissez-faire in industrial relations and opposed any state interference in collective bargaining. Lowi deplores that such privatization hampers the Labor Department's ability "to govern responsibly, flexibly, and determinatively."[44] In a similar vein, Richard Kuisel contends that the French Labor Department was established in 1906 as a concession to socialists and that trade unions sought its help in settling industrial disputes in their favor.[45]

The pluralist accounts of labor departments overlook important variations in the implementation of industrial relations policies. In some crucial instances, the British Labor Ministry took sides. While claiming neutrality and impartiality, the Labor Ministry was part of, and could not escape from being, a political arrangement that was congenial to employers' interests. Rodney Lowe failed to draw the appropriate conclusions when he remarked that in Britain "state intervention was used to preserve, not to change, the status quo."[46] Though pluralism prevailed in the immediate postwar years, the German Labor Ministry gained the power to ride roughshod over both employers and unions in 1923 and sided alternately with them when it saw fit.

Furthermore, from an epistemological standpoint, pluralism has lost ground in recent years.[47] Somewhat ironically, while stressing public opinion and democratic rules, Charles Lindblom acknowledges the existence of a ruling socioeconomic class and concedes that businessmen are a powerful interest group with disproportionate influence.[48] They control the means of production and investment decisions, possess unmatched resources, manage the economy as "public" officials and are not subject to democratic control. What is missing in pluralist analysis is a general description of political economy that takes cumulative inequality in political and economic power and officials' capacity to implement their own policies into account.[49] Pluralism was the starting point and goal of the British and German Labor Ministries, but, as will be shown later, it was by no means the only political process in interwar industrial relations.

### Labor Departments as Social Democratic Beachheads

Social democratic theorists argue that working-class power redirects the state in favor of workers. Policy-making is the result of socialist penetration of the state and parliamentary strength.[50] Some studies on the welfare state show that working-class strength (operationalized as union membership and centralization) and duration of left political parties in power (number of years during which labor parties controlled the cabinet) are the strongest indicators of "generosity, universality, and redistributions of old-age pensions."[51]

This perspective is relevant here since Social Democrats controlled the government and the Labor Ministry in the early years of the Weimar Republic and during the tenure of Social Democratic Labor Minister Rudolf Wissell between 1928 and 1930. This model predicts that in Weimar Germany, union strength and the presence of the Social Democratic party (SPD) in the cabinets and Parliament should have had a major impact on interwar industrial relations policy. As the founder and leader of the first coalition governments, the SPD found itself in a commanding position in both the executive and legislative branches. The socialist Trade Unions as the pillar of support of the cabinets led by socialist chancellors and forged the postwar industrial relations policy that favored free collective bargaining.

However, I shall show that contingencies such as the enormous tasks of demobilization and postwar reconstruction mitigated the influence of the SPD and that subsequent economic crises whittled away the power of the working class. Organized labor was not the architect of state arbitration policy. As a matter of fact, the labor movement opposed the state arbitration decree when Labor Minister Heinrich Brauns promulgated it in October 1923. Likewise, social democratic theory hardly applies to Britain, where the two interwar Labour governments were short-lived and constrained by labor syndicalism. Except for a short period of time, trade unions and labor parties were far from being the key actors in the making of industrial relations policies in both countries, just as they were not the agents of early social insurance innovation.[52]

## Labor Departments as Agents of Capitalist Class Cohesion

Structuralist neo-Marxists contend that the state is capitalist by nature. Of all the theoretical efforts, Nicos Poulantzas is the one scholar who systematically grapples with the volatile nature of the capitalist state by imposing a structuralist neo-Marxist framework.[53] Poulantzas argues that while relatively autonomous from capitalists,[54] the state is structurally dependent on capitalists and the capitalist system for economic production and public order.[55] As an appendage to the capitalist mode of production, the state inevitably serves capitalists' long-term interests and denies their short-term benefits for the sake of continuous capital accumulation. The state creates a united political class among capitalists, regulates their conflicts, improves employers' bargaining position vis-à-vis workers, and enhances their economic competitiveness in international trade.[56] At the same time, the state disorganizes the working class through various legal, economic, political, and repressive means. Public officials resort to repression of organized labor, make "provisional compromises," or dole out economic concessions.[57] This "guarantee to the economic interests of certain dominated classes" consolidates the long-term rule of the dominant classes and neutralizes working-class threats to the bourgeois democracy.[58] Moreover, the state apparatus is a "strategic field"[59] permeated by class struggles and influenced by a capitalist power bloc.[60] Competing factions of capitalist classes battle for the exercise of political power and the right to represent the common interests of all politically dominant classes.[61] Elaborating on Poulantzas's theory, Gøsta Esping-Andersen and his coauthors theorize that the state undertakes structural reforms of the state organizations that have become the objects of class struggles. In doing so, the state "insulate[s] critical functions from working class influence," and neutalizes class struggles.[62] This model stresses ubiquitous class struggles and the inherent capitalist nature of any political regime and policies in industrial democracies.

From the class perspective, labor departments advance the interests of capitalists in various guises. Nancy DiTomaso argues that the dominant class neutralized the U.S. Department of Labor, "a response and solution to class struggle," and turned it into an instrument of class control designed to isolate the "political demands of subordinated classes."[63] Created in response to workers' demands, the Department's main function was to defuse workers' challenges that threaten the political domination of capitalists and their accumulation of capital. Consequently, the Department became "a highly decentralized, fragmented, and ineffectual agency."[64]

David Abraham contends that the German Labor Ministry bought off the working class during the Weimar era because capital was unable to form a stable power bloc and needed the support of the Social Democratic party. From 1924 onwards, the Labor Ministry was the chief vehicle for the promotion of "a general social compromise" between capital and organized labor.[65] Labor Ministers Heinrich Brauns and Rudolf Wissell generously dispensed "material gains" such as wage hikes, social insurance, and public-housing programs[66] and used compulsorily binding arbitration to protect organized labor in industrial disputes. These views reinforce the notion that state agencies are part of a state apparatus that acts as a functional mechanism to maintain the equilibrium of capitalism.

An exclusive focus on class to explain policy shifts does not do justice to either the British Labor Ministry or the German Labor Ministry. Like it's pluralist counterpart, the neo-Marxist interpretation overemphasizes the primary role of a fixed set of actors and fails to theorize the effects of contexts on the contest for political power. Poulantzas's endeavor to account for the relative autonomy of the capitalist state turns out to be class-reductionist. Abraham's structuralist neo-Marxist analysis of Weimar Germany brushes important policy variations aside and is valid only when applied to certain historical contexts. While emphasizing dominant class manipulation of labor departments, DiTomaso and others gloss over the strong working-class demand for free collective bargaining and minimal state intervention. Historian Gerald D. Feldman points out that German heavy industry, the dominant faction of capitalists, was "at the very least a crucial veto group in the Weimar Republic, as well as a major destabilizing force politically," but "it is perfectly true that economic power does not easily or automatically translate itself into political influence, and did not do so in the Weimar Republic."[67] Harold James stresses the fact that big industry had less leverage over public policies in domestic politics than in foreign policy issues.[68] Though they received subsidies from the Republic, employers perceived the interventionist welfare state (Sozialstaat) that promulgated acts such as the 1927 Unemployed Insurance law and the 1930 state arbitration decree as hostile to them. Therefore, James states, one must be "sceptical of theories that either claim too powerful a role for industry in the Republic or assert that the preponderance of heavy industry dictated a conservative growth path of the Weimar economy."[69] Thus, the British and German Labor Ministries involve complex processes that go beyond the purview of any single theory.[70]

A satisfactory neo-Marxist explanation would have to account for the fact that the British and German Labor Ministries' biases toward employers were historically specific outcomes of certain societal conditions rather than results of the Ministries' internal structures. They acquiesced to employers (1) when organized labor gravely threatened order in Britain, as in the 1921 coal miners strike and the 1926 General Strike, and (2) when the Weimar regime was hard-pressed to rebuild the postwar economy in the early 1920s and when the economy fell on hard times in the Depression of 1929-1933. But these agencies also gave in to working-class interest groupings (1) when organized labor demanded, in less broadly calamitous times, that the British and German states incorporate organized labor demands into the postwar industrial relations policy that was sensitive to a plurality of interests, and (2) when the statist Labor Ministry of Heinrich Brauns of the Catholic Center party intervened to protect the German trade unions against employers' attacks in the name of class harmony in 1924-1930.

## *Labor Departments as Corporatist Brokers*

The corporatist state is a cross between its pluralist and neo-Marxist counterparts. According to Philippe C. Schmitter, state corporatism brings employers and organized labor together in a structure of institutionalized cooperation, and grants leaders of powerful organizations the exclusive right to represent their constituencies "in exchange for observing certain controls on their selection of leaders and articulation of demands and supports."[71] In this arrangement, state officials broker between union leaders and management representatives; these three sets of actors strive to stabilize the economy and to stamp out industrial conflicts.

Keith Middlemas argues that the British Labor Ministry from the 1910s to the 1970s was a major promoter of "corporate bias." State corporatism, which was promoted by Lloyd George in the 1920s and lasted until the mid-1960s,[72] allowed both employers and trade unions to behave as "estates of the realm" with the authority to negotiate with the government and to foster consensus on the goals of the state.[73] The concept of state corporatism captures, to some extent, the effort of the political establishment to restore and maintain the bourgeois order during the interwar period. Yet, the attempt to fit state corporatism onto the British industrial system is unconvincing. Rodney Lowe rightly points out that the concept by no means applies to the British case and that factual errors undermine Middlemas's claim of corporate bias.[74] And, according to Colin Crouch, if there was corporatism in Britain, "the incipient neo-corporatism is best regarded as fragile or brittle."[75]

Charles Maier's seminal work on the restoration of bourgeois Europe traces the establishment of Weimar Germany's corporatist framework. The executive branches took initiatives whereas Parliament took a back seat as "a collective notary."[76] Focusing on the national governments and the return of bourgeois rule after the Great War, he cursorily discusses the role of the Labor Ministry as a broker between capitalists and trade unions in an effort to maintain "equilibrium in the marketplace."[77] "Bargaining moved outside the chamber to unofficial party or coalition caucuses, and to government ministries that tended to identify with major economic groupings, such as the Weimar Republic's Ministry of Labor."[78] Corporate pluralism not only consolidated bourgeois rule but also "rewarded labor leadership."[79] Along the same lines, Johannes Bähr contends that as a vehicle of "an anti-liberal, backward corporatist order,"[80] the Labor Ministry imposed the state arbitration decree of 30 October 1923 to protect both organized labor and employers.[81] The state arbitration decree was "an authoritarian-corporatist experiment by a neomercantilist state"[82] to regulate industrial relations after the attempt at societal corporatism had failed. This strong-state tradition had its roots in the authoritarian culture of Prussia and ultimately led to the downfall of the Weimar democracy.[83] In this scheme, German corporatism is seen as a regulator of conflicts among powerful interest blocs.

This corporatist theory is appealing, but falls short of explaining the two cases at hand. The state corporatist system was fragile as it relied on constantly buying off private interests. In his classic study of the interwar German economy, historian Harold James argues that "the failure of the economy discredited not only the corporatist mechanism of resolving conflicts (since it failed to fulfill this object), but also the interest blocs which used it. A machinery and institutions designed to regulate conflicts were in the end destroyed by it."[84]

The three studies mentioned above do not trace policy shifts in industrial relations. Nor do they theorize the conditions for such policy shifts. Corporate pluralism cannot be applied to the whole period under study because employers attacked the system of forced arbitration with vehemence during the interwar years. Contrary to Charles Maier's assertion about the German Labor Ministry's connection to certain major economic groupings, the Labor Ministry identified with neither organized labor (although it took actions to save the trade unions from employers' attacks and financial crises) nor employers. Veering back and forth, the Labor Ministry favored employers at the expense of workers in 1923-1924 and 1930-1933, and severely alienated the business community between 1924 and 1930. These facts point to the statist nature of the German Labor Ministry.

## Labor Departments as Statist Sites

A revitalized body of statist research that draws its inspirations from Max Weber, Otto Hintze, and Alexis de Tocqueville challenges the above "society-centered" explanations of state behavior.[85] The "state-centered" perspective focuses on the organization, resources, and power of the state itself. The state is an actor in its own right and strives to maximize its interests by pursuing policies largely independent of class or group interests.[86] Politicians and bureaucrats promote, above all, their ideological objectives, political missions, and career interests. They build their administrative base and hone their interventionist will,[87] provide solutions to problems and improve or readjust existing policies that are found to be wanting,[88] and are "crucial in giving concrete substance to new policy initiatives and in elaborating already established approaches."[89] The state evolves according to its own logic of organization and infighting among state managers, which shape the subsequent development of state institutions.[90] State structures determine "the ways in which class interests and conflicts get organized into (or out of) politics in a given time and place."[91] In her latest work, Theda Skocpol, the major figure in the statist orientation, insists that states are "sites of autonomous action, not reducible to the demands and preferences of any social groups."[92]

The statist approach identifies two conditions under which the state becomes autonomous. First, the state aims to enhance its international position in the competing state system. This objective bolsters state managers' position vis-à-vis domestic actors especially in times of war.[93] Warfare forces rulers to increase their control over the territory, to impose tax levies, and to create a national standing army.[94] As Charles Tilly argues, "state structure appeared chiefly as a by-product of rulers' efforts to acquire the means of war; and second by insisting that relations among states, especially through war and preparation for war, strongly affected the entire process of state formation."[95] Second, the state pursues national objectives in major social and economic crises. Skocpol and others show that the U.S. New Deal was an autonomous set of policies fashioned by state officials. This set of legislation empowered new agencies to pursue their objectives of resolving the problems generated by the Depression. Skocpol claims that the state is the key "to any satisfactory explanations of the New Deal – and to other episodes, past, present, and future of political response to economic crisis within capitalism."[96]

The statist perspective has yet to gain adherents among those who study labor departments.[97] I argue that in some contexts, the British and German Labor Ministries pursued policies that were independent of class and group interests, and that their policies were inextricably linked to state managers' interests. The German Labor Ministry looks like a perfect statist example of a "strong" site independently initiating the iron-fisted state arbitration decree of 1923. The labor minister and his twenty state arbitrators had the power to unilaterally impose binding awards on both employers and trade unions or extend them to other segments of industry. Pursuing geopolitical objectives, British politicians and bureaucrats stifled the Labor Ministry's active promotion of conciliation bodies. Statist theory provides a powerful explanation for a major difference between the two cases: the extent to which political leadership of all stripes expanded or stunted each labor ministry's administrative capacities.[98]

Yet, like other powerful-group theories, the statist focus on organizational resources can only explain part of the veering and tacking of the British and German Labor Ministries. The concept of state capacity fails to convey the ambiguity of power. The British Labor Ministry was deficient in administrative capacity, but it was actually a strong agency, able to repress labor while maintaining a facade of neutrality and impartiality. The Labor Ministry's apparent abstention in industrial relations turned out to be a policy of strong intervention in disguise. A showcase "strong" state agency, the German Labor Ministry was unable to impose its will in major industrial disputes. The British and German Ministries defy the easy but erroneous categorization of "weak" and "strong" state agencies.

In order to make a convincing case, this book blends narrative with theory-testing. I set the above-mentioned arguments against alternative hypotheses and marshall the necessary evidence to choose between them. Pluralist theory is expected to stand up to comparative scrutiny of historical cases when sundry forces such as organized labor and employers have direct influence on industrial relations policy at the formulation and implementation levels and exact concessions from the state. Social democratic expectations are fulfilled when the political left effects changes in industrial relations policy in favor of organized labor. The expectations of neo-Marxist theory are most likely to be realized when employers use their resources to redirect industrial relations policy in their favor and at the expense of organized labor. State corporatist theory stands when there is concrete evidence of structural arrangements that incorporate both employers and trade unions and allow both of them to draw benefits from industrial relations policy. Statist theory works best when state managers subordinate industrial relations policy to their own goals and build an administrative system that is impervious to external control.

Much strenuous tailoring is needed to squeeze the British and German Labor Ministries' shifts in policy formulation and implementation into existing models of the state. While capturing the pluralist pattern in Britain and the statist mode of intervention in Germany, national political culture framework misses the twists and turns that industrial relations policies went through during the interwar years. The powerful-group theories – pluralist, social democratic, neo-Marxist, corporatist, and statist – overstate the influence of a specific group or class that makes and benefits from state policies at the expense of other equally important features.[99] These theories of the state are approximate, albeit not ideal, benchmarks, for the analysis of state agencies.[100] As such, they fail to come to grips with complex historical reality: State and societal actors gain and lose power under specific conditions.


## Historical Contingencies and Global Cultural Context

Contingency studies have emerged to resolve the debates that are sharply polarized in terms of "class vs. interest groups" and "state vs. society" concepts and Marx vs. Weber. Some scholars argue that the state is unevenly developed and that its autonomy varies with time. Robert Alford and Roger Friedland cogently point out that "it is a mistake to assume a priori that one logic, one aspect, and one dimension are primary and the others are secondary, peripheral, or transitory. Theories should not prejudge the relations between levels of analysis but *should specify the conditions both of autonomy and constraint.*"[101] The contingency analyses combine pluralist stress on interest groups and electoral voice, structural neo-Marxist insistence on dominant-class constraints, and statist emphasis on state managers' autonomy.

Some important studies comprehend all perspectives from the viewpoints of single, lofty neo-pluralism. Alexander Hicks proposes an integrated explanation of welfare spending by including actors and forces emphasized by competing theories. He shows that his comprehensive explanation is far superior to fragmented theories, which fall short of producing decisive conclusions outside special circumstances. He concludes that the competing models exaggerate their differences and overlook the potential contributions of a pluralistic resource theory, and calls for "an integrative theoretical alternative" that is "as open to the importance of 'class' and 'state' as it is to 'interest group' and 'electorate'."[102] To refute monocausal explanations, Michael Mann proposes a multiple-factor theory[103] that captures the different histories of the states, i.e., the four types of polymorphous crystallizations (capitalist, military, representative, and national).[104] The polity-centered model of Theda Skocpol synthesizes the state-centered studies with pluralist propositions. Public opinion, powerful interest groups, and limitations of state power figure prominently in her causal explanations of political conflicts and outcomes.[105] In a similar vein, historical institutionalism focuses on institutional configurations such as rules of electoral competition, constitutional rules, party systems, relations among government agencies, and structure and organization of economic actors such as trade unions and business associations[106] and their impacts on political outcomes. This fine-grained, middle-range analysis promises to deliver a more nuanced and differentiated perspective on the state.

Similarly, neo-Marxists attempt to include contingencies in their analyses. Bob Jessop contends that the state is an institutional ensemble and that its biases are determined by the "changing balance of forces."[107] The nature of the state is contingent, "indeterminable relative to any one theoretical schema." Jessop goes so far as to state that the complexity of the state cannot be captured by "the many forms of marxism."[108] In his study of the welfare state in the German Empire, George Steinmetz elaborates on Jessop's notion of contingent necessity. Steinmetz uses different causal mechanisms and combinations of causal mechanisms to account for local, regional, and central policy-making from 1871 to 1914. Since the objects of study in historical sociology are too complex to be subsumed under any parsimonious explanations, he argues that "it is necessary to combine more than one "state theory" in order to account for a single state, rather than treating alternative theories as mutually exclusive."[109] Harland Prechel develops a contingency theory of business unity to account for complex changes in state business policy over forty-nine years and provides "a more inclusive explanation of capital-state relations.[110] Prechel identifies several contingencies and their effects on state autonomy and the influence of the U.S. steel industry: recessions and depressions lead the state to favor steel industry capitalists; times of steady economic growth reduce the influence of steel industry; and periods of rapid economic development diminish capitalists' dependence on the state for capital accumulation, curtailing state autonomy.[111]

Though increasingly highlighting the role of contingent events in their class analyses, neo-Marxists use contingencies to strengthen their claim that the state favors dominant classes due to the structural constraints of capitalism. Fred Block acknowledges that war, reconstructions, and depression are tipping points that inordinately increase state power. In these crisis periods, the state emerges as a "historical subject" – an independent actor pursuing its own interests and political agenda – in order "to strengthen the nation's position in the world-system and to preserve internal order."[112] But he insists that in the last instance, state managers are "bound by the capitalist context, dependent on capitalist production, and subject to capitalist influence."[113]

Despite its contributions, the contingency literature still does not explain how and why the the states and state agencies shift their policies in favor of some groups simultaneously or alternately. Still missing is a coherent way of theorizing the connections between crucial events and the orientation of state policies, and of systematically comparing and contrasting state agencies to support its contingency arguments. Critics lash out at the alleged tendency to cobble together a pastiche of various theories and to offer no great improvements on what can be found in the existing literature.[114] Furthermore, most recent studies have not adequately examined states' relationships to both dominant and subordinate classes at the same time.[115]

While building on the insights drawn from contingency studies, I do not aim to provide an account of a multiplicity of factors. Nor do I vote for greater indeterminacy in interpreting states' actions. Instead, my work is a modest effort to explain how and why various political processes, rather than a single kind of political process selected by theoretical fiat, become ascendant at particular times under particular historical circumstances. I endeavor to inductively derive a contingency theory of labor department intervention through an in-depth examination of the two cases at hand. I formulate an alternative conception of state agencies and suggest hypotheses about political processes and their impacts on policy-making.


**The Chameleon State**

The central thesis of this study is that state agencies are multifaceted organizations. Like chameleons changing colors, they alter their policy formulation and implementation according to historical conditions. Rather than being inherently beholden to certain interests, state agencies switch sides – supporting either organized labor or business depending on the contexts – or are geared to much more than one group at a time. While formulating and implementing policies according to their interests, state managers do so only in the context of other state and societal actors' preferences, demands, and institutional expressions and bases.[116] Only in certain selected contexts will state agencies satisfy the interests of single social categories such as interest groups, capitalists, or state managers. They cannot maximize the interests of any single group outside these special contexts. The state in capitalist societies is a complex entity, adapting to the changing environment and simultaneously or alternately siding with various, often competing, actors. My contingency theory confronts complex reality head-on by positing that state agencies are more adaptive structures than the existing theories have acknowledged.

This perspective forces the analyst to examine state agencies in various situations and to explain their ability or inability to respond to the environment. Fluctuations, reversals, and inconsistencies are part and parcel of chaotic and incoherent politics in capitalist societies. At the most concrete, empirical level, the British and German Labor Ministries had to deal with the pressures and demands of dominant classes intent on keeping their leverage, organized labor's firm stand on syndicalist autonomy and demand for state intervention, other state actors who disagreed about goals and means, and the larger cultural contexts in which state actions are embedded. The two agencies were vulnerable to internal or external pressures and used strategies such as neutrality, repression, mediation, arbitration, and horse-trading to manipulate the environment to achieve their goals.

The key to understanding the chameleonic nature of the state is state managers' perceptions and responses to changing circumstances. State managers shift their policy when they perceive that contingencies change the balance of power or increase the reliance of the state on certain groups. Based on their reading of the environment, state managers adopt what Peter Hall calls new policy paradigms, frameworks of ideas and standards, and resolve problems by changing "the hierarchy of goals and set of instruments employed to guide policy."[117] Though explaining radical policy overhauls in terms of changing frameworks of ideas and standards, Hall's framework falls short of theorizing the contexts in which a broad array of actors wins or loses political contests. My argument stresses how a crisis changes the balance of power and the perceptions of state managers, which in turn causes a shift in policy.[118] In Britain and Germany, state managers moved back and forth among three paradigms – liberal-democratic arrangement, capitalist order, and nation-state survival. Threats to postwar reconstruction generated liberal-democratic rhetoric and practices. Threats to capitalism gave rise to a vocabulary of order, and threats to the nation to that of survival in the state system.

The research on mostly economic firms in organizational studies provides three organizational reasons for the changes in the behavior of state agencies. First, structural contingency theory suggests that organizations change their structure and improve efficiency[119] when firm managers perceive that some contingencies threaten their survival. Survival in an unpredictable environment is a paramount priority.[120] The pioneering study by Lawrence and Lorsch indicates that there are different ways to organize in order to deal with different environmental conditions. Different external conditions require state agencies to adopt various "organizational characteristics and behavior patterns."[121] As Neil Fligstein cogently puts it, "[a]ctors who control organizations, be they in the employment of the state or firms, must interpret their organizational fields and then make policies based on their reading of those fields. This policy, by necessity, will be bounded by the internal logic of their organizations, what those actors know, how they perceive the world, and what they define as appropriate organizational behavior."[122]

Second, resource dependence theorists show that organizations are vulnerable to external manipulation because of their dependence on the environment for key resources, and that firm managers are able to use various strategies – coopting or giving concessions to external actors – to maintain their autonomy.[123] Resource dependence theory is used to shore up neo-Marxist theory as a middle-range theory. It is argued that the dominant class gains influence when the state is asymmetrically dependent on capitalist resources.[124] This use of resource dependence theory is, in my view, too narrow. In this book, I attempt to show the conditions under which the state agencies are asymmetrically dependent on resources controlled by organized labor as well as capitalists and the conditions under which state agencies alter the environment so that they can pursue their own goals.

Third, the international cultural environment shapes the kind of responses that state agencies can adopt.[125] The wider contextual conditions for chameleonic state agencies are their social construction at the global level. Despite national and cultural differences, state agencies are, to use Peter Katzenstein's terminology, embedded in "international and domestic societies,"[126] and therefore act in a similar way in accordance with the global institutional context and cultural norms.[127] Neo-institutionalists argue that these external contexts and norms spell out the boundaries of legitimate behavior and limit the range of possible outcomes. State agencies have to fit with pre-conceived normative understandings of "the 'right' ways of doing things," which are "the most powerful brakes on radical transformations."[128]

I contend that the unexpected uniformity in policy shifts in Britain and Germany had its source in the liberal world order. According to John Meyer and his associates, the world polity – a set of principles, norms, and rules – legitimates the state as the carrier of modern progress and justifies its policies in terms of promoting the collective good of the nation as a whole. Accordingly, state managers' "action is highly structured by institutionalized rules,"[129] which prescribe the types of responses that state agencies can resort to in times of crises.[130] The liberal world order sanctions interventions to keep domestic peace, to maintain a respectable position in the world, and to trump liberal democracy when necessary. As John Ruggie points out, starting from the interwar period, the international regime, labelled as "embedded" liberalism, legitimated actions of modern states to contain domestic economic and social dislocations created by markets. Though consolidated after WWII, this embedded liberalism emerged between the two world wars and began supplanting what he called orthodox liberalism, which had given free play to unrestrained market forces.[131] Thus, following standard institutional scripts, British and German state managers adopted free collective bargaining in the aftermath of the Great War, but switched to an exclusionary mode to protect capitalism against threats and pursued policies to support the state when the nation was threatened.

This book acknowledges that national political culture shaped the divergent historical trajectories of the British self-determination and German state arbitration policies in industrial relations. But I contend that national political culture fails to account for cross-national similarities. I show that the global cultural context, rather than national political tradition, explains the similar policy shifts in both Britain and Germany. In other words, this study underlines the importance of cultural meanings and practices that are beyond the boundaries of nation-states and defined by the larger international cultural environment.

Contingencies are defined as crucial historical events that have momentous impacts on state policies because they facilitate or hinder dominant classes, organized labor, and state agencies to achieve their goals by shifting the balance of power within and between them. These events are perceived by historians and social scientists as pivotal due to the size and degree of severity of social crises, such as strikes and lockouts, and the impacts of economic and political crises on historical trajectories.

In particular, the British and German state agencies had to deal with contingencies such as major industrial conflicts (the coal miners strike of 1921, the General Strike of 1926 in Britain, the coal conflict in the Ruhr of May 1924, the Ruhr iron and steel conflict of October 1928 in Germany), economic crises (the inflation of 1922-1923 and the Great Depression in 1929-1933 in Germany), watershed events (the First World War and postwar reconstruction), and peacetime geopolitical threats to the nation. These historical events generated inclusionary, exclusionary, and autonomous processes that not only determined variations across cases but also shaped the various shifts within state policies.[132] Each process became salient under specific historical conditions and yielded outcomes in favor of or at the expense of state managers, organized labor, and employers.

Inclusionary processes are a series of actions that allow sundry forces such as organized labor and employers to shape policy formulation, implementation, and outcome. As a result of such processes, state agencies are responsive to societal demands and search for compromises to resolve differences. As Theodore Lowi points out, syndicalism needs to be taken into account in examining minimal state intervention in industrial relations. In fact, organized labor's desire to safeguard its cherished trade autonomy imposed limits on the interwar British and German Labor Ministries. Despite its theoretical weaknesses, pluralist theory rightly stresses factors that are missing in a neo-Marxist account that privileges the role of dominant classes and in a statist interpretation that underscores the role of state managers. In post-WWI Britain and Germany, the Labor Ministries formulated the self-determination policy in an inclusionary way: They allowed employers and trade unions to solve industrial disputes without state intervention. Britain pursued the non-interventionist policy during the entire interwar period. Germany implemented a similar policy until 1923 and even thereafter solved the thorniest industrial disputes in a manifestly pluralistic way. To explain policy shifts, a broad theoretical framework such as pluralism allows for a broad range of actors and interests – "a truly multivocal – or pluralistic – frame for political inquiry."[133] This study in part uses a pluralist model to account for the impacts of sundry forces on policies and administrative capacities. Under some conditions, organized labor gains the upper hand vis-à-vis the state.[134]

Exclusionary processes are those actions that allow dominant classes to shape or gain from state policies and to produce outcomes that are biased against the working class. When such processes are ascendant, state agencies become capitalist and shift policies in favor of capital. To some extent, both the British and German Ministries fit the structuralist neo-Marxist mold of capitalist state agencies. They exercised functions designed to mollify and divide organized labor through tactical concessions and repressive measures. The British Ministry was "weak" in helping organized labor or in pursuing highly independent initiatives, but "strong" in organizing disadvantaged employers and repressing militant workers in large-scale industrial conflicts. Minimal state intervention turned out to be detrimental to the working class in major industrial conflicts. The seemingly autonomous German Ministry swung to the side of employers in times of grave economic crises. The identification of exclusionary processes under certain historical conditions is important, for employers did not always have the upper hand in the interwar period. For instance, while having access to center-right coalition governments from 1924 to 1928 and benefiting from corporate welfare, German big industry had, as Harold James underscores, limited influence on political events. Its power varied. "It was greatest in the winter of 1929-30 as the political system began to shift from a system of interest brokerage ... to one where a very small number of people ... tried to remain in control"[135] as a result of the Depression.

Autonomous processes are those actions that allow national leaders to pursue geopolitical and domestic-ordering goals, even at the expense of groups and classes. In such processes, national interests become paramount and lead to the decline or increase in the influence of labor departments relative to that of other state actors. State policies go through shifts, which need not be cataclysmic, but sometimes are, as suggested by Fred Block's concept of tipping points – processes that go so far that the state is freed from dominant classes for a phase of the New Deal, or takes over the economy and subjugates capitalist forces in the wartime Third Reich.[136] Autonomous processes weakened the British Labor Ministry and strengthened its German counterpart in industrial relations.

In a nutshell, I advance four tentative, general propositions regarding the connections between contingencies, global context, and political processes.

First, the First World War and postwar reconstruction were two contingencies that increased the reliance of the states on sundry forces such as organized labor and employers and that transformed the British and German Labor Ministries into arenas for interest-group politics. Inclusionary processes were typically ascendant in interwar Britain and also prevailed until 1923 in Weimar Germany. Moreover, despite its statist features, for the sake of maintaining order, the German Labor Ministry resorted to pluralistic means to solve major industrial conflicts such as the coal conflict in the Ruhr of May 1924 and the Ruhr iron and steel conflict of October 1928.

Second, contingencies such as crises of international economic relations and domestic political instability compelled state managers to protect national interests and override the interests of employers and organized labor. These autonomous processes diminished the British Labor Ministry's room to maneuver, while they strengthened the German Labor Ministry's position in industrial relations. The Labor Ministries asserted state interests above all else when Britain's sterling supremacy in the world was in doubt and when, in Germany, the breakdown of collective bargaining, leadership paralysis, and threats from radical movements threatened political order. However, this autonomy is entwined with or circumscribed by inclusionary and exclusionary processes.

Third, threats to capitalist property relations and related public order increased the states' asymmetrical dependence on capitalists and reduced the British and German Labor Ministries to agents of capitalist class cohesion. At critical junctures such as economic crises and threats to the political order, the Ministries switched to a class mode in order to protect the capitalist economy. Britain contained union power and militancy in the large-scale 1921 coal miners strike and the General Strike of 1926. Germany favored employers in response to the inflation of 1922-1923 and the Depression of 1929-1933.

Fourth, the complex behavior of the British and German Labor Ministries was in fact socially constructed at the global level. Influenced and legitimized by the liberal world order, the British and German Labor Ministries responded to contingencies by shifting policies in a uniform way. The two cases show that there is an international agreement about the conditions under which the states can trump liberalism.

My contingency approach contributes to the state literature by providing a framework to help analysts identify and organize historically grounded causal accounts of particular policy shifts. This work highlights the bases of alternative public policies and argues that state policies ride on the alternate or simultaneous ascendance of inclusionary, exclusionary, and autonomous processes. Moreover, my theoretical effort is to link particular contingencies to political processes. I provide a tentative contingency theory that is based on nineteen years of two countries' experience and derive propositions that are generalizable across the two cases. These propositions are tentative. They need to be further tested and refined with the help of additional cases.

Thanks to the rich and detailed information stored in archives, I am able to conceive historical situations as a three-way chess-game between the state, employers, and workers. The game evolves and changes according to historical contingencies and the processes unleashed by them. As I shall try to show in this book, while culture determines the dominant pattern of state intervention in the two countries, the interplay between contingencies and inclusionary, exclusionary, and autonomous processes shape the various shifts within state policies. This approach does not assume a priori the weight of state and societal actors. They are all agents of history. The task is to identify the switches and explain their effects on the balance of power among state managers, employers, and organized labor.


## Theory-Building and Archival Data

I use both secondary and archival sources to support the above propositions. Studies on the British and German Labor Ministries by, say, Rodney Lowe and Johannes Bähr, and authoritative works by Gerald D. Feldman on the interwar period provide essential information about the British and German Labor Ministries. An extensive body of literature contains the abundant information on industrial relations policies, national politics, employers, and organized labor. These secondary sources are invaluable in understanding the intricacies of industrial relations policies in both Britain and Weimar Germany, and providing rich information on large-scale industrial conflicts pitting employers and large numbers of workers against each other over issues such as wage rates, working hours, and working conditions.

These monographs are, however, insufficient for a historical comparative analysis, since intimate knowledge of what state managers did, thought, and debated among themselves and with employers and union leaders is required. To elucidate the shifting nature of the British and German Labor Ministries, I traveled to the archives in Britain and Germany and sifted through the documents generated by the Labor Ministries and other state agencies during the period under study. Only archival sources highlight infighting among politicians and bureaucrats and their ties to societal actors, and substantiate my claims about policy shifts in certain historical conditions. This work draws on archival sources such as internal correspondence among officials within the Labor Ministries, and their correspondence with other state officials, employers' organizations, and trade unions. These primary sources, supplemented with memoirs and speeches by officials, bring to light the policy formulation, decision-making, and crisis management of the ministerial leadership and their conflicts with other state actors, employers, and organized labor, and bring into sharp relief the changes in their industrial relations policies over time.[137]

The archival sources are not new to historians, although they are not well-known among social scientists in the U.S. Rather than attempting to unearth new materials, my goal was to personally assess and carefully use some British and German archival data to construct a historically sensitive, comparative, theoretical account[138] and to adjudicate between rival explanations provided by some historians and social scientists.

## Notes


1. Peter Hall, "Policy Paradigms, Social Learning, and the State: The Case of Economic Policymaking in Britain," *Comparative Politics* 25 (April 1993), p. 292.
2. Some of the major theoretical clashes can be found in the following works: C. Wright Mills, *The Power Elite* (New York: Oxford University Press, 1956), Ralph Miliband, *The State in Capitalist Society* (New York: Basic Books, 1969); Nicos Poulantzas, *Pouvoir politique et classes sociales* (Paris: Librairie François Maspero, 1968); Theda Skocpol and Edwin Amenta, "Did Capitalists Shape Social Security?" *American Sociological Review* 50, (1985), pp. 572-575; Jill Quadagno, "Two Models of Welfare State Development: Reply to Skocpol and Amenta," *American Sociological Review* 50, (1985), pp. 575-578; G. William Domhoff, "The Wagner Act and Theories of the State: A New Analysis Based on Class-Segment Theory," in *Political Power and Social Theory*, ed. M. Zeitlin (New York: JAI Press, 1987).
3. See the sophisticated literature on the evolution of welfare states: Ann Orloff, *The Politics of Pensions: A Comparative Analysis of Britain, Canada, and the United States, 1880-1940* (Madison: University of Wisconsin Press, 1992); Peter Baldwin, *The Politics of Social Solidarity: Class Bases of the European Welfare States* 1875-1975(Cambridge: Cambridge University Press, 1990); Gøsta Esping-Andersen, *The Three Worlds of Welfare Capitalism* (Princeton: Princeton University Press, 1990); and P. Flora and A. J. Heidenheimer, eds., *The Development of Welfare States in Europe and America* (New Brunswick: Transaction, 1981).
4. Theda Skocpol and Kenneth Finegold, "State Capacity and Economic Intervention in the Early New Deal," *Political Science Quarterly* 97, (1982), p. 271.
5. Jess Gilbert and Carolyn Howe, "Beyond 'State vs. Society': Theories of the State and New Deal Agricultural Policies," *American Sociological Review* 56, (1991), p. 209.
6. Gerald D. Feldman and Imgard Steinisch, "Notwendigkeit und Grenzen sozialstaatlicher Intervention: Eine vergleichende Fallstudie des Ruhreisenstreits in Deutschland und des Generalstreits in Großbritannien," *Archiv für Sozialgeschichte* 20. B., (1980), p. 57.
7. See Reinhard Bendix, *Work and Authority in Industry: Ideology of Management in the Course of Industrialization* (Berkeley: University of California Press, 1956) and Victoria E. Bonnell, *Roots of Rebellion: Workers' Politics and Organizations in St. Petersburg and Moscow, 1900-1914* (Berkeley: University of California Press, 1983).
8. Stephen D. Krasner, *Defending the National Interests: Raw Materials Investments and U.S. Foreign Policy* (Princeton: Princeton University Press, 1978).
9. Rodney Lowe, *Adjusting to Democracy: The Role of the Ministry of Labour in British Politics, 1916-1939* (Oxford: Clarendon Press, 1986); Robert Middlemas, *Politics in Industrial Sociiety: The Experience of the British System since 1911* (London: A. Deutsch, 1979); Charles Maier, *Recasting Bourgeois Europe: Stabilization in France, Germany, and Italy in the Decade after WWII* (Princeton: Princeton University Press, 1975); Johannes Walter Bähr, *Staatliche Schlichtung in der Weimarer Republik: Tarifpolitik, Korporatismus und industrieller Konflikt zwischen Inflation und Deflation, 1919-1932* (Berlin: Colloquium Verlag, 1989); and David Abraham, *The Collapse of the Weimar Republic: Political Economy and Crisis* (New York: Holmes and Meier, 1986).

10.  Richard Biernacki, *The Fabrication of Labor: Germany and Britain, 1640-1914* (Berkeley: University of California Press, 1995), p. 16.

11.  Frank Dobbin, *Forging Industrial Policy: The U.S., Britain, and France in the Railway Age* (Cambridge: Cambridge University Press, 1994), p. 22. His analysis leaves out Germany.

12.  *Ibid.*, p. 11.

13.  John Saville, "The British State, the Business Community, and the Trade Unions," in *The Development of Trade Unionism in Great Britain and Germany, 1880-1914*, eds. Wolfgang J. Mommsen and Hans-Gerhard Husung (London: Allen & Unwin, 1985), pp. 315-324.

14.  Rodney Lowe, "The Ministry of Labour, 1916-1924: A Graveyard of Social Reform?" *Public Administration* 52, (1974), p. 433.

15.  Ludwig Preller, *Sozialpolitik in der Weimarer Republik* (Stuttgart: Franz Mittelbach Verlag, 1949), pp. 512 and 515.

16.  Ibid., pp. 522-523.

17.  Frieda Wunderlich, *Labor Under German Democracy: Arbitration, 1918-1933* (New York: New School for Social Research, 1940), p. xii.

18.  Johannes Walter Bähr, *Staatliche Schlichtung*, p. 9.

19.  Geoff Eley, ed., *Society, Culture, and the State in Germany, 1870-1930* (Ann Arbor: The University of Michigan Press, 1996), p. 3.

20.  Ibid., p. 7 and George Steinmetz, "The Myth of an Autonomous State: Industrialists, Junkers, and Social Policy in Imperial Germany," in *Society, Culture, and the State in Germany*, pp. 259, 260, and 304.

21.  Hans Luther, *Politiker ohne Partei: Erinnerungen* (Stuttgart: Deutsche Verlags-Anstalt, 1960), p. 93.

22.  Roger Davidson and Rodney Lowe, "Bureaucracy and Innovation in British Welfare Policy, 1870-1945," in *The Emergence of the Welfare State in Britain and Germany*, ed. W. J. Mommsen (London: Croom Helm, 1981), pp. 272 and 277.

23.  W. S. Adams, "Lloyd George and the Labour Movement," *Past and Present* 3, 1953, p. 61.

24.  Chris Wrigley, *A History of British Industrial Relations, 1875-1914* (Sussex: Harvester Press, 1982), pp. 142-146.

25.  Roger Davidson, "Social Conflict and Social Administration: The Conciliation Act in British Industrial Relations," in *The Search for Wealth and Stability*, ed. T. C. Smout (London: Macmillan, 1979), p. 189.

26.  Frederick Leggett, "The Settlement of Labour Disputes in Great Britain," in *Meeting of Minds: A Way to Peace Through Mediation*, ed. Elmore Jackson (New York: McGraw-Hill, 1952), p. 63.

27.  Charles Wrigley, *A History of British Industrial Relations*, p. 152. Wrigley attributes the discontinuity to improvisation and the absence of policy guidelines, which contributed to the fact that "little was learnt from previous experiences" after 1910.

28.  George Steinmetz, *Regulating the Social: The Welfare State and Local Politics in Imperial Germany* (Princeton: Princeton University Press, 1993), p. 43.

29.  Ibid., p. 52.

30.  Kenneth O. Morgan, *Consensus and Disunity: The Lloyd George Coalition Government, 1918-1922* (Oxford: Oxford University Press, 1979), p. 55.

31.  Thomas Jones's letter to Maurice Hankey (19 January 1920), in *Whitehall Diary, 1916-1925*, Vol. 1, ed. Keith Middlemas (London: Oxford University Press, 1969a), p. 98.

32.  RAM 3151, 17 January 1929, italics mine, pp. 269-273.

33.  RAM 3148, 8 June 1925, p. 12.

34.  Carl Severing, *Mein Lebensweg*, Vol. 2 (Köln: Greven Verlag, 1950), p. 172.

35.  Robert A. Dahl, *Who Governs? Democracy and Power in an American City* (New Haven: Yale University Press, 1961), pp. 85-86.

36.  Theodore J. Lowi, *The End of Liberalism: Ideology, Policy, and the Crisis of Public Authority* (New York: W. W. Norton, 1969), p. 71.

37.  Edward O. Laumann and David Knoke, *The Organizational State: Social Choice in National Policy Domains* (Madison: The University of Wisconsin Press, 1987).

38.  David Truman, *The Government Process: Political Interests and Public Opinion* (New York: Knopf, 1971).

39.  David Truman, *The Government Process*; Robert A. Dahl, *Who Governs?* and Charles E. Lindblom, *Politics and Markets: The World's Political-Economic Systems* (New York: Basic Books, 1977).

40.  Rodney Lowe, *Adjusting to Democracy*, p. 126.

41.  Ibid., p. vii.

42.  Ibid., p. 244.

43.  Ibid., p. vii and pp. 248-249.

44.  Theodore J. Lowi, *The End of Liberalism*, p. 102.

45.  Richard F. Kuisel, *Capitalism and the State in Modern France* (Cambridge: Cambridge University Press, 1981), p. 251. See also Albert Peyronnet, *Le Ministère du Travail 1906-1923* (Paris: Berger-Levrault, 1924) and Jean-André Tournerie, *Le Ministère du Travail: origines et premiers développements* (Paris: Edition Cujas, 1971).

46.  Rodney Lowe, *Adjusting to Democracy*, p. 119.

47.  John F. Manley, "Neo-Pluralism: A Class Analysis of Pluralism I and Pluralism II," *American Political Science Review* 77, (1983), pp. 368-383.

48.  Charles E. Lindblom, *Politics and Markets*, pp. 179-180.

49.  Charles E. Lindblom, "Another State of Mind," *American Political Science Review* 76, (1982), pp. 9-21.

50.  Walter Korpi, *The Democratic Class Struggle* (London: Routledge and Kegan Paul, 1983).

51.  Theda Skocpol and Edwin Amenta, "States and Social Policies," *Annual Review of Sociological Research* 12, (1986), pp. 139-143.

52.  Ibid., p. 142.

53.  Nicos Poulantzas, *Pouvoir politique et classes sociales*, p. 207.

54.  See the Poulantzas-Miliband debates: Ralph Miliband, "The Capitalist State: Reply to Nicos Poulantzas," *New Left Review* 59, (1970), pp. 53-60 and "Poulantzas and the Capitalist State," *New Left Review* 82, (1973), pp. 84-92; Nicos Poulantzas, "The Problem of the Capitalist State," *New Left Review* 58, (1969), pp. 67-78 and "The Capitalist State: A Reply to Miliband and Laclau," *New Left Review* 95, (1976), pp. 63-83.

55.  Nicos Poulantzas, *Pouvoir politique et classes sociales*, p. 313.

56.  Fred Block, "The Ruling Class Does Not Rule: Notes on the Marxist Theories of the State," *Socialist Revolution* 33, vol. 7, 3, (May-June 1977), pp. 16-24 and "Beyond Relative Autonomy: State Managers as Historical Subjects," *The Socialist Register*, eds. Ralph Miliband and John Saville (London: Merlin Press, 1980), pp. 230-232; Jill S. Quadagno, "Welfare Capitalism and the Social Security Act of 1935," *American Sociological Review* 49, (1984), pp. 632-647; Jenkins, J. Craig and Barbara G. Brents, "Social Protest, Hegemonic Competition, and

Social Reform: A Political Struggle Interpretation of the Origins of the American Welfare State," *American Sociological Review* 54, (1989), pp. 891-909; and Michael Goldfield, "Worker Insurgency, Radical Organization, and New Deal Labor Legislation," *American Political Science Review* 83, (1989), pp. 1257-1282.

57.   Nicos Poulantzas, *State, Power, Socialism* (London: New Left Books: 1980), p. 140.

58.   Nicos Poulantzas, *Pouvoir politique et classes sociales*, p. 206.

59.   Nicos Poulantzas, *State, Power, Socialism*, p. 138. Here I adopt Poulantzas's revised view of the capitalist state as a site of class conflicts.

60.   Nicos Poulantzas, "The Problem of the Capitalist State," pp. 67-78.

61.   Nicos Poulantzas, *Pouvoir politique et classes sociales*, p. 151 and pp. 262-270.

62.   Gøsta Esping-Andersen, Roger Friedland, and Erik Olin Wright, "Modes of Class Struggle and the Capitalist State," *Kapitalstate* 4-5, (1976), pp. 190-192 and p. 213.

63.   Nancy DiTomaso, "Class Politics and Public Bureaucracy: The U. S. Department of Labor," in *Classes, Class Conflict, and the State*, ed. Maurice Zeitlin (Mass: Winthrop, 1980), p. 135.

64.   Ibid., p. 141. See also Gøsta Esping- Andersen et al., "Modes of Class Struggle," pp. 186-220.

65.   David Abraham, *The Collapse of the Weimar Republic:* p. 244.

66.   Ibid., pp. 42 and 244.

67.   Gerald D. Feldman, *Iron and Steel in the German Inflation, 1916-1922* (Princeton: Princeton University Press, 1977), p. 465.

68.   Harold James, *The German Slump: Politics and Economics, 1924-1936* (Oxford: Clarendon Press, 1986), pp. 171-174.

69.   Harold James, *The German Slump*, p. 169.

70.   George Steinmetz, "The Myth and the Reality of an Autonomous State: Industrialists, Junkers and Social Policy in Imperial Germany," *Comparative Social Research* 12, (1990), pp. 239-293. See also Tien-Lung Liu, "On Whose Side is the State? The German Labor Ministry, 1918-1933," *Journal of Historical Sociology* 10, (1997), pp. 361-388.

71.   Philippe C. Schmitter, "Still the Century of Corporatism?" *Review of Politics* (January 1974), p. 13.

72.   Robert Keith Middlemas, *Politics in Industrial Society*, p. 18.

73.   Ibid., p. 127. There are too many inaccuracies in the historical evidence presented by him and few references to primary sources, as Lowe points out in "The Ministry of Labour: Fact and Fiction," *Bulletin of the Society for the Study of Labour History* 41, (1980), p. 24.

74.   Rodney Lowe, "The Ministry of Labour: Fact and Fiction," p. 25.

75.   Colin Crouch, *Industrial Relations and European State Traditions* (Oxford: Clarendon Press, 1993), p. 134.

76.   Charles S. Maier, *Recasting Bourgeois Europe*, p. 354.

77.   Ibid., p. 387.

78.   Ibid., p. 10.

79.   Ibid., p. 15.

80.   Johannes Walter Bähr, *Staatliche Schlichtung*, p. 8.

81.   Ibid., p. 348.

82.   Ibid., p. 8.

83.   Ibid., pp. 353-355.

84.   Harold James, *The German Slump*, p. 4.

85. Peter B. Evans, Dietrich Rueschemeyer, and Theda Skocpol, eds., *Bringing the State Back In* (Cambridge: Cambridge University Press, 1985).

86. Alfred Stepan, *The State and Society: Peru in Comparative Perspective* (Princeton: Princeton University Press, 1978); Theda Skocpol, "Political Response to Capitalist Crisis: Neo-Marxist Theories of the State and the Case of the New Deal," *Politics and Society* 10, (1980), pp. 155-201; *Protecting Soldiers and Mothers: The Political Origins of Social Policy in the United States* (Cambridge: Belknap Press of Harvard University, 1992); and Tien-Lung Liu, "States and Urban Revolutions: Explaining the Revolutionary Outcomes in Iran and Poland," *Theory and Society* 17, (1988), pp. 179-209.

87. Stephen D. Krasner, *Defending the National Interests: Raw Materials Investments and US Foreign Policy* (Princeton: Princeton University Press, 1978).

88. Hugh Heclo, *Modern Social Politics in Britain and Sweden: From Relief to Income Maintenance* (New Haven: Yale University Press, 1974), pp. 303-305.

89. Ibid., p. 304.

90. Theda Skocpol and Kenneth Finegold, "State Capacity and Economic Intervention in the Early New Deal," *Political Science Quarterly* 97, (1982), pp. 255-278; and Ann Orloff and Theda Skocpol, "Why not Equal Protection? Explaining the Politics of Public Social Spending in Britain, 1900-1911, and the United States, 1880s-1920," *American Sociological Review* 49, (1984), pp. 726-750.

91. Theda Skocpol, "Political Response," p. 200.

92. Theda Skocpol, *Protecting Mothers and Soldiers*, p. 42.

93. Theda Skocpol, "Political Response," pp. 155-201.

94. Charles Tilly, "Reflections on the History of European State-Making," *The Formation of National States in Western Europe*, ed. Charles Tilly (Princeton: Princeton University Press, 1975), pp. 3-83.

95. Charles Tilly, *Coercion, Capital, and European States, AD 990-1992* (Cambridge: Blackwell Publishers, 1992), p. 14. See also Bruce D. Porter, *War and the Rise of the State: The Military Foundations of Modern Politics* (New York: Free Press, 1994).

96. Theda Skocpol, "Political Response" p. 201.

97. Most debates are on the U.S. welfare state: Jill Quadagno, "Welfare Capitalism and the Social Security Act of 1935," *American Sociological Review* 49, (1984), pp. 632-647 and Theda Skocpol and Edwin Amenta, "Did Capitalists Shape Social Security?" *American Sociological Review* 50, (1985), pp. 572-575.

98. Gregory Hooks, "From an Autonomous to a Captured State Agency: The Decline of the New Deal in Agriculture," *American Sociological Review* 55, (1990), pp. 29-43.

99. For example, Krasner states that his book *Defending National Interests* "tries to demonstrate the superiority of an alternative approach, a statist image of foreign policy," p. 6.

100. This argument is consistent with that of Gregory Hooks, who argues that state theories are strong ideal types that need to be watered down when applied to concrete cases. See his article, "The Weakness of Strong Theories: The U.S. State's Dominance of the World War II Investment Process," *American Sociological Review* 58, (1993), pp. 37-53.

101. Robert A. Alford and Roger Friedland, *Powers of Theory: Capitalism, the State, and Democracy* (Cambridge: Cambridge University Press, 1985), p. 390,

emphasis mine. Aslo see Steven Lukes, *Power: A Radical View* (London: Anchor Press, 1974).

102. Alex Hicks and Joya Misra, "Political Resources and the Growth of Welfare in Affluent Capitalist Democracies, 1960-1982," *American Journal of Sociology* 99, (1993), pp. 699 and 703. A similar argument can be found in Edwin Amenta and Bruce G. Carruthers, "The Formative Years of U.S. Social Spending Policies: Theories of the Welfare State and the American States during the Great Depression," *American Sociological Review* 53, (1988), pp. 661-678.

103. Michael Mann, *The Sources of Social Power: The Rise of Classes and Nation-States, 1760-1914*, Vol. 2 (Cambridge: Cambridge University Press, 1993), p. 87.

104. Ibid., p. 81.

105. See Theda Skocpol's discussion of the central role of women's groups in the making of social policies in *Protecting Soldiers and Mothers*, p. ix and pp. 50, 54, and 57.

106. Ellen Immergut, "The Rules of the Game: The Logic of Health Policy-Making in France, Switzerland, and Sweden," in *Structuring Politics: Historical Institutionalism in Comparative Perspective*, eds. Sven Steinmo, Kathleen Thelen, and Frank Longstreth (Cambridge: Cambridge University Press, 1992), pp. 57-81. Her analysis of health care policy in France, Switzerland, and Sweden is an outstanding example of historical institutionalism. She proposes a theory of shifting veto points to show that Swiss policy-makers, for instance, are fearful of their policy proposal reaching the referendum stage, a potential veto point and an area of institutional vulnerability, because interest groups opposed to reform can easily mobilize opposition against policy innovation.

107. Bob Jessop, *State Theory: Putting the Capitalist State in its Place* (Pennsylvania: The Pennsylvania State University Press, 1990), p. 353.

108. Ibid., p. 12.

109. George Steinmetz, *Regulating the Social: The Welfare State and Local Politics in Imperial Germany* (Princeton: Princeton University Press, 1993), pp. 15 and 17.

110. Harland Prechel, "Steel and the State: Industry Politics and Business Policy Formation, 1940-1989," *American Sociological Review* 55, (1990), p. 649.

111. Harland Prechel, "Steel and the State," p. 651.

112. Fred Block, "Beyond Relative Autonomy," p. 233.

113. Ibid., p. 228.

114. For instance, instead of formulating an alternative, coherent theoretical framework, Gregory Hooks merely matches a specific theory to an institutional context which happens to give prominence to various business interests or the objectives of the military. See his article, "The Weakness of Strong Theories," pp. 37-53.

115. The contingency studies in major sociology journals focus on either capital and the state (see Harland Prechel, "Steel and the State"; Gregory Hooks, "The Weakness of Strong Theories" ) or the state and labor (Jill Quadagno, "Social Movement and State Transformation). Gilbert and Howe ("Beyond 'State' vs. 'Society'") does pay attention to the struggles of tenants, the influences of wealthy, white farmers, and their impacts on state policies, but their focus is not on employers and trade unions.

116. Graham Allison, *Essence of Decision: Explaining the Cuban Missile Crisis* (Boston: Little Brown, 1971).

117. Peter Hall, "Policy Paradigms, Social Learning, and the State: The Case of Economic Policymaking in Britain," *Comparative Politics* 25, (April 1993), p. 284.

118. Ibid, pp. 284-285. For an article-length treatment of my argument, see Tien-Lung Liu, "Policy Shifts and State Agencies: Britain and Germany, 1918-1933," *Theory and Society* 27, (1998), pp. 43-82.

119. James Thompson, *Organization in Action* (New York: McGraw-Hill, 1967); Paul R. Lawrence and Jay W. Lorsch, *Organization and Environment* (Cambridge: Harvard University Press, 1967); and Charles Perrow, "A Framework for Comparative Organizational Analysis," *American Sociological Review* 32, (1967), pp. 194-208.

120. Lex Donaldson, *American Anti-Management Theories of Organization: A Critique of Paradigm Proliferation* (Cambridge: Cambridge University Press, 1995), p. 33.

121. Paul R. Lawrence and Jay W. Lorsch, *Organization and Environment*, p. 14.

122. Neil Fligstein, *The Transformation of Corporate Control* (Cambridge: Harvard University Press, 1990), p. 10.

123. Jeffrey Pfeffer and Gerald Salancick, *The External Control of Organizations: A Resource Dependence Perspective* (New York: Harper and Row, 1978).

124. Harland Prechel, "Steel and the State," pp. 649-651. His organizational state perspective mainly rests on the resource dependence theory. See also Gregory Hooks, "The Weakness of Strong Theories," pp. 37-53.

125. See Stephen D. Krasner, "Structural Causes and Regime Consequences: Regimes as Intervening Variables," in *International Regimes*, ed. Stephen D. Krasner (Ithaca: Cornell University Press, 1983), p. 8; and Robert O. Keohane, *After Hegemony: Cooperation and Discord in the World Political Economy* (Princeton: Princeton University Press, 1984), p. 26.

126. Peter J. Katzenstein, ed., *The Culture of National Security: Norms and Identity in World Politics* (New York: Columbia University Press, 1996), p. 22.

127. John W. Meyer and Brian Rowan, "Institutionalized Organizations: Formal Structure as Myth and Ceremony," *American Journal of Sociology* 83, (1978), pp. 340-363; and Paul DiMaggio and Walter W. Powell, *The New Institutionalism in Organizational Analysis* (Chicago: University of Chicago Press, 1991).

128. Glenn R. Carroll and Michael T. Hannan, eds., *Organizations in Industry: Strategy, Structure, and Selection* (New York: Oxford University Press, 1995), p. 25.

129. John W. Meyer, John Boli, and George M. Thomas, "Ontology and Rationalization in the Western Cultural Account," in *Institutional Structure: Constituting State, Society, and the Individual*, eds. George M. Thomas, John W. Meyer, Francisco O. Ramirez, and John Boli (New York: Sage Publications, 1987), p. 12. See also John Meyer, John Boli, George M. Thomas, and Francisco Ramirez, "World Society and the Nation-State," *American Journal of Sociology*, 103, (1997), pp. 144-181.

130. Ibid., 15. Katzenstein argues that "the domestic and international environments of states have effects; they are the arenas in which actors contest norms and through political and social processes construct and reconstruct identities." See his book, *The Culture of National Security*, p. 25.

131. John Gerard Ruggie, "International Regimes, Transactions, and Change: Embedded Liberalism in the Postwar Economic Order," in *International Regimes*, ed. Stephen D. Krasner (Ithaca: Cornell University Press, 1983), pp. 195-232.

132. Charles Tilly, *Big Structures, Large Processes, Huge Comparisons* (New York: Russell Sage, 1984), pp. 116-124.

133. Alex Hicks and Joya Misra, "Political Resources and the Growth of Welfare," p. 703.

134. Jill Quadagno shows that social movement activists transformed the programs of the U.S. Labor Department in the 1960s. See her article "Social Movements and State Transformation," pp. 616-634.
135. Harold James, *The German Slump: Politics and Economics, 1924-1936* (Oxford: Clarendon Press, 1986), p. 189.
136. Fred Block, "Beyond Relative Autonomy," p. 234.
137. Roberto Franzosi points out that the quantative data used in the studies on strikes and labor movement rarely tell the story about the key actors such as the state and employers. See his book, *The Puzzle of Strikes: Class and State Strategies in Postwar Italy* (Cambridge: Cambridge University Press, 1995).
138. Such an approach is commonplace. For example, Charles Maier's magisterial work on interwar Europe is a historical synthesis using corporatist theory and based on secondary works.

# Chapter Two

# The British and German Labor Ministries

## Similarities and Differences

The major aim of this book is to show that the British and German Labor Ministries went beyond the classical portrayals of a "weak laissez-faire state" (Britain) and a "strong interventionist state" (Germany). Though the British Labor Ministry pursued the policy of self-determination during the entire interwar period, this pluralist policy pattern was punctuated by actions that defended dominant class interests and geopolitical objectives. The German Labor Ministry aggressively intervened in industrial relations in the name of public interests between 1923 and 1930, and yet its state arbitration policy was shot through with pluralistic compromises and protection of capitalist interests. These two patterns, permeated by contradictory tendencies in the stage of either formulation or implementation, lie at the heart of this comparative historical study.

What is most puzzling about the seemingly divergent British and German experience in the interwar period is their strikingly similar menus in their pro-labor, pro-capital, and autonomous industrial relations policies. Though different in many aspects, the two labor ministries responded uniformly to certain crucial contingencies, which brought about similar political processes and outcomes. Paradoxically, the weak was strong, and the strong weak, in certain circumstances, blurring the clear-cut line between

---

strength and weakness. My comparative strategy identifies common causes for similar outcomes and rules out competing explanations.[1] The contrast is designed to generate an alternative explanation and to yield some insights that can be useful for the building of a general theory of the state. I solve the puzzle by identifying the conditions under which state policies uniformly shift in favor of some groups or classes in both cases. One important enterprise of comparative historical sociology is, according to Charles Tilly, to present an analysis capable of telling "a tale of diversity in unity, of unity in diversity, of choice and consequences."[2]

## Can Labor Strength Explain Policy-Making?

The two maximally divergent labor ministries can be compared because of important similarities. Labor politics was a priority issue on the national political agenda of the day. Both labor ministries were faced with an unprecedented level of industrial conflicts such as mammoth strikes, aggressive lockouts, and radical movements during the interwar years. In his landmark study on interwar bourgeois Europe, historian Charles Maier wrote that "labor questions became some of the most crucial tests of political stability"[3] in Weimar Germany. Germany went through a difficult period, rocked by revolutionary situations such as the Spartacus uprisings of January 1919 in urban areas and large-scale, destabilizing industrial conflicts such as the coal conflict in the Ruhr in May 1924 and the Ruhr iron and steel conflict in October 1928. The number of workers involved in disputes was staggering, reaching 1,428,116 in 1920. The rampant inflation of 1923 put 28.3 percent of union members out of work in December 1923.[4] Political transition and domestic turmoil required concrete arrangements such as the Stinnes-Legien agreement between capital and organized labor in 1918 and the state arbitration decree of 30 October 1923 (Table 1).

Britain, a case Maier did not study, experienced in some interwar years a degree of industrial militancy unparalleled in the country's previous conflicts.[5] Strikes multiplied, and the number of strikers reached 1,799,000 in 1920.[6] The unemployed totaled two million in June 1921; between 1919 and 1922, the unemployment rate went from under 1 percent of the labour force to 17.5 percent.[7] To achieve their political and economic goals, trade unions resorted to direct action (mass mobilization) in the 1919-1921 coal miners strikes and in the 1926 General Strike, the climax

*Table 1:* Industrial Disputes in Weimar Germany

| Year | Number of Industrial Disputes | Workers Involved (in thousands) | Days Lost (in thousands) |
|---|---|---|---|
| 1913 | 2,464 | 655 | 11,761 |
| 1914 | 1,223 | 238 | 2,844 |
| 1915 | 141 | 48 | 46 |
| 1916 | 240 | 423 | 245 |
| 1917 | 562 | 1,468 | 1,862 |
| 1918 | 532 | 716 | 1,453 |
| 1919 | 3,719 | 2,761 | 33,083 |
| 1920 | 3,807 | 2,009 | 16,755 |
| 1921 | 4,455 | 2,036 | 25,874 |
| 1922 | 4,785 | 2,566 | 27,734 |
| 1923 | 2,046 | 1,917 | 12,344 |
| 1924 | 1,973 | 2,066 | 36,198 |
| 1925 | 1,708 | 1,115 | 2,936 |
| 1926 | 351 | 131 | 1,222 |
| 1927 | 844 | 686 | 6,144 |
| 1928 | 739 | 986 | 20,339 |
| 1929 | 429 | 268 | 4,251 |
| 1930 | 353 | 302 | 4,029 |
| 1931 | 463 | 297 | 1,890 |
| 1932 | 648 | 172 | 1,130 |
| 1933 | NA | NA | NA |

*Source*: B. Mitchell, *European Historical Statistics*, (New York: Columbia University Press, 1975), pp. 182 and 187.

of British labor militancy and the most disruptive strike in the history of European industrial relations.[8] Three-and-a-half million workers walked out during the strike.[9] Colin Crouch noted that "the relatively advanced pluralist system of Britain was on the brink of its general strike of the following year, the single biggest instance of industrial conflict in the countries and period covered by this study" namely, 13 countries over a period of 120 years.[10] The specter of the November 1917 Bolshevik revolution haunted the British establishment and pushed Prime Minister Lloyd George to contemplate using military might to tame strikers.

The extent of industrial conflicts and economic imperatives necessitated negotiations such as the National Industrial Conference in 1919 and the Mond-Turner Talks from 1928 to 1933 in Britain (see Table 2, Figures 1, 2, and 3). Prime Minister Lloyd George wrote to Labor Minister Robert Horne on 3 April 1919 that "the industrial question is perhaps the greatest of all the problem with which we are faced. There is no cut and dried or rough and ready method of solving it"[11] and that "the Ministry of Labour on the 11th November [1918] became the 'Ministry of Munitions of Peace,' upon which primarily fell the immense responsibility"[12] of helping veterans and workers to return to normal life. The government toyed with the idea of a "reorganization of industrial government,"[13] and Lloyd George promised the Labour party leaders in March 1917 that "bigger things" would come since "[t]he whole state of society is more or less molten and you can stamp upon that molten mass almost anything."[14]

*Table 2:* Industrial Disputes in Britain

| Year | Number of Industrial Disputes | Workers Involved (in thousands) | Days Lost (in thousands) |
|---|---|---|---|
| 1913 | 1,497 | 689 | 11,631 |
| 1914 | 972 | 447 | 9,878 |
| 1915 | 672 | 448 | 2,953 |
| 1916 | 532 | 276 | 2,446 |
| 1917 | 730 | 872 | 5,647 |
| 1918 | 1,165 | 1,116 | 5,875 |
| 1919 | 1,352 | 2,591 | 34,969 |
| 1920 | 1,607 | 1,932 | 26,568 |
| 1921 | 763 | 1,801 | 85,872 |
| 1922 | 576 | 552 | 19,850 |
| 1923 | 682 | 405 | 10,672 |
| 1924 | 710 | 613 | 8,424 |
| 1925 | 603 | 441 | 7,952 |
| 1926 | 323 | 2,734 | 162,233 |
| 1927 | 308 | 108 | 1,174 |
| 1928 | 302 | 124 | 1,388 |
| 1929 | 431 | 533 | 8,287 |
| 1930 | 422 | 307 | 4,399 |
| 1931 | 420 | 490 | 6,983 |
| 1932 | 389 | 379 | 6,488 |
| 1933 | 357 | 136 | 1,072 |

*Source:* B. Mitchell, *European Historical Statistics*, p. 185 and 190.

***Figure 1:*** Number of Industrial Disputes in Britain and Germany, 1913-1933

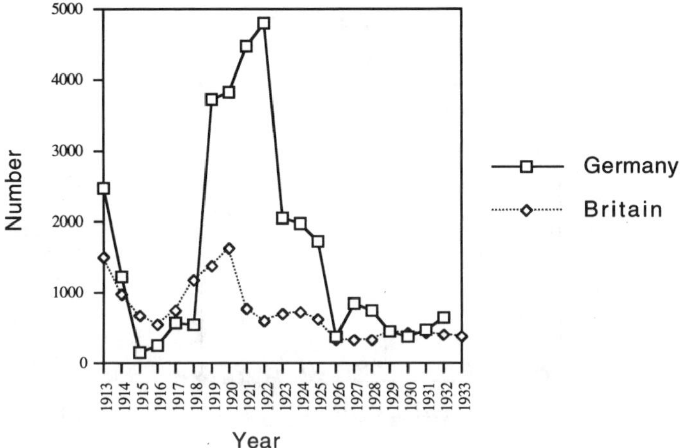


*Source:* B. Mitchell, *European Historical Statistics,* pp. 182, 185, 187, and 190.

***Figure 2:*** Workers Involved in Industrial Disputes in Britain and Germany

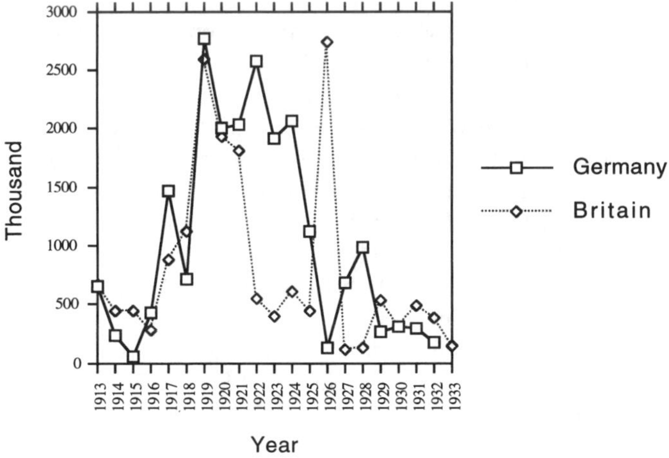


*Source:* B. Mitchell, *European Historical Statistics,* pp. 182, 185, 187, and 190.

***Figure 3:*** Days Lost Due to Industrial Disputes in Britain and
Germany

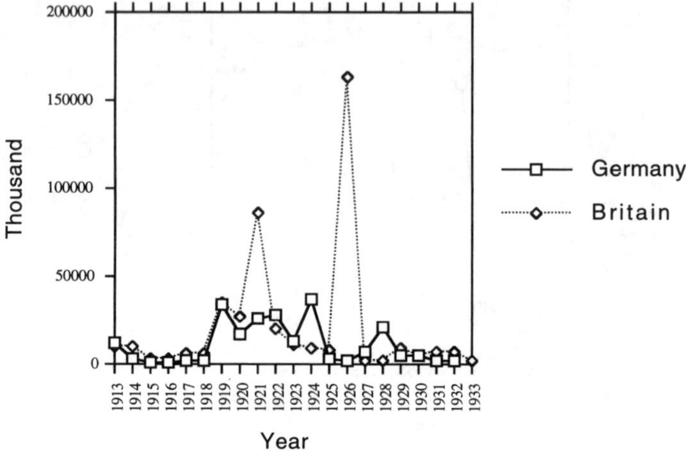


*Source:* B. Mitchell, *European Historical Statistics,* pp. 182, 185, 187,
and 190.

Union density was similar in both countries, and therefore seems
unlikely to have accounted for the differences in British and German labor policies. Organized labor comprised 31 percent (Britain)
and 26 percent (Germany) of total employment in 1930, which "was
remarkably similar in Europe"[15] between the two world wars.

Trade unions ran parallel courses, going through similar periods of dramatic growth after the war and drastic decline after
1920. The war enhanced the bargaining power of unions, and
postwar liberalization swelled their ranks: From 6.6 million in
1918 to 7.8 million in 1919 and 8.3 million in 1920 in Britain, and
from 3.5 million in 1918 to 8.5 million in 1919 and 9.2 million in
1920 in Germany. Both British and German trade unions were
hard hit by the economic slump and were no match for employers'
power thereafter; at that time, union membership dropped to
around four to five million (Table 3 and Figure 4).[16] Union funds
were depleted. As a result, organized labor could not act as effec-
tively as it wished. Twice, the Trades Union Congress backed out
of conflicts with the state and employers. After its defeat in the
1926 General Strike, it was forced to adopt a conciliatory stand
toward employers.

The three major German trade unions, for their part, were so overwhelmed by employers' attacks that they sought protection from the Weimar government. Given the similar predicaments of trade unions in the two countries, the differences in state autonomy and capacity were crucial in determining the political and economic leverage of the labor movement in industrial relations. The German government stepped in and sided with labor from 1924 to 1930, whereas the British state used force to settle industrial disputes, leaving organized labor out in the cold during the entire interwar period.

*Table 3:* Trade-Union Membership in Britain and Germany (in millions)

| YEAR | BRITAIN | GERMANY | YEAR | BRITAIN | GERMANY |
|------|---------|---------|------|---------|---------|
| 1913 | 4.31 | 3.00 | 1924 | 5.54 | 4.78 |
| 1914 | 4.14 | 4.77 | 1925 | 5.50 | 4.92 |
| 1915 | 4.35 | 1.21 | 1926 | 5.21 | 4.74 |
| 1916 | 4.64 | 1.23 | 1927 | 4.91 | 5.30 |
| 1917 | 5.49 | 1.65 | 1928 | 4.80 | 5.79 |
| 1918 | 6.53 | 3.51 | 1929 | 4.85 | 5.91 |
| 1919 | 7.92 | 8.52 | 1930 | 4.84 | 5.66 |
| 1920 | 8.34 | 9.27 | 1931 | 4.62 | 4.50 |
| 1921 | 6.63 | 9.00 | 1932 | 4.44 | NA |
| 1922 | 5.62 | 9.08 | 1933 | 4.39 | NA |
| 1923 | 5.42 | 6.84 | | | |

*Sources*: The German data from 1913-1917 are from Dietmar Petzina et al., *Sozialgeschichtliches Arbeitsbuch*, p. 111. The 1918-1930 data are from Michael Schneider, "Höhen, Krisen und Tiefen: Die Gewerkschaften in der Weimarer Republik 1918 bis 1933," in *Geschichte der deutschen Gewerkschaften von den Anfängen bis 1945*, pp. 324, 371, and 395. The British data are from Department of Employment and Productivity, *British Labour Statistics*, Table 196, Membership of Trade Unions, 1892-1968, p. 395.

German and British employers held similar attitudes toward the economic system and industrial relations as did German and British organized labor. In both countries, employers wanted a return to prewar economic liberalism and minimal state intervention. After the war, the government depended on business confidence to resuscitate the war-shattered economy and to regain the competitive edge in international markets. The leading

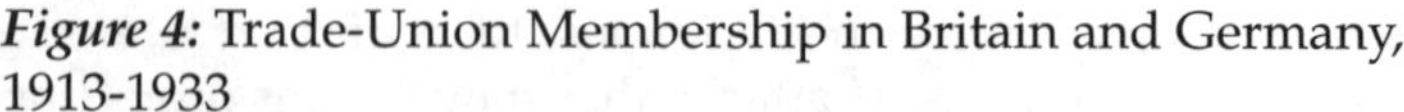

*Figure 4:* Trade-Union Membership in Britain and Germany, 1913-1933

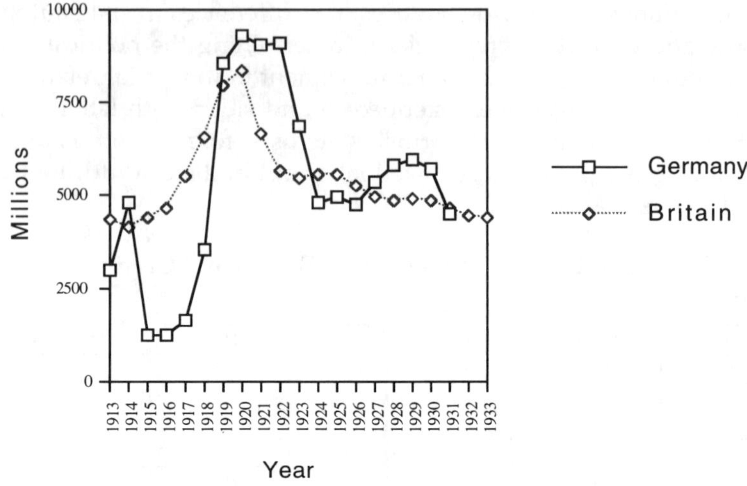


*Sources*: The German data from 1913-1917 are from Dietmar Petzina, Werner Abelshauser, and Anselm Faust, eds., *Sozialgeschichtliches Arbeitsbuch, Band III: Materialien zur Statistik des Deutschen Reiches 1914-1945*, (München: Verlag C. H. Beck, 1978), p. 111. The 1918-1930 data are from Michael Schneider, "Höhen, Krisen und Tiefen: Die Gewerkschaften in der Weimarer Republik 1918 bis 1933," in *Geschichte der deutschen Gewerkschaften. Von den Anfängen bis 1945*, Ulrich Borsdorf, ed.,(Köln: Bund-Verlag, 1987), pp. 324, 371, and 395. The British data are from Department of Employment and Productivity, *British Labour Statistics: Historical Abstract, 1886-1968*, (London: H. M.'s Stationary Office, 1971), Table 196, Membership of Trade Unions, 1892-1968, p. 395.

socialist trade unions, namely the British Trades Union Congress and the German socialist Trade Unions, pushed for evolutionary social reforms within the capitalist context, and shied away from the radical wing of the labor movement and its demands to initiate fundamental changes in industrial relations at the expense of the employers.

The British and German Ministries are the most comparable of labor ministries in terms of both their similarities and differences. No other pairs can match the one I have chosen for this study. The selection is based on a literature review of several labor ministries. The French Labor Ministry and the U.S. Department of Labor during the same period are relatively close to, and therefore not adequate contrasts to, the British case. With similar levels of capacity, they are not ideal cases for the formulation of alternative explanations. Nor are they used to contrast with the German Labor Ministry for two reasons. First, the archival documents of the French Labor Ministry between the wars vanished or were destroyed.[17] Second, the U.S. Department of Labor and the German Ministry cannot be juxtaposed due to several extreme dissimilarities. The U.S. Department was created before the First World War, and the strengths of American organized labor and socialist political parties could not match those found in Weimar Germany.

## The Cases: Maximizing the Differences

This book demonstrates the validity of the contingency theory of state intervention across countries by maximizing the differences between the two cases at hand. Created in 1916 and 1919 respectively, the British and German Labor Ministries differed radically in industrial relations policies, administrative capacity, and historical contexts during the interwar years. As I describe below, the interwar British Labor Ministry is known to have possessed very limited monitoring capacities in industrial relations, whereas the German Labor Ministry stood out as an aggressively interventionist powerhouse. These "weak" and "strong" state agencies seem readily to support a wide range of theories of the state fashioned by pluralists, social democrats, neo-Marxists, corporatists, and statists.

### *The British Labor Ministry: A Featherweight Agency?*

The wartime and interwar British Labor Ministry turned out to be an empty shell, without teeth, disoriented, weak, and ever of little consequence. Pursuing the policy of "self-determination," Labor Ministry officials remained on the sidelines in industrial relations. They played the role of mediator and assisted in the formation of voluntary joint conciliation bodies in the context of a wave of industrial conflicts, unemployment, a strongly felt imperative to return to the economic regime of 1914, pound devaluation, the Treasury's drive to rein in government expenditures, a twelvefold increase in the national debt, loss of markets to Germany and the U.S., and a precipitous decline of the British empire.[18] During the entire interwar period, state intervention was minimized so that employers and organized labor could settle industrial disputes on their own.

The top government leaders of all political stripes had little faith in the agency and belittled the role of labor ministers in British politics and society during the interwar years. In a candid letter to Winston Churchill, Prime Minister Lloyd George voiced his concern about the Ministry's future course: "The organization of the place [Labor Ministry] is very imperfect and there is a lack of grip which is more than ever required during a period of reconstruction. And, machinery apart, the purposes for which the department exists are inevitably so general that acumen and balance of judgement are in a high degree required to prevent developments on lines which may prove *undesirable and even mischievous*."[19] A year after it began functioning, Churchill, then Secretary of War in 1918, questioned the Labor Ministry's existence and had not a single good word for the state agency when Lloyd George asked him to recommend a candidate for the position of labor minister:

> I cannot think of anybody for Labour. I do not myself hold with the existence of such a Ministry. Arbitration and conciliation are the functions of an impartial department like the Board of Trade. Factories etc. are well managed by the Home Office. Labour policy belongs to the government. But since the office has been created and is looked upon as a Ministry of 20 pence for labour men, I cannot see why Roberts shall not continue. He is honest and preachy and loyal.[20]

The Labor Ministry was consistently treated as a "second rate" state agency by the wartime and interwar governments:[21] The Coalition government under Lloyd George (1916-1922), the Conservative governments led by A. Bonar Law (1922-1923) and Stanley Baldwin (1923-1924), the Labour government headed by J. Ramsay MacDonald (1924), the Conservative government of Stanley Baldwin (1924-1929), and the Labour government of J. Ramsay MacDonald (1929-1931). This state of affairs remained unchanged as the Conservative party was in power for most of the period, though sometimes under the guise of Coalition or National governments.

By and large, the Labor Ministry was the product of wartime expediency: it lacked a well-defined mission and had a difficult time finding its rightful place in the British state. Labor ministers and Ministry officials aspired to play an important role in postwar reconstruction and made plans accordingly before the end of the war. However, their efforts were frustrated by "interdepartmental friction," "overlapping," "dual authority,"[22] and the lack of "a fully fledged Ministry."[23] Labor Minister John Hodge complained that Lloyd George's decision to create the Ministry of Reconstruction in August 1917[24] threatened to "do away with much of the *raison d'être* of a Ministry of Labour"[25] and that taking away the industrial side of reconstruction would destroy "the chief objects for which the Ministry of Labour was created." He deplored that behind symbolic trappings, "the Labor Ministry is *not intended to be a reality, but is a mere piece of make-believe.*"[26] The Labor Ministry's officials protested against "the absolutely intolerable position ... of having to surrender part of its staff" and put off its own demobilization plan to an infant agency such as the Ministry of Reconstruction.[27] Hodge also complained about the creation of National Service Department in 1917 to manage the distribution of manpower.[28] In a memorandum to the Prime Minister, he argued that the National Service Department was "clearly less qualified to undertake the work now in question than is the Employment Department [of the Labor Ministry], which alone possesses the necessary staff, premises, and organization."[29] He protested against the proposal to transfer Employment Exchanges to the National Service Department:

> Its transfer to another department would reduce the Ministry of Labour to a mutilated fragment, with no very obvious reason for further existence, and it would further be necessarily regarded as a definite indication that the problems of demobilization, for dealing with which the exchanges are an essential piece of machinery and in which Labour is vitally interested, are not after all to be any concern of the Ministry of Labour .... I should deeply deplore if my advent to office were marked by such a surrender of the legitimate rights of Labour."[30]

The eight labor ministers lacked prestige and political clout in the government circle, were the lowest-paid among cabinet-ranking officials, were looked down upon by most politicians, and held an average tenure of eight months.[31] None of the labor ministers stayed in office long enough to leave his mark on ministerial organization and policy. They came and went at dizzying speed through the cabinet's revolving door (Table 4 and Figure 5). Recruited during the war for the newly created post, the first two former labor leaders turned labor ministers, John Hodge from December 1916 to August 1917, and George H. Roberts from

August 1917 to January 1919, had shown their true conservative colors. Once acting chairman of the Labour party, Hodge held views closer to those of the Conservative party and disliked unofficial strikes. Roberts, a right-wing labor leader of the Typographical Association and supporter of the war, joined the Conservative ranks in 1922.[32] The sixth minister, T. Shaw, a socialist cotton union leader, was a "passage bird," whose short tenure of ten months (January to November 1924) gave him little time to perform his functions in the short-lived first Labour government of Ramsay MacDonald.[33] Shaw could not stand the more progressive and major British labor organization, the Trades Union Congress, which he saw as "suspicious of every reform offered by government and employer" and was "too fast in seeking ultimate ideals (such as nationalization)."[34] The eighth minister, Margaret Bonfield, of working-class origin and chairwoman of the TUC in 1923, was more a pragmatic administrator spurning partisanship than a fervent politician championing labor interests.[35]

The remaining four ministers had Conservative leanings or membership. Robert Horne (January 1919 to March 1920) had, in the words of Harold Butler, "little affection for progressive social policies. His foot instinctively sought the brake rather than the accelerator."[36] Unsurprisingly, after becoming Chancellor of the Exchequer in 1921-1922, Horne went along with the Geddes Committee's recommendations by curtailing the Labor Ministry's conciliation activities. T. J. Macnamara (March 1920 to October 1922), a Coalition Liberal, and Montague Barlow (October 1922 to March 1923) were kindred spirits of their predecessors. The longest-tenured minister (November 1924 to June 1929), Arthur Steel-Maitland, a Conservative social reformer and chairman of the Conservative party from 1910 to 1916, was an ineffective leader and a minor figure in the cabinet. He failed to protect the interests of the Labor Ministry and lost the fight against Winston Churchill, the Conservative party's right wing, and the National Confederation of Employers' Organizations over the measures destined to punish trade unions in the wake of the 1926 General Strike.[37]

In the absence of stable ministerial leadership, civil servants became the dominant voice in the agency.[38] They shaped the views, decisions, and policies of the successive ministers. Their voices were most frequently heard in the archival documents – e. g., W. C. Bridgeman, Parliamentary Secretary; Harold B. Butler, Assistant Secretary; W. W. Henderson, Private Secretary; A. W. Watson, Head of Establishments; Horace J. Wilson, Head of Indus-

*Table 4:* Tenure Lengths and Party Affiliations of British Labor Ministers

| | From | | | To | | | |
| Cabinets | Month | Day | Year | Month | Day | Year | Labor Ministers |
| --- | --- | --- | --- | --- | --- | --- | --- |
| Coalition Gvt. H. Asquith (Liberal) | 5 | 25 | 1915 | 12 | 5 | 1916 | None |
| Coalition Gvt. Lloyd George (Liberal) | 12 | 6 | 1916 | 10 | 19 | 1922 | J. Hodge (Labour) 10 December 1916<br><br>G. Roberts (Labour) 17 August 1917<br><br>R. Horne (Conservative) 10 January 1919<br><br>T. J. Macnamara (Liberal) 19 March 1920 |
| Conservative Gvt. A. Bonar Law | 10 | 23 | 1922 | 5 | 20 | 1923 | Montague-Barlow (Conservative) 31 Oct. 1922 |
| S. Baldwin | 5 | 22 | 1923 | 1 | 22 | 1924 | |
| Labour Gvt.<br><br>J. R. MacDonald | 1 | 22 | 1924 | 11 | 3 | 1924 | T. Shaw (Labour) 22 Jan. 1924 |
| Conservative Gvt. Stanley Baldwin | 11 | 4 | 1924 | 6 | 4 | 1929 | A. Steel-Maitland (Conservative) 6 November 1924 |
| Labour Gvt. J.Ramsay MacDonald | 6 | 5 | 1929 | 8 | 24 | 1931 | Margaret Bondfield 7 June 1929 |

trial Relations Department; and David Shackleton, a former union leader, Permanent Secretary. David Shackleton feared to be seen as biased toward one side at the expense of the other. Horace Wilson outright supported the Treasury's economic and administrative orthodoxy.[39] The Labor Ministry's Permanent Secretary had a wide latitude in the administration of the agency. By special general order from the Labor Minister, David Shackleton assumed the title of Chief Labour Adviser in charge of the formulation and execution of the Labor Ministry's general labor policy as well as

*Figure 5:* Tenure Lengths of British Labor Ministers

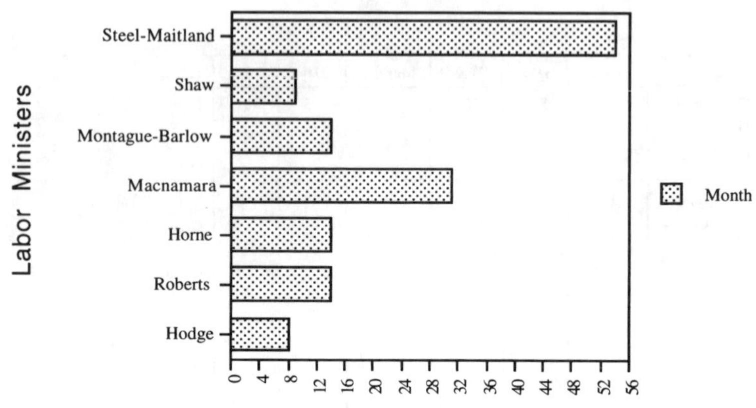


policies on "negotiations ... employment, wages and hours, disputes, Trade Boards, Joint Industrial Councils and industrial organization."[40] Horace Wilson was Permanent Secretary from 1921 to
1930 and became Prime Minister Baldwin's confidant.[41] Shackleton and the other officials reorganized the Labor Ministry, fought
against jurisdictional overlapping with other public agencies (e.g.,
the National Service Department), tried hard to stave off budget
cuts from the Treasury and the Geddes Committee, and resisted
the intruding control of the Treasury over the Ministry's policy-
making. These officials tried in vain to protect their authority in
industrial relations and to safeguard their autonomy from other
state institutions.

*The German Labor Ministry: An Interventionist Stronghold?*

In Weimar Germany, the Labor Ministry was a major beneficiary
of the strong presence of the Social Democratic party. In the aftermath of the First World War and domestic turmoil, the SPD
founded the Weimar Republic in November 1918 and became a
political force to be reckoned with throughout the interwar years.
The SPD was part of every cabinet (except the ones led by Fehrenbach and Cuno) between 1919 and 1923, and its leaders Philipp
Scheidemann, Gustav Bauer, and Herman Müller led the first four
cabinets. Though out of power from 1923 to June 1928, the SPD

nevertheless played a crucial role in politics, as the successive cabinets could not govern without its vote in Parliament. The SPD obtained 100 seats in the parliamentary elections of 4 May 1924, 131 on 7 December 1924, 153 in 1928, and 143 in 1930. The SPD reassumed power between 1928 and 1930 when it won 29.8 percent of the vote and Herman Müller formed the Grand Coalition cabinet with the Catholic Center party, the Democratic party, and the Populist party.

The First World War was a watershed for Germany. Having lost the war, the Wilhelmine monarchy crumbled. A democratic regime emerged in the ruins of military defeat. The interwar period was marked by political and economic crises such as the Kapp putsch of 13 March 1920, war reparations, the hyper-inflation of 1922-1923, the breakdown of collective bargaining in the 1920s, and the rise of conservative power with the onset of the Depression. These contexts profoundly marked politics and society between the two wars. From 1919 to 1923, the Labor Ministry followed the policy of self-determination established by organized labor and employers at the end of the war. Employers and unions joined hands to keep the state out of industrial relations. However, the Labor Ministry became an interventionist powerhouse when it issued the state arbitration decree of 30 October 1923. The decree empowered the Labor Ministry to police industrial relations. The labor minister and his state arbitrators imposed solutions on both parties when they failed to reach an agreement.

The Labor Ministry was unique in its scope and strength of administrative capacity. It had jurisdictions over a vast array of policies – social insurance, veterans' benefits, health insurance, public assistance, pubic housing, labor and child welfare, job creation, and unemployment compensation. Moreover, Articles 7, 9, 151, 157, 161, and 163 of the new Weimar Constitution increased the Labor Ministry's power in the demobilization of defeated troops and postwar reconstruction. Because of the Weimar regime's emphasis on Sozialpolitik, the Labor Ministry carried out social policies that had been denied to organized labor before the collapse of the monarchy. Sozialpolitik, a set of measures to improve the living and working conditions of the working class, was a top priority item on the national political agenda. Labor Minister Heinrich Brauns excluded the Finance and Economy Ministries from labor matters to such an extent that they had to ask for the Labor Ministry's permission before contacting or negotiating with the trade unions – and were allowed to do that, only in the presence of a

Labor Ministry official.[42] The Labor Ministry went beyond its federal duties by taking over the labor responsibilities of the Länder
and Communes and centralizing the administration of regional
affairs. But overcentralization and administrative overload later
forced the Labor Ministry to relieve itself of the duties not essential
to a federal ministry.[43] During the interwar years, the question at
issue for the German Labor Ministry was not overlapping jurisdiction, the Achilles' heel of the British Labor Ministry, but overcentralization and arrogance toward other government agencies.

All the interwar coalition governments, except the presidential
cabinets starting on 30 March 1930, recognized the SPD's strength
in the Reichstag and the importance of trade unions. They
reserved the post of labor minister for former union leaders from
either socialist or Catholic Center camps. From 1919 to 1930, three
were from the Social Democratic party, a pillar of the new republican regime, and two from the Catholic Center party, an indis-
pensable ally in the coalition governments. They were succeeded
by independents when Conservatives seized political power and
set out to dismantle the Labor Ministry's arbitration power from
1930 to 1933.

While the Social Democratic party played a critical role in
founding the Labor Ministry, its labor ministers left no significant
imprint on the state agency or industrial relations policy in the
early postwar years (Table 5 and Figure 6). The instability of the
four coalition governments cut their tenure short. The urgent
needs to rebuild the economy and solve the problems of demobilization limited the capacity of the first four cabinets led by Social
Democratic chancellors to shape industrial relations. Gustav
Bauer, vice-president of the General Commission of the General
Federation of German Trade Unions (ADGB, or socialist Trade
Unions) headed the Labor Ministry for four months in 1919 before
assuming the chancellorship (1919-1920). He had great plans and
promised to carry out a socialist program that would address the
long-standing grievances of the working class.[44] Bauer became
chancellor on 21 June 1919, and this appointment increased the
political significance of the Labor Ministry. Alexander Schlicke,
the socialist leader of the German Iron and Steel Workers' Association (Deutscher Metallarbeiter Verband), had a short tenure in
three successive cabinets (1919-20). In fact, neither Bauer nor
Schlicke in the first four Weimar cabinets had the time or a well
thought-out plan to develop the new state agency.[45] Socialist control of the Labor Ministry lasted only a year and a half, until the

fall of the Müller cabinet in 1920. Heinrich Brauns excepted, the average tenure of Weimar labor ministers was one year.

Heinrich Brauns was the most active labor minister with the longest tenure (25 June 1920 to 12 June 1928). As a radical of the populist, left-wing faction of the Catholic Center party and a leader of the reformist Popular Society for a Catholic Germany, Brauns was an activist priest who led the Catholic labor movement aimed at improving the welfare and working conditions of industrial workers. Brauns's career as Labor Minister started abruptly. He filled the post left vacant by Social Democrats only because the Social Democratic party had declined to join the Fehrenbach cabinet in 1920, and after Chancellor Fehrenbach had secured Bishop Schulte's permission to let Brauns exercise a public function. As Brauns himself explained in 1938: "I was forced to take over the Labor Ministry … as the Social Democrats refused to join the government …. I had to accept the offer because no one could find a suitable Minister and those nominated were rejected by the workers' organizations."[46] Brauns oversaw the passage of the most important pieces of labor legislation of the Weimar Republic, such as the labor exchange and labor court laws, the state arbitration decree, work jurisdiction, the Unemployment Insurance Act of July 1927, and working hours. Unlike his British colleagues, he directed the staff with a heavy hand and had a thorough knowledge of labor and welfare issues. He vigorously thrust the Labor Ministry to the forefront of state arbitration. His stature, authority, and program were unequalled by other German and British labor ministers and civil servants.

Rudolf Wissell (27 June 1928 to 30 March 1930) replaced Brauns in June 1928. He was Social Democratic economy minister in 1919, former state arbitrator under Brauns, and a union bureaucrat who advocated planned economy. Ironically, this Social Democratic labor minister presided over the decline of the Labor Ministry. While defending the state arbitration system against employers' attacks,[47] Wissell was unable to keep the Labor Ministry's authority in industrial relations intact. Wissell and the other socialist labor ministers never counted for much in the development and strengthening of ministerial capacities. They came and went, leaving few traces on the organizational make-up and policy orientations of the new Ministry.

The fall of the Müller cabinet in 1928 and the emergence of presidential cabinets allowed conservatives to choose labor ministers subservient to the policies of Chancellor Heinrich Brüning,

**Table 5:** Tenure Lengths and Party Affiliations of German Labor Ministers

| Cabinet | Coalition | From | | | To | | | Minister | Party |
|---|---|---|---|---|---|---|---|---|---|
| | | Month | Day | Year | Month | Day | Year | | |
| Philip Scheidemann SPD | Weimar Coalition: SPD+DDP +Zentrum | 2 | 15 | 1919 | 6 | 20 | 1919 | Gustav Bauer | SPD |
| Gustav Bauer I SPD | Same as above | 6 | 30 | 1919 | 10 | 3 | 1919 | Alexander Schlicke | SPD |
| Gustav Bauer II SPD | Same as above | 10 | 3 | 1919 | 3 | 26 | 1920 | Alexander Schlicke | SPD |
| Hermann Müller I SPD | Same as above | 3 | 26 | 1920 | 6 | 20 | 1920 | Alexander Schlicke | SPD |
| Constantin Fehrenbach Zentrum | Bourgeois Coalition: DDP+ Zentrum+ DVP | 6 | 20 | 1920 | 5 | 4 | 1921 | Heinrich Brauns | Zentrum |
| Joseph Wirth I Zentrum | Weimar Coalition: SPD+DDP +Zentrum | 5 | 9 | 1921 | 10 | 22 | 1921 | Heinrich Brauns | Zentrum |
| Joseph Wirth II Zentrum | Weimar Coalition: SPD+DDP +Zentrum | 10 | 26 | 1921 | 11 | 13 | 1922 | Heinrich Brauns | Zentrum |
| Wilhelm Cuno Independent | Bourgeois Coalition: DDP+ Zentrum+ DVP | 11 | 22 | 1922 | 8 | 12 | 1923 | Heinrich Brauns | Zentrum |
| Gustav Stresemann DVP | Grand Coalition: SPD+DDP +Zentrum+ DVP | 8 | 13 | 1923 | 10 | 2 | 1923 | Heinrich Brauns | Zentrum |

## Table 5 Continued

| Cabinet | Coalition | From | | | To | | | Minister | Party |
|---------|-----------|-------|-----|------|-------|-----|------|----------|-------|
| | | Month | Day | Year | Month | Day | Year | | |
| Gustav Stresemann DVP | Bourgeois Coalition: DDP+ Zentrum+ DVP | 10 | 6 | 1923 | 11 | 23 | 1923 | Heinrich Brauns | Zentrum |
| Wilhelm Marx I Zentrum | Same as above | 12 | 1 | 1923 | 1 | 15 | 1925 | Heinrich Brauns | Zentrum |
| Hans Luther I Independent | Right Coalition: Zentrum+ DVP+ DNVP | 1 | 15 | 1925 | 12 | 5 | 1925 | Heinrich Brauns | Zentrum |
| Hans Luther II Independent | Bourgeois Coalition: DDP+ Zentrum+ DVP | 1 | 20 | 1926 | 5 | 12 | 1926 | Heinrich Brauns | Zentrum |
| Wilhelm Marx II Zentrum | Same as above | 5 | 17 | 1926 | 12 | 17 | 1926 | Heinrich Brauns | Zentrum |
| Wilhelm Marx III Zentrum | Same as above | 1 | 29 | 1927 | 6 | 12 | 1928 | Heinrich Brauns | Zentrum |
| Hermann Müller II SPD | Grand Coalition: SPD+DDP +Zentrum+ DVP | 6 | 28 | 1928 | 3 | 27 | 1930 | Rudolf Wissell | SPD |
| Heinrich Brüning I & II Zentrum | Presidential Cabinet | 3 | 30 | 1930 | 5 | 30 | 1932 | Adam Stegerwald | Zentrum |
| Franz von Papen Zentrum | Presidential Cabinet | 6 | 2 | 1932 | 12 | 2 | 1932 | Hugo Schäffer | None |
| Kurt von Schleicher Independent | Presidential Cabinet | 12 | 2 | 1932 | 1 | 30 | 1933 | Friedrich Syrup | None |

*Note*: There were 19 governments between 13 February 1919 and 28 January 1933; they lasted 8.5 months on average.

*Figure 6:* Tenure Lengths of German Labor Ministers

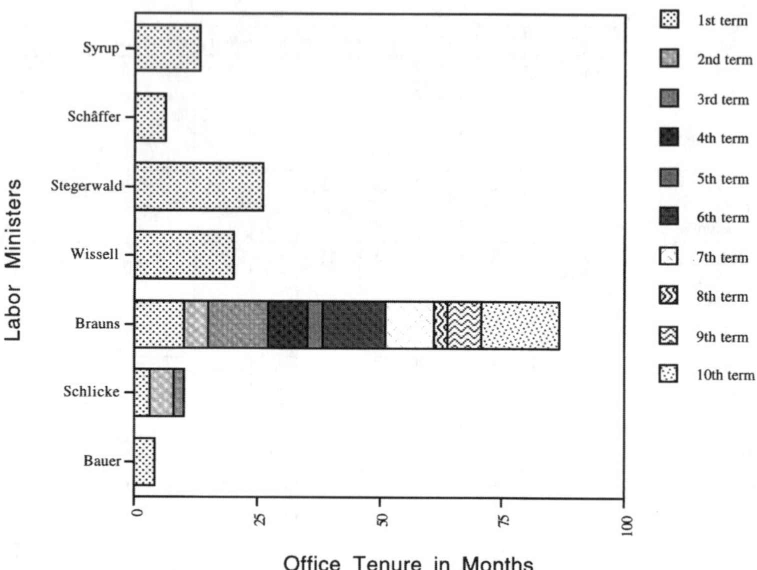



Franz von Papen, and Kurt von Schleicher. Adam Stegerwald, a Catholic Center labor minister, played no significant role, despite his 26-month stint (30 March 1930 to 2 June 1932) at the Labor Ministry. He was succeeded by two independents, Hugo Schäffer and Friedrich Syrup, who lost all semblance of independence in the last years of the Weimar Republic.

The following three chapters demonstrate that despite differences in culture and the power of key actors, the British and German Labor Ministries responded to contingencies in a similar way. Certain contingencies are crucial in explaining policy shifts. The task is to ascertain the conditions under which a political process became ascendant and shaped the policy outcomes of the British and German Labor Ministries. My goal is to explain changes in the state's boundaries and actions and their outcomes within and across cases in greater historical detail. More precisely, I look for the historical conditions under which the state established labor departments, allowed organized labor to reorient industrial relations policies, strengthened employers' leverage in industrial disputes, and facilitated state managers' pursuit of geopolitical objectives at the expense of industrial relations policy.

# Notes

1. Morris Zelditch, "Intelligible Comparisons," in *Comparative Methods in Sociology*, ed. I. Vallier (Berkeley: University of California Press, 1971), pp. 267-307; Victoria E. Bonnell, "The Uses of Theory, Concepts and Comparison in Historical Sociology," *Comparative Studies in Society and History* 22, 2, (1980), pp. 164-166; Theda Skocpol, "Emerging Agendas and Recurrent Strategies in Historical Sociology," in *Vision and Method in Historical Sociology*, ed. Theda Skocpol (Cambridge: Cambridge University Press, 1984), pp. 356-390; Adam Przeworski and Henry Teune, *The Logic of Comparative Social Inquiry* (New York: Wiley, 1970); and Charles Ragin, *The Comparative Method: Moving Beyond Qualitative and Quantitative Strategies* (Berkeley: University of California Press, 1987).

2. Charles Tilly, *Coercion, Capital, and European States, AD 990-1992* (Cambridge: Blackwell Publishers, 1992), p. 33.

3. Charles Maier, *Recasting Bourgeois Europe: Stabilization in France, Germany, and Italy in the Decade after WWI* (Princeton: Princeton University Press, 1975), p. 582.

4. Michael Schneider, "Höhen, Krisen und Tiefen: Die Gewerkschaften in der Weimarer Republik, 1918 bis 1933," in *Geschichte der deutschen Gewerkschaften von den Anfängen bis 1945*, ed. Ulrich Borsdorf (Köln: Bund-Verlag, 1987), p. 346.

5. James E. Cronin, *The Politics of State Expansion: War, State, and Society in Twentieth-Century Britain* (New York: Routledge, 1991).

6. James E. Cronin, "Labour Insurgency and Class Formation: Comparative Perspectives on the Crisis of 1917-1920 in Europe," *Social Science History* 4, (1980), p. 128.

7. Trevor Barnes, "Special Branch and the First Labour Government," *Historical Journal* 22, 4, (1979), p. 950.

8. Alan Fox, *History and Heritage: The Social Origins of British Industrial Relations System* (London: Allen & Unwin, 1985), pp. 292.

9. Eric L. Wigham, *Strikes and the Government, 1893-1981* (London: Macmillan, 1982), p. 66.

10. Colin Crouch, *Industrial Relations and European State Traditions* (Oxford: Clarendon Press, 1993), p. 153.

11. F 27/6/15.

12. F 27/6/25, 19 September 1919.

13. Lab 2, 212/11, 28 June 1917.

14. Quoted in Bentley B. Gilbert, *British Social Policy, 1914-1939* (Ithaca: Cornell University Press, 1970), p. 5.

15. John D. Stephens, *The Transition from Capitalism to Socialism* (New Jersey: Humanities Press, 1980), pp. 115-116.

16. Michael Schneider, "Höhen, Krisen und Tiefen: Die Gewerkschaften in der Weimarer Republik, 1918 bis 1933," in *Geschichte der deutschen Gewerkschaften von den Anfängen bis 1945*, ed. Ulrich Borsdorf (Köln: Bund-Verlag, 1987), pp. 324, 371, and 395. The British data are from the Department of Employment and Productivity, *British Labour Statistics: Historical Abstract, 1886-1968* (London: H. M.'s Stationary Office, 1971), Table 196, p. 395. Britain and Germany shared many similarities, as Sidney Pollard points out. See his analysis, "The Trade Union and the Depression of 1929-1933," in *Industrielles System und poli-*

*tische Entwicklung in der Weimarer Republik*, eds. Hans Mommsen, Dietmar Petzina, and Bernd Weisbrod (Düsseldorf: Droste Verlag, 1974), pp. 237-248.

17.  Jean-André Tournerie, *Le Ministère du Travail: origines et premiers développements* (Paris: Editions Cujas, 1971), pp. 11-12.

18.  Eric Hobsbawm, *Industry and Empire: From 1750 to the Present Day* (London: Penguin Books, 1990), pp. 207-224.

19.  F 9/2/22, 31 March 1920, pp. 302-303, italics mine.

20.  F 8/2/49, 26 December 1918.

21.  V. L. Allen, *Trade Unions and the Government* (London: Butler & Tanner Ltd., 1960), p. 63.

22.  Lab 2 212/18, pp. 5-7.

23.  Lab 2 212/9, 7 November 1917, p. 8.

24.  Lab 2 212/ML 1367/6, pp. 1-2. Lloyd George directed the Labor Ministry to provide personnel and assistance to the new Minister of Reconstruction by virtue of the New Ministries Bill in August 1917. These instructions were included in a Lloyd George's letter to the Labor Minister.

25.  Lab 2 212/18, 30 May 1917, p. 2.

26.  Lab 2 213/5, 20 August 1917, italics mine.

27.  Lab 2 212/ML 1367/6, 2 August 1917.

28.  Lab 2 242/Ml 1105, 19 January 1917.

29.  F 27/5/4, 23 July 1917.

30.  Lab 2 213/5, 20 August 1917.

31.  Rodney Lowe, *Adjusting to Democracy: The Role of the Ministry of Labor in British Politics, 1916-1939* (Oxford: Clarendon Press, 1986), p. 53.

32.  Ibid., p. 28.

33.  I found few traces of T. Shaw's archives at the Public Record Office in London. But the absence of papers of the first Labour Government does not mean that it did not have a policy.

34.  Rodney Lowe, *Adjusting to Democracy*, p. 85.

35.  A description of these labor ministers can be found in Ibid., pp. 28-36.

36.  Harold Butler, *The Confident Morning* (London: Faber & Faber, 1950), p. 141.

37.  Rodney Lowe, *Adjusting to Democracy*, p. 33.

38.  V. L. Allen, *Trade Unions and the Government*, p. 63 and Rodney Lowe, *Adjusting to Democracy*, p. 242.

39.  Rodney Lowe, *Adjusting to Democracy*, pp. 63-64.

40.  Lab 2 1718/CEB 186/3/1920.

41.  Max Beloff, "The Whitehall Factor: The Role of the Higher Civil Service, 1918-39," in *The Politics of Reappraisal*, eds. G. Peele and C. Cook (London: Macmillan, 1975), p. 212.

42.  Uwe Oltmann, "Reichsarbeitsminister Heinrich Brauns in der Staats—und Währungskrise von 1923/24: Die Bedeutung der Sozialpolitik für die Inflation, den Ruhrkampf und die Stabilisierung," Dissertation (Kiel, 1968), p. 53.

43.  Martha Driessen, *Die Entwicklung der Reichsarbeitsbehörden, 1919-1924*, (Köln, 1932), p. 13.

44.  Ernst Deuerlin, "Heinrich Brauns – Schattenriß eines Sozialpolitikers," in *Staat, Wirtschaft und Politik in der Weimarer Republik: Festschrift für Heinrich Brüning*, eds. Ferdinand A. Hermens and Theodor Schieder (Berlin: Duncker und Humboldt, 1967), p. 82.

45.  Hubert Mockenhaupt, *Weg und Wirken des Geistlichen Sozialpolitikers Heinrich Brauns* (München: Verlag Ferdinand Schöningh, 1977), p. 166.

46. Hubert Mockenhaupt, *Heinrich Brauns*, p. 162.

47. Gerald D. Feldman and Imgard Steinisch, "Notwendigkeit und Grenzen sozialstaatlicher Intervention: Eine vergleichende fallstudie des Ruhreisenstreits in Deutschland und des Generalstreits in Großbritannien," *Archiv für Sozialgeschichte* 20. Bd., (1980), p. 99.

# Chapter Three

# The First World War, Postwar Reconstruction, and the Pluralist States

For decades before the First World War, the British and German states were hostile to the working-class demand for a centralized, cabinet-ranking Labor Ministry and for greater influence on industrial relations policy. During these prewar years, trade unions and socialist political parties tried in vain to use their numerical and political strengths to press for the creation of a labor department. Conventional theories of the state argue that policy-making is the result of stronger groups such as the working class, socialist political parties, capitalists, or state managers. In this chapter, I intend to show that two contingencies and their effects on the balance of power, rather than the actors' strengths, compelled the state to establish a centralized labor ministry and to pursue a postwar industrial relations policy in favor of organized labor. The first contingency, the First World War, swept away all obstacles to institutional innovation. The second contingency, postwar reconstruction, strengthened the increasing influence of organized labor. Under these two conditions, the British and German Labor Ministries became pluralist mirrors, reflecting the desires of trade unions above all, and those of employers to pursue free collective bargaining without government interference.

---

Notes for this chapter begin on page 82.

## Organized Labor and the Prewar Struggles for a Labor Ministry

Relatively speaking, labor departments are newcomers in the history of states. Centralized, cabinet-ranking agencies specialized in labor affairs emerged only in the twentieth century: in 1906 for France, in 1913 for the United States, in 1916 for Britain, and in 1919 for Germany, to name a few. Historically, their belated appearance is connected to industrialization and the concomitant rise of the working class as a political force in capitalist economies. Changed and changing demographics, urbanization, the ravages wrought by capitalism on workers, and the persistent and pressing calls of social reformers all converged to force the political elite to reconceptualize the traditional functions of the government, and eventually to recognize that it would no longer be possible to leave organized labor out of the realm of public administration. In response to these changes, the hard-pressed governments had legislation passed to protect workers from employers' abuses. They started instituting labor agencies within existing departments or ministries. But, throughout the nineteenth century and until the early twentieth century, there existed nearly insurmountable obstacles to the creation of centralized labor ministries with cabinet status. However, as the labor movement kept on with its pressures, and as the socioeconomic and political influence of organized workers became more and more irresistible in industrialized countries, the national political leadership had no choice but to accede to some of the demands, including the demand for a labor department.

For decades prior to the First World War, the British and German collectivist trade-union leaders and socialist political parties campaigned for a centralized, cabinet-ranking labor ministry. In their view, such a state agency would achieve important goals of the labor movement. A centralized labor ministry would regulate working conditions equitably and more efficiently than decentralized agencies dispersed within existing departments or ministries. A cabinet-ranking labor minister would represent workers in a pro-employer state and truly reflect the concerns of the working class.

Many attempts were made to establish such a beachhead in the government in both countries. Since the 1800s, the British Labour party and collectivist trade-union leaders envisioned a centralized labor agency to administer unemployment programs, regulate working conditions, consult labor opinion, and nationalize the economy.[1] The Labour party's 1903 electoral platform included a centralized labor ministry. Ben Tillett, leader of the Dockers' union and a notable advocate of new unionism (a more militant kind of movement to form general industrial unions), advocated government assistance and labor representation in the state. Ernest Bevin, the Trades Union Congress president, urged the creation of a labor ministry with full cabinet rank as early as 1905. Sidney and Beatrice Webb, the leading theorists of the Labour party, proposed greater coercive power for the state in industrial relations and a labor ministry to serve as a center for employment exchanges.[2] The TUC reaffirmed Bevin's draft resolution again in September 1915.[3] Ernest Bevin saw the labor ministry as an agency gathering data on the number of employed and unemployed, regulating factories, administering exchanges and registration agencies, directing a National Department of Industrial Arbitration and Conciliation, and a Labour Legal Department dealing with "Trade Union law … and all Acts affecting the industrial life of the workers." Bevin pointed out the advantages of such a centralized ministry: "Delegates will know the difficulty we experience in going to one Department after another in regard to our interests. We often have to end up where we began, before we can get all our wants attended to."[4]

In Germany, the idea of a centralized, cabinet-ranking labor department was first suggested by an academic in 1871[5] and then advocated by the Social Democratic party. In 1877, the SPD's Fritzsche-Bebel bill proposed a labor protection agency within the Health Department as a means to boost state presence in industries. In 1885, Social Democrats escalated their parliamentary struggle for an Office of Labor. The Grillenberger-Bebel bill intended to centralize the administration of all labor matters, to collect statistics on the working class[6] and manage employer-labor relations, in a single agency with a status equal to that of the Health Department or the Insurance Department. Similar in substance, the Pachnicke-Rösicke bill was reintroduced on 12 December 1898.

However, the creation of a labor ministry remained the object of struggles among the tripartite actors in industrial relations until the First World War. The state adamantly opposed the institutional innovation proposed by collectivist trade-union leaders, the British Labour party, and the German Social Democratic party. The political elite of both countries considered a centralized, cabinet-ranking labor ministry as envisioned by the labor movement to be a threat to propertied interests and their associated political power.

The British Parliament torpedoed all efforts to realize the idea of a centralized, cabinet-ranking labor department. Conservatives and Liberals in Parliament killed off a series of fifteen bills that proposed a labor ministry, combining the function of labor with either those of commerce or those of the relief of destitution.[7] In 1892, by promoting the legal recognition of trade unions, Prime Minister William Gladstone dismissed Liberal reformers' novel but "progressive" idea of a labor department to monitor an increasingly important area of economic life and the problem of unemployment. The 1894 Minority Reports of the Royal Commission on Labour made a similar proposal, but nothing came of it.[8] The Webbs' proposal in the 1909 Minority Report of the Poor Law Commission withered and died quietly, and the 1904 and 1908 amendments to the Royal Address to Parliament to set up such an organization were aborted.[9]

The most vigorous opposition to the idea of a labor ministry came from the major center of labor policy-making: the Labour Department of the Board of Trade (BOT). The Board's Labour Department articulated employers' fear that a cabinet-ranking labor department would intensify class struggles. In the name of impartiality, Llewellyn Smith, trade unionist turned Commissioner for Labour at the BOT, and his colleagues advocated a ministry that combined commerce and labor in the 1890s. They argued that a pro-union labor minister would be biased toward the working class, distort industrial policy, and damage "the free market individualism of the Board of Trade."[10] Conflicts would inevitably arise in the cabinet between "a Minister of Labour supposed to stand for the 'labour' side of each economic question and a Minister of Commerce taking the other side." As Smith put it very succinctly, the idea of a labor minister with a separate ministry was "unsound."[11] Smith's opinion carried great weight. It was better, so the argument ran, that several departments managed the interests of the working class, for the combined influence of several ministers and their views "are likely to carry greater weight because they represent in a way the nation as a whole." A centralized ministry would be suspected of class bias: "A Minister of Labour would represent the views of a class and his representation would necessarily be somewhat discounted by this fact."[12] On Smith's advice, the government kept the decentralized structure.

In Germany, the government's perception of a threat posed by the rising and increasingly influential German Social Democratic party and trade unions caused it to stifle efforts to reform labor administration. Between 1910 to 1917, the bourgeois-conservative majority at the Reichstag killed off or rebuffed a series of Social Democratic bills for an Office of Labor, or Reichsarbeitsamt (RAA).[13] While recognizing trade unions at the height of the war, the embattled monarchy ignored the continuing call of the Social Democratic party, the largest party in the Reichstag, for an RAA within the Department of Interior in spring 1917.

The Wilhelmine monarchy adopted repression as the centerpiece of its industrial relations policy.[14] To fight workers' struggles for political inclusion, the Anti-Socialist Law from October 1878 to January 1890 banned associations, meetings, and publications associated with the Social Democratic party, and restricted the rights of trade unions. Even after the repeal of the law in 1890, the regime denied official recognition to trade unions and paid only lip service to an 1890 royal decree "to allow for workers' participation in solution of common concerns in the negotiations with employers and state agencies and in the protection of their interests."[15] As the Labor Ministry's official memoir later pointed out: "But no actions ever followed these words. Not once did state agencies act on this royal decree."[16] The Imperial Department of Interior managed trade and social policies besides its other domestic functions, chiefly police and repressive duties, and buttressed employers' absolute authority in workplaces. The State Ministries of Interior protected employers and strike-breakers from strikers. Police harassed the SPD and socialist Trade Unions' meetings, blacklisted and arrested union activists, dispersed picket lines, and encouraged business to dismiss union members.[17] Employers used blacklists and lockouts, set up pro-employer work associations, and refused to negotiate with the three major trade unions – the socialist Trade Unions, the Liberal Hirsch-Duncker Unions, and the Christian Trade Unions. With the help of strongly repressive laws, the Supreme Court of the Reich curtailed trade union activities and excluded the unions from policy formulation. The monarchy harshly repressed strikes, such as the Ruhr miners strike of 1912, and emphasized containment to stem the tide of anti-capitalist labor movement before the onset of the First World War. Along with other public policies,[18] industrial relations policy was aligned with the interests of capitalists. The Imperial government could not tolerate a "progressive" institution, one that recognized industrial relations as a legitimate area of government administration and labor issues as worthwhile.

Nevertheless, while the legislation for a labor agency languished for years in Parliament, the executive branch became more receptive to the idea when the Ministry of Interior saw the need to lessen its workload, overburdened by the war. The Ministry of Interior combined all the functions of an Interior Ministry, Labor Ministry, and Economy Ministry. It had traditionally administered all labor affairs and had earned a reputation as "the Monster," "the Mammoth Organization," and "the Political Octopus" ("Wasserkopf") for its management of three vast domains: internal security, economy, and social policy. Despite the urgent need for bureaucratic reforms, the government rejected the SPD's renewed call for an RAA within the Ministry of Interior in spring 1917, and, instead, decided to create a Federal Economy Department (Reichswirtschaftsamt, or RWA) that would deal with both economic and social policies.[19] The RWA briefly exercised its functions until the RAA was finally set up by the reformists in 1918.

Both the British and German states preferred to stem the tide of workers' challenges by carrying out important reforms to improve workers' living and working conditions. Ruling the country with an iron hand and political astuteness, Otto von Bismarck established the first social insurance system in the world to coopt workers into the Wilhelmine regime and to undermine working-class organizations such as the mutualist funds, the SPD, and trade unions.[20] Reforms such as accident insurance, sickness insurance, and old-age pensions were legislated by 1887.[21] Britain initiated social insurance through a coalition forged between the Liberal government of Lloyd George and the Labour party. Though advances were made in welfare and working conditions, the issue of a centralized, cabinet-ranking labor ministry remained a dead letter till the outbreak of the Great War.

## The First World War and the Emergence of Labor Ministries

The First World War abruptly changed the balance of power among state managers, employers, and workers in Britain. Military mobilization and armaments production forced the British government to increase its reliance on the working class and to change its industrial relations policy. In May 1915, the government appointed Arthur Henderson as its Labour Adviser with a seat in the cabinet to oversee industrial disputes. However, Henderson, a

Labour party man, was "unhelpful" in conciliation and arbitration due to the existence of many departments dealing with labor. As the war dragged on, Prime Minister Lloyd George hastily set up the Labor Ministry in December 1916 in return for working-class support for the war and the formation of a coalition government of national unity. Thanks to the First World War, the Labour party obtained a unique opportunity to bargain from a position of strength. Representing his party, Arthur Henderson demanded a labor minister's seat in the war cabinet for the Labour party, a labor ministry that would consolidate the labor agencies of the Board of Trade and the Ministry of Munitions,[22] and nationalization of the mines and shipping industry.[23] The Labour party saw the chance to serve "the national interests and the possibility of Labour securing a greater opportunity to mould policy and exercise authority in important administrative positions."[24] A sizeable minority within the party ranks refused to participate in a Liberal bourgeois government, but party leaders ignored the dissenting voices. According to George Askwith, a high-ranking government official, "the Ministry of Labour was settled in a few minutes, or even less, when Mr. Lloyd George heard the conditions under which the Labour party would be prepared to support him politically."[25]

In Germany, the Wilhelmine monarchy made concessions to the working class during the war, but the centralized, cabinet-ranking Labor Ministry emerged only with military defeat and the creation of the Weimar democracy. As in Britain, the demands of the First World War for personnel and materials forced the monarchy to adjust its industrial relations in favor of trade unions. The military realized that a labor office was needed to deal with food problems and mobilization of workers in war and military production. Faced with dwindling human and material resources after 1916, Carl Duisberg, a captain of the chemical industry, supported the plan, and the League of German industrialists petitioned for such a state agency.[26]

In these circumstances, trade unions wrested several concessions from the government. To obtain labor support for the war and total mobilization of labor reserves, the War Office led by General Wilhelm Groener allowed elections of trade-union representatives to the workers' committees in factories. The government passed the Auxiliary Service Act of 5 December 1916, which radically altered the relationships between organized labor and the state. The law recognized trade unions, required employers to negotiate with trade-union leaders as the sole representatives of their workers, introduced wage contracts into Germany's industrial relations, and rescinded the industrial code protecting strike-breakers in March 1918.[27] But the monarchy stopped short of creating a labor department and enacting the Labor Law demanded by organized labor.[28]

The prospects of a military defeat accelerated institutional change in Germany. The new chancellor, Max von Baden, who was charged by the military with negotiating an armistice with the Allied forces in late summer and fall of 1918, launched a spate of reforms to save the monarchy from collapse. Chancellor von Baden created the Imperial Office of Labor within the Department of Interior on 4 October 1918, a month before the Armistice on 11 November 1918.[29] The RAA was a political formula used to coopt prominent socialist politicians into the parliamentary monarchy and to satisfy a persistent demand of the Social Democratic party, which had claimed the post of State Secretary for the Reich Office of Labor. Gustav Bauer, vice-president of the General Commission of the socialist Trade Unions, was appointed to the post of the Labor Office's state secretary. Philipp Scheidemann took the post of minister without portfolio.[30] The bourgeois-conservative parties opposed the inclusion of socialists,[31] but, as Vice-Chancellor von Payer argued, the RAA was a last-ditch attempt to pacify the working class and a solution to the outsized functions of the Reich Economy Office of the Department of Interior.

However, the timing of the creation of the two Labor Ministries meant that the government and organized labor used the newly created agencies to advance their own immediate political goals, rather than to effect changes in industrial relations. Lloyd George conceived a "real Ministry of Labour,"[32] created "without protracted preliminary inquiries or planning,"[33] as merely a means to incorporate the working class in military mobilization. It was not intended to be a vehicle to promote the welfare of the working class or to advance new social policies. Lloyd George railroaded the New Ministries and Secretaries Act through Parliament and instructed two of his men – W. G. S. Adams, Secretary to the Prime Minister and Editor of War cabinet Reports from 1916 to 1918, and Alfred Zimmern, a professor of international politics[34] – to work on the transfer of labor-related departments and their duties from the Board of Trade to the Labor Ministry. Besides the transfer, "no details were arranged,"[35] and officials skipped the necessary step of consulting with organized labor on the organization of the new Labor Ministry.

Discord among trade-union leaders over the Labor Ministry's functions prevented the Labour party from exerting any influence on its organization. As a whole, trade-union leaders were divided on the issue of a labor ministry and resisted any further interference in collective bargaining. While collectivist trade-union leaders sought greater participation in government affairs, syndicalist leaders feared that the Labor Ministry would drastically curtail the political and economic power of their trade unions and would subject them to coercive regulations.[36] Thus, J. H. Thomas, General Secretary of the National Union of Railwaymen, a popular and shrewd union leader, passed up the chance to mold a new ministry when Lloyd George offered him the job of labor minister. Thomas did not consider the opportunity a worthwhile one in the promotion of working-class interests. He responded that he "could render more assistance to the nation and also the best interests of labour ... by remaining outside the Ministry [of Labour]."[37] Thereupon, Lloyd George appointed a conservative Labourite trade-union leader, John Hodge, to that position and chose a moderate union bureaucrat, David Shackleton, a former president of the Trades Union Congress, as Permanent Secretary. The Labour party was more interested in getting a seat in the cabinet than in shaping industrial relations policy through the control of the Labor Ministry. It turned out that the labor movement's call for a labor department was, as Lowe states, merely "a political slogan designed to draw the attention to a particular grievance rather than a serious attempt to adapt the machinery of government to new responsibilities."[38]

The discredited German monarchy used the Imperial Office of Labor to accommodate the representation needs of the SPD politicians and trade-union leaders, giving itself a facelift in the transition to a postwar political order. As a conservative sarcastically pointed out, in the rush to build a coalition, the government offered "new positions ... for the leaders of political parties.... One does not look for people for the posts, but the posts for the people."[39] Indeed, the Imperial Office of Labor represented a desperate attempt to muster Social Democratic support for a transitional government, to rein in the revolutionary impulse of workers and soldiers alike, and to gain credibility at the negotiating table with the Allies: "The new government must appear to the outside world as having essentially acquired a face other than that of the old regime, which did not gain the trust of foreign government and that of our foes.... It is a must to include in the government the prominent personalities from various political factions."[40]

The issue of Social Democratic participation in a repressive regime drove a wedge between collectivists and syndicalists in Germany. Gustav Bauer urged his colleagues to take up positions in the government and to run economic and social affairs. Yet, his fellow trade-union leaders, Carl Legien, president of the socialist Trade Unions, and Theodore Leipart, adamantly disagreed with him. Syndicalist in belief, they disapproved of Bauer's unequivocal commitment to state intervention. Legien even threatened to resign in this bitter dispute over ideological differences; the socialist Trade Unions refused to let Bauer return to his trade-union post after he had lost his government position in 1920.[41] The controversies were more ideological than practical. Indeed, the RAA was essentially a means to pacify the working class. Labor Secretary Bauer lacked any broader mandate to initiate reforms. He worked on orderly transition to a postwar order and demobilization and took on the minor duties of gathering information on matters such as strikes, lockouts, and working-class conditions in major cities.[42] The RAA was short-lived, as the old regime collapsed in November 1918.

The November revolution of 1918 swept the monarchy away and opened a new era in industrial relations. Initiated by the revolt of sailors on 3-5 November 1918 in Kiel, the socialist revolution and formation of soldiers' and workers' councils brought the Social Democratic party to power. Friedrich Ebert proclaimed the Weimar Republic and became its first president on 9 November 1918. In the wake of the radical changes in the political system, the centralized German Labor Ministry with full cabinet rank emerged on 10 February 1919. The war fostered a consensus on the need of a labor department, and it became a reality as a result of changes in regime – from authoritarian monarchy to constitutional monarchy to democratic republic. The Social Democrats and trade unions had taken 41 years to resolve the "issue of the creation of a social agency … as old as the German Empire"[43] and to put a Social Democrat, Gustav Bauer, in charge of the centralized, cabinet-ranking Labor Ministry of the Weimar Republic.

Unlike the monarchy, the Social Democratic government set out to implement its Sozialpolitik, a set of legal safeguards and insurance plans designed to protect and improve workers' conditions and to strengthen the Social Democratic hold on the labor movement against Bolshevik and anarchist groups. The Weimar Labor

Ministry became an antidote to anything resembling the soldiers' and workers' councils, the Spartacus uprisings, and military repression of January 1919. However, as will be shown below, economic reconstruction and demobilization prevented the Social Democratic government from realizing its socialist goals, not to mention having its Labor Ministry introduce radical changes in industrial relations.

In sum, the First World War shifted industrial relations policy in favor of organized labor. The state and employers were forced to make concessions since the conduct of the war relied on workers' cooperation in warfare and armaments production. The war and postwar reconstruction elevated organized labor into a major political force. Trade-union membership doubled in Britain, from four million in 1913 to eight million in 1919, and dramatically increased in Germany, from three million in 1918 to seven million in 1919. The British state promulgated the Representation of the People Act in 1918, which enfranchised the working class, enlarged the electorate from five-and-a-half to 21 million, and granted suffrage to nine million women.[44] German workers not only gained full political rights, but also dominated German politics through the socialist Trade Unions and the Social Democratic party.

## Reconstruction and Labor Power in Industrial Relations

While the First World War increased the bargaining power of organized labor, postwar reconstruction was a crucial contingency that compelled the British and German Labor Ministries to incarnate some essentials of a "pluralist" state. Trade unions became a major player in the shaping of postwar industrial relations policies and, because of their hold on the workforce and central role in the rebuilding of the economy, were able to forcefully eschew strong state initiatives.

### Britain: Syndicalism and Self-Determination

An unprecedented wave of labor militancy bolstered the bargaining power of trade unions vis-à-vis the British government. With the end of the war and decontrol of the labor market, workers aggressively protested against the hardships endured during the war. The British rank-and-file movements among munitions, engineering, shipbuilding, and railway workers staged wildcat strikes. Drawing their inspiration from the successful 1917 revolution in Russia and revolutionary insurrections in Berlin, Munich, and Budapest, they agitated for changes in the economic system.[45] Discontent grew as unemployment reached two million in June 1921. Industrial strikes in both the public and private sectors and the police strike alarmed the government. During the railway strike of September-October 1919, Prime Minister Lloyd George told the Railway Executive Committee that there were "plenty of troops available" against workers who "were working for a complete change in the social order," and that "the strike really amounted to civil war." He would mobilize the country "to support the Government in resisting the attempt made by Cramp [a union leader] and his fellows to destroy the whole fabric of society."[46] Lloyd George contemplated "us[ing] machine guns and drop[ping] bombs"[47] in the 1919-1921 miners strikes. A civil war psychosis prevailed.[48]

Faced with a surge of strikes, the Lloyd George government proposed a system of compulsory arbitration that would allow the Industrial Courts to make collective bargaining awards and to enforce the Courts' awards to the parties involved, making them legally binding on industry.[49] The government further promised to make collective agreements legally binding on unorganized employers (as in Germany) if the Trades Union Congress would accept binding arbitration; a kind of statist or structural neo-Marxist labor regime seemed to be in the offing.

However, organized labor used its new-found strength to decisively reject the government's plan to preserve the wartime system of wage arbitration. Trade unions and Labour party representatives rejected binding arbitration and restrictions on the right to strike. Trade-union leaders never had faith in the state machinery.[50] They preferred to rely on their own networks of unions, self-help societies, and the Labour party to press for improved pay and working conditions. From the vantage point of guild-socialism, the Labor Ministry was a means to solve the pressing issue of unemployment, not to step up state intervention in industrial disputes. The syndicalist leaders kept the Labor Ministry at arm's length and never came to its defense when the Treasury and the Geddes Committee cut its programs and budget. Labor Minister T. J. Macnamara conceded that his power was limited by the staunch opposition of the Trades Union Congress, which particularly underscored its independence from state arbitration:

Under the Industrial Courts Act where the Ministry of Labor has power in certain circumstances to institute a Court of Inquiry without the consent of the disputing parties, the element of compulsion was regarded *with such suspicion* that report of the Court takes only the nature of a recommendation and is not an award. Trades Union Congresses have repeatedly defeated resolution in favor of some measure of compulsion. The attitudes of both capitalists and trade unions were crucial in determining the home rule policy of the Ministry of Labour.[51]

The issue of compulsory arbitration popped up occasionally, but never became an official policy."[52] The trade-union leadership and rank and file were unwilling to make a deal with the government at the 1919-1921 National Industrial Conference (NIC), a key attempt to defuse social turmoil and to promote cooperation between employers and unions in the immediate aftermath of the war. The assertion of self-determination prevented the Labor Ministry from carving out a niche in the postwar reconstruction and demobilization. Labor Minister Robert Horne was the chairman of the NIC, but left no mark on such issues as working hours, national minimum wage, unemployment, and cooperation between employers and employed. He played a negligible role and had little influence on Lloyd George, who turned down the NIC Joint Committee's proposals on working hours and minimum wages, and dissolved the new body on 19 July 1921. Horne did not even make "a pretense at consultation" with the NIC after the railway and mine strikes had subsided.[53]

Industrial relations policy was by no means "capitalist," in the sense of being formulated by employers or the capitalist state and benefiting only them. Some sections of the Labour party were hostile toward the increased presence of the state in industrial relations. George Barnes, a trade-union leader and member of the parliamentary Labour party, urged the Ministry's abolition and the elimination of its officials:

I believe there is a good deal that might be abolished in the Labour Department as there is in other Departments. I am one of those who believe that so far as the mass of employers and workmen are concerned they ought to be left to adjust their own differences. They know more about them than anybody else, and there is a danger that if we do too much or hold out the hope to either side of doing too much in regard to industrial disputes we may tend *to foment them rather than adjust them. If you have a number of men fussing around looking for trouble they are sure to get it* .... I am suggesting that *some of these officials, at all events, might be eliminated and set to earn their living in a more useful capacity* .... My point is that in looking around for disputes, disputes are

made. It would therefore be better to dispense with many of these people who are doing no good to themselves nor anybody else.[54]

Employers had a similar attitude. The Federation of British
Industries (FBI) and the National Confederation of Employers'
Organizations (NCEO) pressed the government, which came under
the "pressure of business interests, the clamour of its supporters,
the noise made by the press,"[55] to dismantle the stringent wartime
regulations of production and the labor market, and insisted on
employers' right to settle industrial disputes on their own. They
opposed state intervention on the ground that it would increase
expenditures. Employers demanded a return to the pre-1914 situation and were gratified when the government repealed the last
wage control regulations, the Wages Temporary Legislation Act.

The reliance on organized labor and employers for postwar
reconstruction compelled Lloyd George to scrap the plan to shape
the rules of industrial relations and to move toward a more passive, non-interventionist stance. The Labor Ministry remained a
powerless intermediary, shackled by two pieces of legislation, the
Conciliation Act of 1896 and the Industrial Courts Act of 20
November 1920. The 1896 Conciliation Act forbade the prewar
Board of Trade and now the Labor Ministry to directly intervene
in labor disputes; its officials were excluded from the trade boards,
which were made up of management and workers.[56] When labor
disputes arose, the Ministry could only conduct an investigation
and appoint conciliators and arbitrators independent of the Ministry. The Industrial Courts Act of 20 November 1920 established
permanent industrial tribunals consisting of representatives of
employers and workers. The Labor Ministry could submit a dispute to an Industrial Court when both parties had consented to its
mediation and after both had failed to reach an agreement
through the existing negotiating machinery in the industry. This
legal arrangement was superfluous since, as the high-ranking
Labor Ministry official Frederick Leggett acknowledged, the
"Industrial Court has never become more than one of many forms
of tribunal and has never reached the status intended for it."[57] The
Labor Minister could appoint an independent single arbitrator or
a Board of Arbitration only when a case was referred to him, and
could not take the matter into his own hands and make a decision
on his own. He had the authority to appoint a Court of Inquiry
into a dispute without the parties' consent, but the Court could
only recommend solutions. Neither the Labor Ministry nor any

other body could impose its will on the parties, let alone enforce the decisions.[58]

At the insistence of organized labor, the British government adopted a stance of neutrality that cut across party lines and conformed to extensive cultural and group preferences for a pluralistic polity. The Labor Ministry devoted itself to the task of assisting in the formation of Whitley councils and permanent conciliation boards. Recognizing the need for workers' participation in determining work conditions, these councils "lay the foundations for a new order of things in the relations between capital and labor."[59] These joint conciliation bodies were entirely free from government influence and staffed by employers and union representatives. The Labor Ministry dismissed compulsory arbitration as a method that would "result in more harm than good, and would be violently opposed by *both employers and trade unions*,"[60] and claimed that it "has always been unpopular in this country, *both with organization of employers and trade unions*,"[61] and "would encourage the production of frivolous complaints and lend unreality to industrial negotiations."[62]

The British labor ministers proclaimed their neutrality throughout the interwar years: "The policy of the Ministry of Labour since the war has been to revert as far as possible and as quickly as circumstances would permit to the prewar attitude of leaving wages and conditions of employment to be settled by negotiation between the employers and the workpeople, or the organizations or joint bodies representing them."[63] During his tenure, Labor Minister John Hodge stressed neutrality in trade board activities. He declared that he was "a strong believer in direct settlement" and in "playing cricket," that is, to be fair to both parties, thus refusing to interfere in Trade Board activities. While meeting a labor delegation, he stated that:

> I can assure you of this that I should be very reluctant indeed to indicate to any Board that they should reconsider a problem that they had considered. I should be very reluctant to do that. As I said at the very beginning I do not think it would be right on my part to have the representations of employers coming to me and making statements and putting forward requests without giving the other side the opportunity of making their statement. If one is going to make the Ministry of Labour a success it can only be done, if I may so put it, – I have put it in that way on many occasions – *by playing cricket, that is, we have got to be fair to both sides* …. If you could do anything out of your own goodness of heart I think it would be very much better than if it were obtained in any other way.[64]

Likewise, G. H. Roberts, the second Labor Minister, resisted the idea of using state machinery to serve the interests of a class. In a meeting with a delegation of the Trades Union Congress, he defended the policy of minimum intervention as "not only proper for the people we represent but also good for the state. It is extremely difficult to require that state machinery shall be used on behalf of one section of the community only." Home rule meant above all that "interventions should be reduced to a minimum" and that "active intervention and the establishment of the elaborate governmental machinery" should be deprecated.[65] The fourth labor minister, T. J. Macnamara, stated that "interventions should be reduced to a minimum" lest they undermine negotiations. British state managers inside and outside the Labor Ministry[66] agreed that the goal of the Ministry was "to strive to the utmost to avoid intervention,"[67] and to leave the resolution of industrial disputes in the hands of voluntary bodies.[68] Self-determination was "in the best interests of the country."[69] Though expressing his sympathy for workers, Permanent Secretary David Shackleton refused to intervene as a workers' delegation requested because he was afraid that "the machinery of the state [Arbitration Courts] would break down" completely. He insisted that he had "no interest except the state" and "interference with the arbitration" would be out of the question;[70] and he further declared that "the department does not adjudicate, it only sees fair play."[71]

Accordingly, the chief industrial commissioners were instructed to avoid intervention at the local level,[72] i.e., to prevent rather than solve industrial conflicts. Stationed in various parts of the country such as Birmingham, Manchester, Leeds, Newcastle, Glasgow, and Cardiff, these officials kept the Labor Ministry informed of disputes at the local level. A ministerial directive urged the chief industrial officers to avoid "any appearance of a desire to intervene in a dispute."[73] The Labor Ministry required them to keep as low a profile as possible, and to act only if invited by one or both parties or on instructions from headquarters.[74] T. J. Macnamara made it clear that "the Conciliation Officers understand perfectly well that it is their business (and their efficiency is measured by the extent to which they make it their business) to be acquainted with matters of importance without anybody concerned knowing that they are acquainted."[75] When invited to mediate, they were expected to encourage both sides to discuss their problems rather than fight over them.[76] Consequently, the Labor Ministry's conciliation proceedings fell dramatically: 1,323 in 1919, 920 in 1920, 272 in 1921, and 167 in 1923.[77]

*Germany: The Dominance of Organized Labor*

In Germany, truly inclusionary processes became operative in industrial relations only after the occurrence of crucial contingencies: crushing military defeat, the abdication of the monarchy, the socialist revolution of November 1918, the foundation of the Weimar Republic on 9 November 1918 by the Social Democratic party, and the Treaty of Versailles of June 1919. The disastrous military defeat shattered the authoritarian legacies of the past and shifted the balance of power in favor of organized labor, which emerged as a major political force in shaping the postwar Weimar democracy. The socialist revolution in Berlin turned the political landscape in Germany upside down. Social Democrats became the important representatives of national interest and filled the offices of President (Friedrich Ebert), Chancellor (Philipp Scheidemann, Gustav Bauer, and Hermann Müller) and gained an important foothold in the key Ministries of Economy (Rudolf Wissell), Food (Robert Schmidt), and Labor (Gustav Bauer) in the first coalition government. As a matter of fact, the SPD was the largest political party represented at the Reichstag (Figure 7), and yet its power was limited to the immediate postwar reconstruction years.

The Social Democratic government intended to keep some forms of compulsory arbitration on the basis of the wartime patriotic Auxiliary Service Law of 5 December 1916, which gave army officers appointed by the War Office arbitration power to chair a conciliation board consisting of an equal number of representatives of employers and workers. Faced with widespread wildcat strikes, Chancellor Gustav Bauer urged the formation of compulsory arbitration courts. Such measures proved necessary as internal security organs reported "the danger of a Communist uprising in Germany."[78] In spring 1919, the Prussian government proposed delaying strikes until means of mediation had been exhausted provided the workers' committee approved such a delay by a majority of three-fourths. In July and October 1919, Chancellor Bauer planned to establish an "obligatory" arbitration court (Schiedsgericht). And in March 1920, the Labor Ministry unveiled a plan to increase state regulation of labor conflicts by establishing local, provincial, and central arbitration boards.[79] After consulting with employers and trade unions, the Labor Ministry drafted a bill

***Figure 7:*** Seats Held by Political Parties at the Reichstag

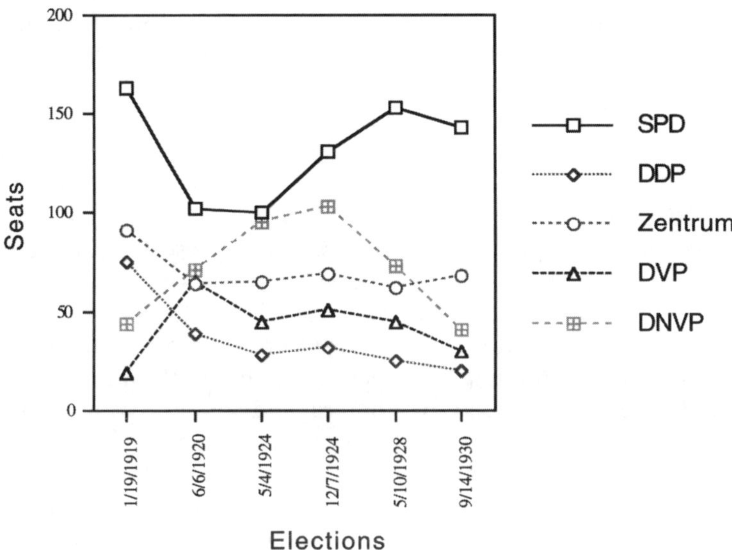


*Source:* Georges Castellan, *L'Allemagne de Weimar 1918-1933* (Paris: Librairie Armand Colin, 1969), pp. 89, 91, 94, 100, and 103.

to set up a permanent compulsory arbitration system in 1921, and submitted it to the National Economic Council for approval. The bill reached the Reichstag, but was shelved with the onset of hyper-inflation.[80]

The crushing military defeat and the pressing need for postwar reconstruction provided organized labor with a unique opportunity to dominate postwar industrial relations policy. Days after the Armistice, employers hurriedly changed course to "cooperate hand in hand with trade unions in order to save what is possible to save."[81] Representing the business community, Hugo Stinnes eagerly made a pact with the socialist Trade Unions President Carl Legien on 15 November 1918 – six days after the socialist revolution in Berlin and four days after the Armistice. The Stinnes-Legien agreement ratified the labor legislations of the revolutionary government of November 1918. Employers recognized the socialist, Christian, and Liberal Trade Unions' leadership as the sole representatives of the rank and file. They also accepted collective bargaining and the eight-hour day in all branches of industry. In exchange, the socialist, Christian, and Liberal Trade Unions consented to respect private property and free enterprise. The rapprochement between employers and workers was, ironically, the by-product of the war. The Imperial government forced employers to recognize the trade unions and sit with their officials on boards established to deal with labor problems during the war. Both employers and trade unions saw advantages in forging an alliance against bureaucratic encroachments and negotiated the terms of that alliance in 1917 and 1918. The accord established free collective bargaining and set up joint conciliation boards to resolve labor disputes. In addition, employers and organized labor established the Central Cooperative Working Association, known as ZAG (Zentralarbeitsgemeinschaft), to discuss policy issues. Most importantly, employers and trade unions joined hands to exclude the state from postwar industrial relations and to contain the threats posed by workers' and soldiers' councils and their factory occupations, which undermined their authority.[82]

As a result, the German Labor Ministry closely fits a pluralist model that focuses on interest groups: It incorporated the demands of organized labor and employers in the early Weimar years. The socialist government put the agreement into law. By the end of 1920, the German Labor Ministry was less "a social Maginot line,"[83] defending the interests of the working class (as described by Charles Maier) than a pluralist mirror reflecting the dominance of organized labor and the desires of both trade unions and employers to establish self-determination. The Stinnes-Legien agreement of 15 November 1918 was a "remarkable corporatist rebellion" and "a silent revolution of associations against the state."[84] The socialist Trade Unions' influence reached its climax in 1920-1922. Its president Carl Legien became a pivot between the central government, coalition parties, and the SPD as his union defeated the Kapp putsch on 13 March 1920 conducted by military troops disenchanted with the Treaty of Versailles. While President Ebert, Chancellor Bauer, and the cabinet fled the capital, the trade unions staged a general strike, brought down the putschists, and rescued the Weimar regime.[85]

While increasing the strength of the socialist Trade Unions, postwar reconstruction prompted the Social Democratic government to postpone the building of socialism and to adopt a more pragmatic line. Faced with the sudden return and demobilization of millions of soldiers and the rapid switch from war production to a civilian economy, the SPD government allied itself with middle-class parties and pursued an orthodox economic policy that encouraged production for exports to support the Mark, to find jobs for six million war veterans, to pay for food, and to solve the problems of coal shortages and transportation bottlenecks.[86] The Social Democratic government opposed the workers' and soldiers' councils, abandoned state control of the economy, devoted its energy to preventing the dreadful rise of an unemployed army of veterans, and voted down the socialization program presented by Rudolf Wissell at the Social Democratic party meetings and the socialist Trades Union Congresses in 1919. The major task of SPD Chancellors Scheidemann (1919), Bauer (1919), and Müller (1920) "was to get from one day to the next."[87] They attempted to govern with impartiality, and avoided meeting union leaders, communicating with them in writing. Consequently, trade-union leaders barely considered the SPD ministers to be their colleagues and complained about the lack of socialist reforms.[88] The rank and file were disappointed in the SPD and refrained from joining the party, whose membership hovered around only a million between 1919 and 1922.

The instability of the Weimar regime was a significant impediment to the Social Democratic Labor Ministers' contributions to industrial relations. Their tenure was short-lived as the four cabinets led by socialist chancellors in the span of a year (1919-1920) lasted only 3.7 months on average. The Weimar Coalition (consisting of the SPD, the Democratic party, and the Catholic Center party) lasted for a total of two-and-a-half years – from 13 February 1919 to 14 November 1922. Gustav Bauer held the office for only four months. His brief stint ended with the fall of the Scheidemann cabinet and his rise to chancellorship on 21 June 1919. That undoubtedly elevated the stature of the labor agency over which he had presided, but it was largely symbolic. Alexander Schlicke, a former leader of the German Iron and Steel Workers' Association, held the post for ten months between 1919 and 1920.

The disastrous consequences of the First World War and the rocky transition to a new political regime set the stage for the ascendance of unprecedented inclusionary processes in Germany. Trade unions and employers managed to keep the state at bay for the first time in Germany's history.

This comparative study of the British and German Labor Ministries suggests that war and postwar reconstruction were two crucial contingencies that gave rise to inclusionary processes in which organized labor played an important role in policy-making. The two cases show that organized labor became ascendant when the state had to rely on its support for war and mobilization. Moreover, this analysis uncovers a major variable missed by structuralist neo-

Marxist arguments: syndicalism in both countries prevented organized labor from converting the labor departments into vehicles of class interests.

## Notes


1.   Rodney Lowe, *Adjusting to Democracy: The Role of the Ministry of Labour in British Politics, 1916-1939* (Oxford: Clarendon Press, 1986.), p. 17.
2.   J. A. M. Caldwell, "The Genesis of the Ministry of Labour," *Public Administration* 37, IV, (1959), p. 384.
3.   Alan Bullock, *The Life and Times of Ernest Bevin*, Vol. 1 (London: Heinemann, 1960), p. 52.
4.   Trades Union Congress, *Report of Proceedings at the 47th Annual Trades Union Congress, Associations Hall, Bristol, 6-11 September 1915* (London: Cooperative Printing Society Ltd., 1915), p. 411.
5.   Reichsarbeitsministerium, *Deutsche Sozialpolitik, 1918-1928. Erinnerungsschrift des Reichsarbeitsministeriums* (Berlin: Mittler & Sohn, 1929), p. 12.
6.   Ibid., p. 14.
7.   Lab 2 865/IR 1008/1921, p. 2.
8.   Rodney Lowe, *Adjusting to Democracy*, pp. 18-20.
9.   Rodney Lowe, "The Ministry of Labour, 1916-1924: A Graveyard of Social Reform?" *Public Administration* 52, (1974), p. 417.
10.   Roger Davidson, "The Ideology of Labour Administration, 1886-1914," *Bulletin of the Society for the Study of Labour History* 40, (1980), p. 29.
11.   Lab 2 213/L 156/1904.
12.   Lab 2 213/L 156/1904, 2 May 1904.
13.   Reichsarbeitsministerium, *Deutsche Sozialpolitik*, pp. 16-17.
14.   Freund Otto Kahn, *Labor Law and Politics in the Weimar Republic* (Oxford: Blackwell, 1981), pp. 8 and 23.
15.   Reichsarbeitsministerium, *Deutsche Sozialpolitik*, pp. 1-2.
16.   Ibid.
17.   Based on Klaus Saul, "Repression or Integration? The State, Trade Unions and Industrial Disputes in Imperial Germany," in *The Development of Trade Unionism in Great Britain and Germany*, eds. Wolfgang J. Mommsen and Hans-Gerhard Husung (London: George Allen & Unwin, 1986), pp. 341-351.
18.   George Steinmetz, "The Myth of an Autonomous State: Industrialists, Junkers, and Social Policy in Imperial Germany," in *Society, Culture, and the State in Germany*, ed. Geoff Eley (Ann Arbor: The University of Michigan Press, 1996), pp. 260 and 304.
19.   Martha Driessen, *Die Entwicklung der Reichsarbeitsbehörden, 1919-1924*, pp. 4-6; Reichsarbeitsministerium, *Deutsche Sozialpolitik*, pp. 14-17; and Wolfgang Siebert, *Die Entwicklung der Staatlichen Arbeitsverwaltung* (Darmstadt: Forschungen zum Staats- und Verwaltungsrecht A 14, 1943), pp. 48-49.

20. George Steinmetz, *Regulating the Social: The Welfare State and Local Politics in Imperial Germany* (Princeton: Princeton University Press, 1993), p. 124.

21. Gaston Rimlinger, *Welfare Policy and Industrialization in Europe, America, and Russia* (New York: Wiley 1971).

22. Chris Wrigley, *Arthur Henderson* (Cardiff: GPC Books, 1990), p. 108.

23. Eric L. Wigham, *Strikes and the Government, 1893-1981* (London: Macmillan, 1982), p. 35.

24. Chris Wrigley, *Arthur Henderson*, p. 109.

25. Lord George Askwith, *Industrial Problems and Disputes* (London: J. Murray, 1920), p. 414.

26. Gerald D. Feldman, *Army, Industry and Labor in Germany, 1914-1918* (Princeton: Princeton University Press, 1966), p. 178.

27. Jürgen Kocka, *Facing Total War: German Society, 1914-1918* (Leamington Spa: Berg, 1984), p. 47.

28. For wartime government-labor relations, see Jürgen Kocka, *Klassengesellschaft im Krieg: Deutsche Sozialgeschichte, 1914-1918* (Göttinghen: Vanderehoeck & Ruprecht, 1978), Gerald Feldman, *Army, Industry and Labor*, and Friedrich Zunkel, *Industrie und Staatssozialismus: Der Kampf um die Wirtschaftsordnung 1914-1918* (Düsseldorf: Droste, 1974).

29. RAM 2854, 1918, p. 2.

30. Dokument Nr. 4, "Sitzung des Interfaktionellen Ausschusses," 1 October 1918, in *Die Regierung des Prinzen Max von Baden. Quellen zur Geschichte des Parlamentarismus und der politischen Parteien*, Erste Reihe, Band 2, eds. Erich Matthias und Rudolf Morsey (Düsseldorf: Droste, 1962), p. 24.

31. Dokument Nr. 12, "Bericht des bayerischen Gesandten Graf Leichenfeld an Ministerpräsident Ritter von Dandl München," 2 October 1918, ibid., p. 42.

32. Lab 2 212/19, 7 November 1917, p. 8.

33. V. L. Allen, *Trade Unions and the Government* (London: Butler & Tanner, 1960), p. 56.

34. Thomas Jones, *Whitehall Diary, 1916-1925*, Vol. 1, ed. Keith Middlemas (London: Oxford University Press, 1969), p. 13.

35. Lord George Askwith, *Industrial Problems and Disputes*, p. 414.

36. Rodney Lowe, *Adjusting to Democracy*, pp. 18-20.

37. Quoted in ibid., p. 28.

38. Ibid., p. 21.

39. Dokument Nr. 38, "Aufzeichnung des Abg. Friedrich Graf von Galen," 10 October 1918, *Die Regierung des Prinzen Max von Baden*, p. 125.

40. Dokument Nr. 17, "Besprechung des Vizekanzlers mit den Bevöllmächtigen zum Bundesrat," 3 October 1918, ibid., pp. 51-52.

41. Heinrich Potthoff, *Freie Gewerkschaften, 1918-1933: Der Allgemeine Deutsche Gewerkschaftsbund in der Weimarer Republik* (Düsseldorf: Droste, 1987), pp. 273-274.

42. RAM 2062, p. 37 and RAM 2059, p. 480.

43. Reichsarbeitsministerium, *Deutsche Sozialpolitik*, p. 12.

44. Alan Fox, *History and Heritage: The Social Origins of British Industrial Relations System* (London: Allen & Unwin, 1985), p. 283. In the December 1910 election, 44 percent of the adult population, mainly workers and women, were ineligible to participate in the democratic process.

45. James E. Cronin, *The Politics of State Expansion: War, State, and Society in Twentieth-Century Britain* (New York: Routledge, 1991), pp. 13-52.

46.  F187/3/1, 27 September 1919.

47.  Thomas Jones, *Whitehall Diary*, p. 99.

48.  Kenneth O. Morgan, *Consensus and Disunity: The Lloyd George Coalition Government, 1918-1922* (Oxford: Oxford University Press, 1979), p. 281.

49.  Rodney Lowe,"The Failure of Consensus in Britain: The National Industrial Conference, 1919-1921," *Historical Journal* 21, (1978a), p. 666.

50.  James E. Cronin, *The Politics of State Expansion*, pp. 37-48.

51.  Lab 2 921/IR/190/22, p. 117, italics mine.

52.  Eric L. Wigham, *Strikes and the Government*, p. 14.

53.  V. L. Allen, *Trade Unions*, pp. 58-59.

54.  Lab2 933/IR549/1922, p. 2, italics mine.

55.  R. H. Tawney, "The Abolition of Economic Controls, 1918-1921," *Economic History Review* 23, (1943), p. 13.

56.  V. L. Allen, *Trade Unions*, pp. 51-53 and 59-62.

57.  Frederick W. Leggett, "The Settlement of Labour Disputes in Great Britain," in *Meeting of Minds: A Way to Peace through Mediation*, ed. Elmore Jackson, (New York: McGraw-Hill, 1952), p. 68.

58.  V. L. Allen, *Trade Unions*, pp. 62-63.

59.  Lab 2 212/11, 28 June 1917.

60.  Lab 2 921/IR/190/22, p. 114, italics mine.

61.  Lab 2 921/IR/190/22, p. 117, italics mine.

62.  Lab 2 921/IR/190/22, italics mine, p. 114.

63.  Lab 2 933/IR 549/1922, 8 March 1922.

64.  Lab 2 212/7, 1917, p. 12, italics mine.

65.  Lab 10/399, 23 November 1917, pp. 208-209.

66.  Lab 2 921/IR 190/22, p. 111.

67.  Lab 2 933/IR 549/1922.

68.  Lab 2 851/IR805/1925, 15 March 1923.

69.  Lab 2 696/15, 25 February 1921.

70.  Lab 10/399, 21 September 1917, p. 12.

71.  Lab 10/399, quoted in Rodney Lowe,"The Ministry of Labour:, 1916-1919: A Still, Small Voice?" in *War and the State: The Transformation of British Government, 1914-1919*, ed. Kathleen Burke (London: Allen & Unwin), p. 116.

72.  Lab 2 933/IR 549/1922.

73.  Lab 2 933/IR 549/1922, 8 March 1922.

74.  Lab 2 1779/MHESTAB 1012/2, 10 December 1918, pp. 3-4.

75.  Lab 2 933/IR 549/1922, 2 March 1922.

76.  Frederick W. Leggett, "The Settlement of Labor Disputes," p. 69.

77.  V. L. Allen, *Trade Unions*, pp. 62-63.

78.  See R43I/2667 F8, 24 February 1921, report from the Reichskommissar der Überwachung der Öffentlichen Ordnung, p. 241, and R43I/2671 F3, report from the Defense Minister to the Chancellor, p. 94.

79.  Ludwig Preller, *Sozialpolitik in der Weimarer Republik* (Stuttgart: Franz Mittelbach Verlag, 1949), pp. 257-258 and Nathan Reich, *Labour Relations in Republican Germany* (New York: Oxford University Press, 1938), p. 125.

80.  Gerard Braunthal, *Socialist Labor and Politics in Weimar Germany: The General Federation of German Trade Union* (Conn.: H. Amden, 1978), p. 151.

81.  Statement made by Carl Duisberg and quoted in Friedrich Zunkel, *Industrie und Staatsozialismus: Der Kampf um die Wirtschaftsordnung 1914-1918* (Düsseldorf: Droste, 1974), p. 173.

82. Gerald D. Feldman,"German Business Between War and Revolution: The Origins of the Stinnes-Legien Agreement," in *Entstehung und Wandel der modernen Gesellschaft: Festschrift für Hans Rosenberg zum 65. Geburtstag*, eds. Gerhard A. Ritter and Hans Rosenberg (Berlin: De Gruyter, 1970), .p. 336; Charles Maier, *Recasting Bourgeois Europe: Stabilization in France, Germany, and Italy in the Decade after WWI* (Princeton: Princeton University Press, 1975),. p. 160; Werner Abelshauser, "Freiheitlicher Korporastimus im Kaiserreich und in der Weimarer Republik," in *Die Weimarer Republik als Wohlfahrtstaat: Zum Verhältnis von Wirtschafts- und Sozialpolitik in der Industriegesellschaft*, ed. Werner Abelshauser (Stuttgart: Franz Steiner Verlag, 1987), pp. 160-161; and Gerald D. Feldman, "Die Freien Gewerkschaften und die Zentralarbeitsgemeinschaft," in *Vom Sozialistengesetz zur Mitbestimmung*, ed. Heinz O. Vetter (Köln: Bund-Verlag, 1975), p. 245. Nathan Reich overstates the fact that employers surrendered to trade union demands and that economic power shifted in favor of labor: *Labour Relations in Republican Germany* (New York: Oxford University Press, 1938), p. 26.

83. Charles Maier, *Recasting Bourgeois Europe*, p. 192. This may be true in comparison with France and Italy, the other cases he studied.

84. Gerald D. Feldman, "The Weimar Republic: A Problem of Modernization?" *Archiv für Sozialgeschichte*, Band XXVI, (1986), p. 15 and Johannes W. Bähr, *Staatliche Schlichtung*, p. 16.

85. See Heinrich August Winkler's excellent account in *Von der Revolution zur Stabilisierung: Arbeiter und Arbeiterbewegung in der Weimarer Republik 1918 bis 1924* (Berlin: Verlag J. H. W. Dietz Nachf., 1984), pp. 294-342.

86. William Carl Mathews, "The Continuity of Social Democratic Economic Policy from 1919 to 1920: The Bauer-Schmidt Policy" in *Die Anpassung an die Inflation*, eds. Gerald D. Feldman, Carl-Ludwig Holtfrerich, Gerhard A. Ritter, and Peter-Christian Witt (Berlin: Walter de Gruyter, 1986), pp. 510-512 and Richard Bessel, *Germany After the First World War* (Oxford: Clarendon Press, 1993), pp. 70-71, 86-87, and 100.

87. Richard Bessel, *Germany After the First World War*, p. 106.

88. Heinrich Potthoff, *Freie Gewerkschaften 1918-1933*, p. 274.

# Chapter Four

# Veering Away from British Pluralism
## Class Interests and Statist Pursuits

The British Labor Ministry was a multifaceted organization that changed its nature in response to outside pressures. On the one hand, the agency professed neutrality and impartiality in industrial relations at the insistence of organized labor throughout the interwar years. On the other hand, as I shall show in this chapter, the dominant pluralist practices in industrial relations were punctuated with blatant promotion of employers' interests and overriding concerns with the international standing of the nation. In crucial circumstances, the British Labor Ministry switched to an exclusionary mode: workers' interests were invariably sacrificed when crises of industrial relations and economic institutions threatened the viability of the capitalist system and the related political order. Labor ministers blatantly joined the political elite in the suppression of workers in large-scale strikes such as the coal miners strike of 1921 and the General Strike of 1926. On other occasions, national leaders' efforts to bolster the international position of Britain stunted the administrative development of the Labor Ministry and subordinated industrial relations policy to geopolitical pursuits. A nuanced and fine-grained analysis is needed to understand the ascendance of exclusionary and autonomous processes in a largely pluralist industrial relations system.

---

Notes for this chapter begin on page 106.

## Capitalist Cohesion and Crises of Industrial Relations and Economic Institutions

### Organizing Employers

In the aftermath of the war, the crisis of economic institutions – culminating in the failure to reach consensus at the National Industrial Conference in 1919 – compelled the British state to act as an agent of capitalist cohesion by uniting a section of employers against organized labor. The Labor Ministry intervened to organize small and medium-size engineering employers into the National Confederation of Employers' Organization (NCEO) in 1919. These employers had been overwhelmed by an upsurge in strikes[1] and the rise of union power and failed to close ranks against organized labor at the Conference. The British Labor Ministry helped the NCEO's fifty members counter the increasing bargaining power of trade unions, and withheld its own support from trade unions. Such assistance, in fact, had a precedent. In 1916, the government had supported the creation of the Federation of British Industries "to the extent of seconding two senior Foreign Office officers to assist it and to ensure that its trade promotion policy did not diverge from its [the government's] own."[2]

However, the capitalist bias of the British Labor Ministry was confined to times of crises. Contrary to a structuralist neo-Marxist interpretation, the two main employers' organizations, the Federation of British Industries and the National Confederation of Employers' Organizations, had little influence on the "relatively autonomous" Labor Ministry: "Business interests, especially the peak national associations, never were as influential as they were believed and feared to be, and there is little evidence that organized industry or business groups ever attempted to utilize extraconstitutional means to alter political outcomes."[3] Though created with the help of government assistance, the NCEO turned its back on the Labor Ministry's welfare programs. Its leaders, Sir Allen Smith (also chairman of the Engineering Employers Federation, 1919-1922), Lord Weir, and Sir James Lithgrow, lambasted the Labor Ministry "as one of the most extravagant and 'socialistically-inclined' departments, whose abolition was essential to national survival."[4] Indignant, Labor Ministry officials stopped rolling out the red carpet for the NCEO leaders and drastically curtailed their access to the Ministry. As Walter Citrine pointed out, the NCEO's influence on the Labor Minister was dismal:

> Forbes Watson [the NCEO leader] usually had a grumble against the Government. He felt that they were keeping his organization too much at arm's length. He envied the ease with which the T.U.C. was received in Whitehall. I thought to myself: 'This is all wrong. Why should the employers not have the same facilities for making direct representations to the Government?' What is more, I did my best to help this along. I sensed that there would be many occasions upon which it would be as well if the Government knew there was an identity of view between our organizations, although our representations might be made separately. I remember on one occasion when Forbes and I were going to the Ministry of Labour, just as we entered the building he turned to me and said, 'We owe this to you,' referring to the fact that we were both received with such facility.[5]

The FBI was "influential neither with government nor with industry,"[6] and was anything but the "General Staff" of industrialists and "the brain center of British capitalism."[7] Walter Citrine, the TUC leader from 1926 to 1945, acknowledged that the image of a "dangerous, conspiratorial organization whose ultimate aim was to establish control by a small business elite over the policies of the industry and the State" was exaggerated.[8] The 1,392 affiliated members of the Federation jealously guarded their autonomy, thwarted any effort of the leadership to centralize the decision-making process, and curtailed the Federation's ability to represent them as a group vis-à-vis the government and trade unions.[9] Furthermore, the FBI and the NCEO could not agree on a common labor policy because of "different economic interests, favoring different strategies and embodying different traditions and attitudes towards labour relations."[10] They settled for a compromise by dividing the tasks between themselves. The FBI agreed to handle economic matters, while the NCEO devoted itself to labor issues.

*Strikes and Repression*

The British state went into capitalist mode especially when crises of industrial relations threatened the economic system and the related political order. In these circumstances, the state relied on illiberal means such as strike-breaking and military force to support employers in their fight against organized labor. The government created the Supply and Transport Committee (STC) in October 1919 as a successor to the wartime Strike Committee. Its major task was to mobilize emergency services to replace strikers and to defeat working-class challenges to the regime and employers. In

1923, the Supply and Transport Organization (STO) was established to replace the STC, which was disbanded due to budget cuts. As a cabinet-level policy-making body buttressed by the Emergency Act of 29 October 1920, the STO was "more than a strike-breaking machine: It became the principal national bulwark against revolution and anarchy."[11] The STO became a formidable weapon in the General Strike of 1926. To counter the disruptive effects of strikes, the state appointed civil commissioners to take over essential services and supervise the transport of supplies.[12] C. E. Penney, Food Controller and a key member of the strike-breaking organization, argued that "the side which is organized wins the fence-sitters in the battle between the loyalists and the revolutionaries."[13] While professing neutrality, Penney was determined "to fight revolution at the same time" to the benefit of one segment of the community at the expense of another."[14] Both the Supply and Transport Organization and the Supply and Transport Committee kept their activities secret from the labor movement and worked with employers, who provided information to the state on coal stocks and transportation.[15] The FBI offered assistance and was "confidentially placed in communication with the Supply Department."[16] In the 1921 coal mines dispute, employers were intransigent toward miners because they knew that the state would activate the Supply and Transport Committee.[17]

The most salient feature of British liberalism in industrial relations is the state's predilection for repression. The successive interwar governments, Conservative, Liberal, and Labour, fell back on the time-honored tradition of declaring a state of emergency and calling in the police and military. Neglecting the Labor Ministry's conciliation and arbitration capacity, the state directed the Home Office to create a "centralized controlled force" of police,[18] which had previously been under the control of local authorities and independent from the Home Secretary prior to 1918 and gained unprecedented power over "the provincial police and their local authorities in emergency"[19] by the 1930s. The government granted police protection to employers and workers who stayed away from strikes.

The military was regularly cast in the role of industrial peacekeeper and adjunct to the centralized police force. The military put down the 1919 Glasgow strike and the rioting and looting on the docks of Liverpool in 1919. The escort of truck convoys by armored cars and soldiers carrying machine guns broke the strikers' blockade of the London docks in 1926. Hardliners within the government made no apology for the use of the military in industrial conflicts. Winston Churchill, Secretary of State for War, "was not prepared to make any distinction between an industrial emergency in time of war and in peace;" he insisted on deploying troops to quell the strike of electrical engineers in February 1919, and ordered the General Headquarters of Great Britain "to prepare a complete scheme and organization of military forces throughout the country to act in aid of the civil authorities, in the event of a national strike of revolutionary character."[20] He used the Territorial Army to crush strikes, although it was not legally meant to be used in industrial disputes. This Army was used to create a Defence Force on 8 April 1921 to counter the Triple Alliance threat. About 70,000 men were enlisted to this end from April onwards. The practice of using the military in industrial conflicts, carried over from the days of limited democracy in favor of the privileged, took on an institutional and cultural life of its own. The neo-Marxist conception of an agent of capitalist cohesion does apply in these specific, extreme contexts. In the following, I elaborate on the capitalist nature of the British Labor Ministry by examining two major industrial conflicts of the interwar period.

## The Coal Miners Strike of 1921

The British coal mines became a major battlefield between employers and trade unions when the government decided to return the mines to private owners on 31 March 1921.[21] After the war, the mines suffered huge financial losses as a result of foreign competition and the sharp plunge of coal prices to below the prewar level on the international market. To rationalize the industry, mine owners undertook measures to cut wages by fifty percent and to nullify all wage concessions that had been made by the wartime government. In defense, the Miners' Federation of Great Britain (MFGB) demanded nationalization of the mining industry and the formation of a National Wages Board,[22] and insisted on national rather than district wage agreements to gain more leverage on employers and to obtain a uniform wage structure. The Federation rejected a compromise offered by state officials, who, in turn, rebuffed the miners' demands. Mine owners then locked out miners on 31 March 1921 nationwide.[23] This lockout set off a national strike called by the Triple Alliance, a coalition of miners, railway workers, and industrial workers.[24]

In the standoff, the government shifted gears in favor of employers. Prime Minister Lloyd George and his cabinet painted the coal miners strike as "political, unconstitutional and revolutionary"[25] and attacked the MFGB and its leader Frank Hodges as "irrational extremists."[26] They launched a full-scale propaganda campaign against the Triple Alliance, which was, in their words, led by anarchists and Bolsheviks bent on undermining the liberal-democratic government.[27] Abandoning the Ministry's nominal neutrality, Labor Minister Robert Horne openly took the side of mine owners. He himself detested the Triple Alliance and "exaggerated the danger of a social upheaval."[28] He favored pro-employer measures such as the increase of domestic coal prices in May 1920, the ending of state subsidies, and the termination of contracts. "[F]inancially logical," Horne's attitude was "industrially disastrous." He was "privately not unwishful for a fight."[29]

The deadlock in negotiations between employers and trade unions compelled the British government to resort to force to end the crisis. Indeed, the 1921 coal miners strike was a textbook example of interwar labor repression. The impressive show of force underlined the fact that "neither the government nor the miners had any use for the conciliation service of the Ministry of Labour."[30] Lloyd George, his cabinet, and Labor Minister Robert Horne resorted to "the call-up of army, navy and air force reservists, the moving of troops into mining areas and the installments of machine gun posts at pitheads, the establishment of supply departments in public parks, the enrollment of special constables and the preparation of a special defence force of some 80,000 armed and uniformed men."[31] The military troops included 56 infantry battalions, 14 of them brought back from the Rhineland and Ireland, and six cavalry regiments,[32] as well as other strike-breaking forces.[33] The cabinet activated the Supply and Transport Organization and invoked the Emergency Powers Act of 29 October 1920 to establish order during the dispute.

Invariably, the working class surrendered whenever the British government and Labor Ministry switched to capitalist mode. Backing down in the face of a formidable show of military deployment, the Triple Alliance leaders negotiated their withdrawal from the strike with Lloyd George on 15 April 1921, known as Black Friday. Although the nationwide strike lasted for seven days and the workers' morale had been high, the Triple Alliance leaders were understandably short on the will to confront the authorities. Contrary to government propaganda, the Triple Alliance had actually never intended to topple the government by means of direct action; it had intended a mass mobilization tactic involving a general strike and demonstrations for the purpose of improving working conditions. The trade union leaders, except for "three out and out revolutionists," were not prone to "violence and revolution," as reported by Professor Laski, a go-between during the strike.[34] The Triple Alliance lost legitimacy among workers and was derided as the Crippled Alliance for the rest of the period under study. Miners struck again, but lost the battle after a ten-week stalemate that drained their strike funds. The Lloyd George government carried the day, and, most importantly, mine owners reaped the benefits: they dictated their own terms and cut wages.

### The General Strike of 1926

The British government sided with employers again in the General Strike of 1926. Once again, the mines were at the center of the dispute. The increasing competition from the U.S., Poland, and the Ruhr region of Germany, the revaluation of the pound sterling by ten percent (which made exports more expensive), diminishing profit, and the return to the gold standard in April 1925 engineered by the Chancellor of the Exchequer Winston Churchill, aggravated the plight of British industry. Losing £1 million a month, mine owners announced their intent to extend working hours and cut wages by 10-25 percent.[35] MFGB President Herbert Smith and powerful trade-union leader Arthur J. Cook rejected the employers' new measures and pressed the government to nationalize the mining industry to save mining from bankruptcy and to protect wage rates from employers' further assaults.

Unlike in 1921, the Conservative government led by Baldwin attempted to defuse the crisis by setting up a Royal Commission to examine reorganization of the mining industry and to provide a subsidy of £23 million for nine months to support existing wages and an average profit. This conciliatory move made on 31 July 1925 came to be known as Red Friday, a sort of a working-class triumph. In fact, as a high-ranking official Philip Cunliffe-Lister remarked,[36] the government merely postponed an imminent confrontation with trade unions because it "was not ready" for it. Prime Minister Baldwin agreed to subsidize both employers and workers until 1 May 1926, while awaiting the report of the Samuel Royal Commission.

However, the Samuel Commission hardly supported the miners. Its recommendations included wage reduction and termination of subsidy. The trade unions spurned the recommendations and any compromises put forth by Herbert Samuel.[37] Negotiations among the government, mine owners, and miners bogged down in April. The government proclaimed a state of emergency on 30 April 1926,[38] and mine owners proceeded to cut wages on 1 May 1926.

The government's support of mine owners set off the largest strike that had ever been organized in Europe. The General Council of the Trades Union Congress declared a general strike on 3 May 1926. One-and-a-half million coal workers struck for nine days.[39] Other industrial workers joined *en masse;* the General Strike mobilized a total of 3.5 million workers. Some 162,233,000 working days were lost due to industrial conflicts in 1926; "about 15 million of these were due to the General Strike but 146,434,000 were due to the lockout of over a million miners."[40]

The 1926 crisis in industrial relations forced the British state to drop the claim of serving the common good with "neutral" responses to social forces. Baldwin and his cabinet construed the General Strike as "a challenge to Parliament, and ... the road to anarchy and ruin"[41] and "a challenge to the constitutional rights and freedom of the nation."[42] Acting on this perception, they threatened to bring the strike to a violent end. Several members of the cabinet – Finance Minister Winston Churchill, Minister of Interior William Joynson-Hicks, and Secretary for India Lord Birkenhead – pushed for the use of force when necessary. Churchill epitomized the hardliners' mentality when he shouted at Thomas Jones: "We are *at war*, we must go through with it."[43] Labor Minister Arthur Steel-Maitland shared Baldwin's antipathy toward the strike, as evidenced in his somber remarks to labor leader Arthur Henderson, who reported: "[I]t was time we [organized labor] were put in our places."[44] He made it clear that the government would proceed with negotiations only when the TUC called off the strike: "The government cannot negotiate until the General Strike has been withdrawn ... their [the government's] position is plain. They hold that the General Strike is unconstitutional and illegal. They are bound to take steps to make its repetition impossible. It is therefore plain that they cannot enter upon any negotiation unless the strike is so unreservedly concluded."[45]

Most importantly, the British state put all its weight behind repression and played down the conciliation role of the Labor Ministry. Steel-Maitland played second fiddle in the Baldwin cabinet. He could not go much beyond obediently carrying out the decisions handed down to him by the Prime Minister and the cab-

inet. Baldwin now and then shunted him aside on important matters relating to the General Strike. Steel-Maitland himself once
complained about not being designated to speak for the government in Parliament: "He [Steel-Maitland] bewailed the fact that
the P. M. had not put him up instead of Winston to reply for the
Government on Monday night, as he knew the course of the negotiations and Winston did not."[46] Likewise, Baldwin often met with
mine owners and union leaders without even asking for Steel-
Maitland's presence.[47] In addition, though Steel-Maitland was
involved ex officio in the process of day-to-day negotiation with
employers and labor representatives, his weak and uninspiring
performance as a negotiatior was worrisome to many. According
to Thomas Jones's diary, "[h]e is most industrious and has laboured
hard to get up the subject, but distrusts himself, turns constantly
to Horace Wilson at his elbow, apologises, protests that he is being
frank and straight, which of course he is trying to be, but the total
impression is one of weakness and cloudiness. As the Conference
proceeded he became less nervous and more lucid and convincing."[48] Jones also wrote in the diary that Stanley Baldwin "needed
*more adequate ministerial support* ... Steel-Maitland] is very conciliatory in manner but ineffective and uncertain. I urged the P. M. to
call in Worthington-Evans or Birkenhead."[49] These two officials
were called in and their influence on the Prime Minister proved to
be larger than that of the Labor Minister. The Labor Minister, ide-
ally a kind of a kingpin in such a situation, found himself on the
sidelines on the key issues.

What is worse, the state was determined to fight to the end.[50]
Industrialist Alfred Mond suggested that Baldwin impose a solution on both employers and trade unions.[51] Baldwin wanted nothing of that sort, however.[52] He sided with the mine owners
because the British mining industry needed wage cuts to stay
competitive in the world market, and he was determined to meet
working-class challenges with brute force. The Conservative government's bias shone through in ways its officials dealt with
employers and labor representatives: "It is impossible not to feel
the contrast between the reception which ministers give to a body
of owners and a body of miners. Ministers are at ease at once with
the former, they are friends jointly exploring the situations."[53] The
Supply and Transport Committee rapidly prepared its strike-
breaking logistics during the nine-month temporary truce; gathering 200,000 commercial vehicles, stocking supplies, increasing
the number of special constables from 98,000 to 226,000, adding

18,000 men to the reserves, and "mobiliz[ing] the military, navy's police and hundreds of thousands of volunteers."[54]

The massive show of military force and strike-breaking organization brought the Trades Union Congress to its knees. The TUC General Council broke with miners on 12 May 1926. Its general secretary, Walter Citrine, accused miners of being "out to justify themselves in the eyes of their own people without any regard at all to the position of the Council, on whom the whole blame, if there is any, will be thrown."[55] The TUC had "no intention to win the General Strike."[56] Citrine conceded that the TUC leaders were more interested in galvanizing the crowd with a few speeches designed "to strengthen the determination of the rank and file to meet whenever trouble might arise"[57] than in planning the logistics of the impending confrontation. To support his claim, he went on to describe a meeting that took place on 4 May 1926: "The rest of the members sit about looking tired, somewhat bored, worried but far from rattled, almost in a state of coma. Some improve the shining hour by reading the *British Worker*, unheeding the peroration of the orator holding the floor. Not much sign here of the alleged revolutionaries who are plotting to overthrow the Constitution and the Government."[58] He insisted that the General Strike "was never aimed against the State as a challenge to the Constitution. It was a protest against the degradation of the standards of life of millions of good trade unionists. It was a sympathetic strike on a national scale."[59] Historians unanimously conclude that the TUC General Council was in reality half-hearted in its fight against the government.

The TUC paid dearly for its surrender. About 500,000 members walked out on the trade unions. Parliament passed punitive legislation, the Trade Disputes and Trade Unions Act of 1927, to punish trade unions for their involvement and to prevent future occurrences by reducing workers' contributions to Labour party funds.[60] Though never enforced, it nevertheless heightened class tensions.

The government's tough stance smashed the political power and exhausted the financial resources of the Miners' Federation of Great Britain (MFGB), once "the largest, most powerful, most cohesive, and most political section of workers,"[61] and the avant-garde in nationwide struggles between 1918 and 1926. As in 1921, miners were left alone and ultimately defeated in November 1926 after a three-month self-sustained strike. Desperate, they accepted longer hours and lower wages, which were even worse than the working conditions before the First World War. The prospect of national settlements became a utopian goal as employers imposed district settlements and restored the basic wages of 1914.

The General Strike of 1926 was a turning point in the balance of power in industrial relations. The working class lost its bargaining power gained during the war and in the immediate postwar years, and languished as a negligible factor in the economic and labor policies of the state from 1926 onwards.[62] The hostility of the state toward labor also killed any plans to establish a central tribunal with power to enforce arbitration measures, which could avoid stalemates and military intervention. The plan never materialized due to opposition of the cabinet and Parliament.[63]

In principle, employers and labor settled their disputes by themselves through collective bargainings and mediation bodies. The Labor Ministry remained on the sidelines when matters could be resolved without much fracas. However, the self-determination principle hit a snag when both sides came to a deadlock. The government then intervened in favor of business, resorting to ultimatum and invariably sending in police, troops, and strike-breaking organizations against strikers. Employers were the biggest beneficiaries of the outcome of these two major industrial conflicts. The self-determination policy, which organized labor advocated, worked to the advantage of employers and put labor at a disadvantage in times of major crises. Thus, the Ministry's commitment to non-intervention was a strong form of state intervention in disguise

## Labour Governments and Industrial Relations Policy

British industrial relations policy changed according to crucial contingencies, rather than according to changes in political power during the interwar years. The Labor Ministry remained powerless under the Labour governments of 1924 and 1929.[64] In 1923, Ramsay MacDonald offered the post of Labor Minister to the leading Labour theoretician Sidney Webb, a widely respected socialist intellectual, but then changed his mind. Sidney Webb had gladly accepted this "unpretentious office with a low salary and no social duties;"[65] however, MacDonald, under the influence of his staff, told Webb on 17 January 1924 that the Ministry was the "Cinderella of the government office," meaning a neglected and meaningless agency below Webb's status. Instead, MacDonald offered him the presidency of the more established Board of Trade, which had more political prestige in government hierarchy.[66] When offering the post of Labor Minister to Sidney Webb on 31 December 1923, MacDonald was blunt about what the Labor Minister could do: "As little legislation as you can do with, please, though you will need some."[67] The Labor Minister was relegated to such an insignificant role in the government that he did not even sit on the cabinet committee appointed by the 1929 Labour Government to consider the repeal of the 1927 anti-union Trade Disputes and Trade Union Act.[68]

The rise of the first Labour Government was hailed as "a red letter day in the history of the [labor] movement."[69] But the two Labour governments had no desire whatsoever to increase the Labor Ministry's political role and administrative capacity. As a result of the Prime Minister's overshadowing role, the Labor Minister never became "the main link between the government and the trade union movement" during the interwar years. He did so only when Ernest Bevin assumed the Ministry's leadership in 1940, in the heat of the Second World War. Labor also had to wait until the Second World War to see the state begin paying more attention to trade-union policy and conciliation with labor.[70]

Ramsay MacDonald, the first Labour Prime Minister, continued the policy of his Conservative predecessors. During MacDonald's leadership in 1924 and again in 1929, the Labor Ministers remained a vassal and the Labor Ministry a marginal weakling. Hurriedly taking office and hastily withdrawing therefrom, Prime Ministers could barely cope with the daily business of running the state machinery, and therefore "had no time for policy development." Ministers tried "to stay afloat in the troubled waters of minority government, without being asked to make much headway towards the far shore of socialism."[71]

Once in power, both the 1924 and the 1929 socialist governments tried to dispel the appearance of any class bias in their actions. They projected themselves as the national governments and, in their effort to stay above class conflicts, avoided favoring trade unions in industrial disputes. The top priority of the governing Labour party was to shed its image of working-class champion and, instead, to protect the public interest. At the center of this concern lay the Labour party's desire to win the heart of the country.[72] In numerous instances, socialist ministers of the 1929-1931 government were more vehemently opposed to class solutions than non-Labour cabinet members.[73] As impatient with strikes as the previous Conservative governments, the 1924 Labour government allowed the strike-breaking Supply and Transport Organization to survive and, for fear of antagonizing the civil service, sought the service of STO's John Anderson when two strikes led by Ernest Bevin and the Transport and Ground Workers' Union broke out in February and March 1924. Using the Supply and Transport Organization, the Labour government came down hard on the strikers in the name of public interest. As Lloyd George eagerly remarked, "Mr. Ramsay MacDonald and his Ministry not only took it [STO] over, but were ready and even anxious to make use of it ... in the two threatened emergencies of 1924."[74] The Labour government kept the Supply and Transport Organization alive and did not change its personnel; nor did it "provide an alternative method of handling emergencies arising from industrial strikes.[75]

In line with the Labour policy of neutrality and impartiality, Labor Minister T. Shaw was careful to avoid being perceived as pro-labor in industrial disputes. His overriding concern was to rule responsibly in the interest of all. He protected his neutrality by first mediating by himself and then summoning a Court of Inquiry. Seven Courts of Inquiry were held in 1924, while only six were held from 1914 (the year of the passage of the Industrial Courts Act) to 1923.[76] Moreover, the Labour government underlined its neutrality when Ramsay MacDonald prohibited his ministers from showing copies of bills to employers and trade unions prior to their introduction in Parliament, and, on 8 April 1924, rejected the request of a deputation from the TUC General Council to examine industrial legislation.[77] The socialist governments left no programmatic change that could thrust the long-dormant and bullied Labor Ministry into a dynamic role in industrial relations. Under the control of T. Shaw, formerly a moderate cotton union leader, the Labor Ministry collided with the TUC, which was "suspicious of every reform offered by government and employer" and was "too fast in seeking ultimate ideals (such as nationalization)."[78] The leadership of a socialist Labor Minister did not, therefore, make a difference in the outcomes of industrial conflicts and in labor legislation. It turned out that the socialist-led Ministry was but a carbon copy of the one under the Conservative governments.

The interwar years abound with instances in which the political and industrial leadership of the labor movement were at odds with each other. During the General Strike of 1926, the TUC failed to mobilize the support of the Labour party and its parliamentary leaders, who, in Sidney Webb's words, "had nothing to do with it [the General Strike]." At the time, Sidney Webb, a parliamentarian, had no sympathy for the TUC. According to his account, the trade-union leaders "and the General Council generally, and Citrine, the new Secretary thereof, are anti-political, jealous of the Labour party, which has outstripped the General Council and old-fashioned trade unionism, especially in regards to getting the limelight."[79] Suspicious of each other, the General Council and the Labour party were not in constant communication with each other during the General Strike.[80]

There was a profound strategic difference between the trade-union leaders turned ministers and those in charge of trade unions. The TUC leaders favored direct action to further their goals, whereas the two Labour governments, dominated by the right-wing faction of labor, advocated political action. Prime Minister MacDonald, whose 1924 Labour government depended on Liberal support in Parliament, abhorred strikes pushing for higher wages, because, in his view, they were liable to impede the legislative work of the new government.[81] The TUC leaders opposed the first Labour government's intervention in industrial disputes, while MacDonald was eager to re-establish public order so as to demonstrate the ability of a socialist government to rule. Furthermore, personal animosity came into play, further straining the tense relationship between TUC officials and Labour party politicians. According to a top TUC official, Fred Bramley, he and MacDonald did not even have five minutes' conversation during the brief Labour government interlude.[82] While trade unions had gleefully hailed the Labour party' s electoral triumphs in the 1924 and 1929 national elections, they had no easy access to the MacDonald governments, which did not even make an effort to set up formal channels for trade unions to use. Beatrice Webb, a shrewd observer of the political scene, remarked in her diary entry on 3 March 1924 that MacDonald, "deep down in his heart … prefers the company of Tory aristocrats and Liberal capitalists to that of the Trade Union officials and the ILP [International Labour party] agitators."[83]

Moreover, the TUC was unable to exert much influence on the government due to its internal weaknesses. Until 1926, the TUC lacked executive power over its members. It could not speak with authority for the individual unions, which "were intensely jealous of their autonomy and afraid of their authority being usurped."[84] The TUC's constituency foiled any attempt to centralize a highly decentralized structure or to establish a coordinated policy. As a federative organization, the TUC could not make decisions without the prior approval of its members and had little influence even on its internal affairs. As its general secretary Walter Citrine observed, the TUC "could not lay down any plan of reorganization which its affiliated unions could be compelled to accept. No matter what the TUC said, the individual unions always had the last word."[85] Only with the defeat of the labor movement in 1926 did the TUC leadership gain more power. The full-time general secretary and the General Council, a central executive body created in 1921, could direct the labor movement from the center. They steered the trade unions away from the self-destructive strategy of direct action in favor of closer cooperation with both the Ministry and employers from 1926 onwards.[86]

The TUC also fell victim to economic downturns. Although it was the largest labor organization, the TUC "never represented more than one-third of the work force after 1921."[87] Its membership fell from 8 million to 4.7 million: 4 million in 1914, 8 million in 1922, and 4.7 million in 1927.[88] In 1921, unionized labor dropped to 37 percent of the labor force, from 54.5 percent previously.[89] Hard hit by mass unemployment, the TUC struggled to remain financially afloat, but, in the end, it accomplished little. Trade-union funds took a sharp plunge: From £12.5 million in early 1926 to £8.5 million at the end of 1926.[90] In view of the TUC's weakness, the Labor Ministry refused to let it be the sole labor representative on government committees.

## Postwar World Leadership Crisis and Autonomous Processes

The British tradition of liberalism in industrial relations was not only shot through with exclusionary processes in favor of employers, but also entwined with the pursuit of international prestige by Lloyd George and the successive interwar governments. The First World War weakened the British hold on the international economy and the ability of the City to act as banker to the world. The U.S. emerged as a formidable competitor and became Britain's creditor.[91] British exports of manufactured goods and foreign investments declined drastically after the war. To recover its prewar glory, the British government attempted to return to the gold standard, which was suspended in 1913 and then abandoned in 1919. As Cain and Hopkins noted in their studies of British imperialism, "[t]he struggle to restore the gold standard demonstrates Britain's determination to repel the challenge of the U.S. and to reassert financial authority on the periphery as well as traditional orthodoxy at home."[92] The quest to maintain financial supremacy in the world dominated the agenda of the day and wreaked havoc on public bureaucracies.

Sterling supremacy could be achieved only by cutting down expenditures at home, eliminating administrative duplication, and cleaning up financial waste created by the war. Thus, Lloyd George imposed the authority of the Treasury over the state machinery with respect to departmental spending, staffing, recruitment, training, promotion of all officials, and policy-making in 1919.[93] He ordered the Treasury and its extension, the Geddes Committee, to cut budgets across the board. The pursuit of world hegemony gave ammunition to the Treasury and the Geddes Committee to eradicate or sharply limit the capacity and growth of the wartime "mushroom ministries" such as the Ministries of Munitions, Reconstruction, Food, and Labor. Permanent Secretary to the Treasury Warren Fisher urged that all "wartime departments" should "be wound up as rapidly as possible and not continued"[94] and pressed the ministries to substantially reduce public expenditures. He vigorously pursued the budget-cutting policy "not merely in special war services which are now dwindling automatically, but also in normal services where they [reductions of expenditure] are more difficult to obtain."[95]

The Labor Ministry's administrative capacity and labor policy were sacrificed at the altar of international financial supremacy.[96] Warren Fischer used his position as the Head of the Civil Service to assert his active participation in the Labor Ministry's policy-making process.[97] In March 1923, Fischer insisted that government agencies consult with the Treasury before submitting policy to the cabinet. He held the right to examine and veto any policy and stressed the principle that "before a decision is invited or reached a proposal should have been subjected to careful and critical examination from the point of view of getting the best value for money and making sure that there is money available."[98] He had the Labor Ministry's own establishments and finance officers act as the watchdogs of the Treasury.[99] In a meeting with employers, Labor Minister G. H. Roberts once conceded that he did not have "unlimited power, even a cabinet Minister has not, and you would be surprised to know that very often for even the most trivial item of expenditure we've got to get Treasury sanction."[100]

Firmly anchored in classical economic orthodoxy, the Treasury and the Geddes Committee were particularly hostile to the Labor Ministry since they opposed any sort of state intervention, even such mild forms as voluntary conciliation bodies.[101] In their belief, wages were to be determined by market forces and should reflect the value of work done.[102] Accordingly, they sought to undermine the network of local conciliators and to block any ideas of arbitration with enforcement power and a coherent national wages policy.[103] The Treasury cut the number of investigating officers working on the establishment of new Trade Boards in 1920 and 1921,[104] reduced the provincial staff of its Wages and Arbitration Department, which was, according to the Labor Ministry, "a small body of experienced and expert mediators and conciliators" and "of great value in enabling the numerous small disputes which arise between employers and workpeople to be dealt with promptly and efficiently."[105] The Labor Ministry was also forced to scale back the work of its statistical department and to close its publicity, intelligence, and exchange policy departments.[106] Humbert Wolfe, the senior administrator of the Trade Boards, fought hard to preserve ministerial power, but in vain. Furthermore, the Treasury's stranglehold weakened ministerial ties to the labor movement. In the name of professionalization, the Treasury banned the hiring of trade union representatives and labor experts. The Labor Ministry's high-ranking officials Askwith, Shackleton, and Wilson opposed the ban.[107] The Treasury got the upper hand in 1920 when it succeeded in preventing labor representatives from acting as permanent local conciliation officers.[108]

The Treasury and the Geddes Committee proposed the abolition of two departments within the Ministry – the Industrial Relations Department and the Employment Exchanges – and even suggested the abolition of the Labor Ministry itself.[109] The Treasury zeroed in on the Industrial Relations Department. In a report to the Geddes Committee, the financial secretary to the Treasury, E. Hilton-Young, argued that the Industrial Relations Department was an unnecessary nuisance. Labor Ministry officials were criticized for their constant interference in management-labor relations and for their high salaries. "This was precisely the kind of Department which the public thought should be suppressed. The work done was no doubt very valuable, but why was it necessary to have special officials to do it?"[110] The Geddes Committee recommended in 1922 the transfer of the functions of the Trade Boards and the Industrial Relations Department to the Board of Trade.[111] It issued a scathing condemnation of the work of the Industrial Relations Department and drew a line between state intervention and conciliation: "With the knowledge that in the end there will be government intervention neither side will have the same incentive to make the final proposals which might lead to a settlement of the disputes and we suggest that the discontinuance of this branch of activity should be considered by the government."[112] In doing so, the Committee dismissed Labor Minister T. J. Macnamara's warning about the effects of such a dismantlement:

> The destruction of the Industrial Relations Department would mean the abandonment not only of the State Scheme of Conciliation and Arbitration embodied in the Conciliation Act and in the Industrial Court Act, but also the abandonment of the Whitley Council Schemes and the other Conciliation machinery which has been developed not by state interference but by judicious consultation with the people concerned during the last 25 years. Under present conditions it is suggested that such action would be the reverse of economy.[113]

Labor Ministry officials reacted swiftly, but their protests fell on deaf ears. In an internal memo to A. W. Watson, head of the Establishments section, a senior official angrily insisted that financial officers "should not deal with a question of policy on grounds of policy."[114] Likewise, another high-ranking official, T. W. Phillips, strongly argued against the Finance Department "taking part in the settlement of policy, in order to ensure that policy is framed with due regard to economy," and feared that "it tends to weaken the sense of responsibility of administrative officers for economy," and to slow down their work.[115] The Labor Ministry officials deplored the situation in which "finance seeks to take its place side by side with the administrative heads of Departments on practically all questions of policy."[116] In spite of the Ministry officials' assertiveness, the Treasury carried the day. Surrendering to the Treasury, Horace J. Wilson, the senior official leading the Industrial Relations Department, announced on 14 July 1925 that:

> Although the primary responsibility for "public economy" rests upon administrative officers both in framing policy and in putting policy into practice ... the Accountant General, as Finance Officer, should participate at an early stage, in discussions leading to the initiation and settlement of administrative policy, with his mind more particularly directed to the financial aspects of that policy.[117]

These autonomous processes – i.e., the Prime Minister's decision to mobilize the Treasury and the Geddes Committee to protect Britain's international supremacy – resulted in neutralizing the Labor Ministry for the sake of political goals. The Industrial Relations Department survived the axe, but it was cut to the bone.

It lost its conciliation capacity. Its headquarters staff decreased dramatically: 112 in January 1919, 116 in August 1920, 90 in March 1921, and 63 in October 1921; and the staff in the provinces were reduced to 54 in October 1921 from 117 in January 1919.[118] In January 1924, only twenty-eight provincial staff members remained. Under the pressure of the Geddes Committee's report on National Expenditure, the Labor Ministry scratched its Whitley Councils, its centerpiece of self-determination policy, and the Joint Industrial Councils Division was folded into the Industrial Relations Department. Ironically, former Labor Minister Robert Horne, who had never protected the Labor Ministry and its conciliation work against the Geddes Committee, "was actually the Chancellor of the Exchequer who commissioned the axe, reducing the Labor Ministry's size by 87 percent.[119] Hence, the Labor Ministry's growth "stopped and contracted" until the outbreak of the Second World War.[120]

More significantly, these maneuvers consolidated Prime Ministers' control over labor affairs, upstaging labor ministers in large-scale conflicts. Between 1918 and 1930, the five prime ministers personally intervened in negotiations between employers and trade unions and reduced the labor ministers to intermediaries. Prime Minister Lloyd George became known as the powerful "auxiliary Minister of Labour" in every important matter. His "views were crucial. The doors of Downing Street, to a wide variety of trade union deputations and delegations, were ever wide open."[121] This pattern of subjugation was repeated across the political spectrum. Conservative Prime Minister Stanley Baldwin (1924-1929) directly negotiated with employers and labor, sidelining his Labor Minister Arthur Steel-Maitland. So did socialist Prime Minister Ramsay MacDonald, who was eager to prove he could govern the nation, in 1924 and 1929. The British Labor Ministry's lack of conciliation and arbitration capacity meant that it could not settle major industrial disputes such as the coal miners strike of 1921 and the General Strike of 1926 and that the political leadership had to squash industrial conflicts through the use of police, military, and legal repression. This deficient intervention capacity thus weakened labor and strengthened capital in large-scale industrial conflicts.

The pursuit of world power and belt-tightening at home benefited the City. The Bank of England and its allies in the financial community opposed state intervention in industrial relations and approved of the budget cuts that weakened the Labor Ministry.

Their interests were anchored in a strong sterling standard and reduction of public expenditures.[122] Financial capital more than welcomed the return to the gold standard in April 1925, though the measure aggravated the plight of British industry. The autonomous processes ultimately promoted the interests of the Bank of England and its allies in the financial community, which, instead of the industrial sector, was the chief societal influence on the British government.[123] As historians point out, in spite of the First World War and deteriorating British influence in the world, the City remained powerful throughout the interwar period: "The City of London retained its independence and its central position in British economic life throughout the interwar period, despite the fall in income from overseas investment and the rise of large-scale manufacturing in Britain. The City was not absorbed into a monopoly capitalist structure dominated by manufacturing in the way that banks had become linked to large-scale industry in Germany and the U.S.; its priorities continued to imprint themselves on economic policy and on the empire, as they had done before the war."[124]

In sum, the decline of British international standing and pursuit of internal peace initiated autonomous processes that dealt heavy blows to the Labor Ministry's feeble administrative capacity in promoting conciliation bodies. These autonomous processes were scattered among – to use Michael Mann's term, "entwined with" – inclusionary and exclusionary processes.[125] However, they are consequential nonetheless. The Labor Ministry's drastic shifts from inclusionary to exclusionary and autonomous processes stand out dramatically.

# Notes


1. G. W. McDonald and H. F. Gospel, "The Mond-Turner Talks, 1927-1933: A Study in Industrial CO-Operation," *Historical Journal* 16, (1973), p. 808.

2. Robert Keith Middlemas, *Politics in Industrial Society: The Experience of the British System since 1911* (London: A. Deutsch, 1979), p. 13.

3. Stephen Blank, *Industry and Government in Britain: The Federation of British Industries in Politics, 1945-1965* (Mass.: Lexington Books, 1973), p. 7.

4. Rodney Lowe, *Adjusting to Democracy: The Role of the Ministry of Labour in British Politics, 1916-1939* (Oxford: Clarendon Press, 1986.), p. 84.

5. Lord Walter Citrine, *Men and Work* (London: Hutchinson, 1964), p. 251.

6. Stephen Blank, *Industry and Government*, p. 21. See also Jonathan Zeitlin, "From Labour History to the History of Industrial Relations," *Economic History Review* XL, 2, (1987), p. 175.

7. Stephen Blank, *Industry and Government*, pp. 30-31.

8. Ibid., p. 7.

9. The 1,392 members included 175 trade associations, 1,202 individual firms, and 15 associations created by the state during the war. See Stephen Blank, *Industry and Government*, p. 15.

10. Howard F. Gospel, "Employers' Labour Policy: A Study of the Mond-Turner Talks 1927-1933," *Business History* 21, 2, (July 1979), pp. 194-195.

11. Keith Jefferey and Peter Hennessy, *States of Emergency: British Governments and Strikebreaking since 1919* (Boston: Routledge & K. Paul, 1983), p. 101.

12. M. C. Shefftz, "The Trade Union and Trade Disputes Act, 1927," *Review of Politics* 29 (1967), p. 390.

13. R. H. Desmarais, "The British Government's Strikebreaking Organization and Black Friday," *Journal of Contemporary History*, (1971), p. 116.

14. Ibid., p. 117.

15. Arthur J. McIvor, "Employers' Organisation and Strikebreaking in Britain," *International Review of Social History* 29, Part 1, 3-4, (1984), p. 644.

16. Cab 27/73, 23 September 1920, p. 133.

17. R. H. Desmarais, "The British Government's Strikebreaking Organization," p. 122.

18. Jane Morgan, *Conflict and Order: The Police and Labour Disputes in England and Wales, 1900-1939* (Oxford: Clarendon Press, 1987), p. 130.

19. Ibid., p. 146.

20. Peter Dennis, "The Territorial Army in Aid of the Civil Power in Britain, 1919-1926," *Journal of Contemporary History* 16, 4, (October 1981), p. 707.

21. The British state was one of the biggest employers in the interwar era. In addition to mines, it controlled the railways until August 1921 and had a financial stake in coal until after the General Strike. See V. L. Allen, *Trade Unions and the Government* (London: Butler & Tanner Ltd, 1960), p. 90.

22. Ibid., p. 188.

23. Kenneth O. Morgan, *Consensus and Disunity: The Lloyd George Coalition Government, 1918-1922* (Oxford: Oxford University Press, 1979), p. 188.

24. See P. S. Bagwell, "The Triple Industrial Alliance," in *Essays in Labour History*, eds. A. Briggs and J. Saville (New York: Macmillan, 1971).

25. K. G. J. C. Knowles, *Strikes – A Study of Industrial Conflict, with Special Reference to British Experience between 1911 and 1947* (Oxford: Basil Blackwell, 1954), p. 109.

26. Kenneth O. Morgan, *Consensus and Disunity*, p. 55.
27. David Wrigley, *Lloyd George and the British Labour Government* (New York: Barnes & Noble, 1976), p. 234.
28. Thomas Jones, *Whitehall Diary, 1916-1925*, vol. 1, ed. Keith Middlemas (London: Oxford University Press, 1969), p. 98.
29. Kenneth O. Morgan, *Consensus and Disunity*, p. 54.
30. Rodney Lowe, "The Ministry of Labour, 1916-1924: A Graveyard of Social Reform?" *Public Administration* 52, (1974), p. 434.
31. K. G. J. C. Knowles, *Strikes*, pp. 108-109.
32. Kenneth O. Morgan, *Consensus and Disunity*, p. 55 and Jane Morgan, *Conflict and Order*, p. 97.
33. Kenneth O. Morgan, *Consensus and Disunity*, p. 55.
34. Thomas Jones, *Whitehall Diary*, Vol. 1, pp. 43 and 53.
35. M. C. Shefftz, "The Trade Union and Trade Disputes Act," p. 389 and Keith Jefferey and Peter Hennessy, *States of Emergency*, p. 91.
36. Thomas Jones, *Whitehall Diary*, vol. 2, p. 325. The union leaders were "badly tricked" by Baldwin's disposition.
37. M. C. Shefftz, "The Trade Union and Trade Disputes Act, 1927," p. 391.
38. Kenneth O. Morgan, *Consensus and Disunity*, p. 118.
39. M. C. Shefftz, "The Trade Union and Trade Disputes Act, 1927," p. 390.
40. Eric L. Wigham, *Strikes and the Government, 1893-1981* (London: Macmillan, 1982), p. 66.
41. Robert Keith Middlemas and John Barnes, *Baldwin: A Biography* (London: Weidenfeld & Nicolson, 1969), p. 412.
42. Thomas Jones, *Whitehall Diary*, vol. 2, 2 May 1926, p. 30.
43. Quoted in Robert Keith Middlemas and John Barnes, *Baldwin*, p. 413, italics mine.
44. Lord Walter Citrine, *Men and Work*, p. 175.
45. Lab 2 1207/IR 745/1926, p. 89.
46. Thomas Jones, *Whitehall Diary*, vol. 2, 5 May 1926, p. 38.
47. Ibid., p. 13.
48. Ibid., 14 April 1926, p. 12.
49. Ibid., 17 April 1926, p. 17, italics mine.
50. Martin Jacques, "Consequences of the General Strike," in *The General Strike 1926*, ed. Jeffrey Skelley (London: Laurence and Wishart, 1976), p. 382.
51. Thomas Jones, *Whitehall Diary*, vol. 2, 23 April 1926, p. 18.
52. Ibid., p. 20.
53. Ibid., 23 April 1926, p.19.
54. K. G. J. C. Knowles, *Strikes*, p. 111.
55. Lord Walter Citrine, *Men and Work*, p. 199.
56. V. L. Allen, *Trade Unions and the Government*, p. 198.
57. Lord Walter Citrine, *Men and Work*, p. 145.
58. Ibid., p. 191.
59. Lord Walter Citrine, *Men and Work*, p. 217.
60. M. C. Shefftz, "The Trade Union and Trade Disputes Acts," pp. 387-406.
61. Martin Jacques, "Consequences of the General Strike," p. 383.
62. Ibid., p. 382. G. A. Phillips argued against Martin Jacques's contention that the working-class defeat was a historical watershed because the labor movement did not suffer in the long run. See G. A. Phillips, *The General Strike: The Politics of Industrial Conflict* (London: Weidenfeld & Nicolson, 1976), p. 280.

63.  Thomas Jones, *Whitehall Diary*, vol. 2, 26 September 1926, p. 87.

64.  Rodney Lowe, "The Ministry of Labour, 1916-1924," pp. 421-422.

65.  Lisanne Radice, *Beatrice and Sidney Webb: Fabian Socialists* (London: Macmillan, 1984), p. 241.

66.  Ibid., p. 242.

67.  Ibid., p. 241.

68.  Rodney Lowe, *Adjusting to Democracy*, p. 111.

69.  PRO 30/69/239; the statement came from a deputation of the Miners' Federation, 1 October 1924.

70.  V. L. Allen, *Trade Unions and the Government*, p. 64.

71.  R. W. Lyman, *The First Labour Government, 1924* (London: Chapman & Hall, 1957), pp. 226-227.

72.  R. H. Desmarais, "Strike-breaking and the Labour Government of 1924," *Journal of Contemporary History* 8, (1973), p. 170 and V. L. Allen, *Trade Unions and the Government*, p. 232.

73.  V. L. Allen, *Trade Unions and the Government*, p. 255.

74.  Chris Wrigley, *Arthur Henderson* (Cardiff: GPC Books, 1990), p. 148.

75.  R. H. Desmarais, "Strike-breaking," pp. 169-170.

76.  V. L. Allen, *Trade Unions and the Government*, p. 235.

77.  Lab 10/1.

78.  Rodney Lowe, *Adjusting to Democracy*, p. 85.

79.  Quoted in Lisanne Radice, *Sidney and Beatrice Webb*, p. 255.

80.  Robert Keith Middlemas and John Barnes, *Baldwin*, p. 412.

81.  Richard W. Lyman, *The First Labour Government, 1924*, p. 233.

82.  V. L. Allen, *Trade Unions and the Government*, p. 236.

83.  Quoted in Lisanne Radice, *Beatrice and Sidney Webb*, p. 243.

84.  Lord Walter Citrine, *Men and Work*, p. 227.

85.  Ibid., p. 221.

86.  Rodney Lowe, *Adjusting to Democracy*, p. 85.

87.  Ibid., pp. 84-87.

88.  G. W. McDonald and Howard F. Gospel, "The Mond-Turner Talks, 1927-1933," p. 814.

89.  Robert Keith Middlemas, *Politics in Industrial Society*, p. 163.

90.  Martin Jacques, "Consequences of the General Strike," p. 382.

91.  Peter Cain and A. G. Hopkins, *British Imperialism: Crisis and Deconstruction 1914-1990* (Longman: London 1993), p. 59.

92.  Ibid., p. 6. On prewar world supremacy, see their accompanying volume, *British Imperialism: Innovation and Expansion, 1688-1914* (Longman: London 1993).

93.  Kathleen Burke, "The Treasury: From Impotence to Power," in *War and the State: The Transformation of British Government, 1914-1919*, ed. Kathleen Burke (London: Allen & Unwin, 1982), pp. 91-97.

94.  Kathleen Burke, "The Treasury," p. 102.

95.  Lab 2 1823/CEB 380/1923, 1 June 1923.

96.  Jonathan Zeitlin develops a realist approach to the state that underlines the importance of geopolitical considerations – i.e., the international role of sterling – for labor policy. See his study, "Shop Floor Bargaining and the State: A Contradictory Relationship," in *Shop Floor and the State: Historical and Comparative Perspectives*, eds. Steven Tolliday and Jonathan Zeitlin (Cambridge: Cambridge University Press, 1985), pp. 26-37.

97. The power of the Treasury was limited during the period of 1854-1914. See Maurice Wright, "Treasury Control, 1814-1914," in *Studies in the Growth of Nineteenth Century Government*, ed. Gillian Sutherland (London: Routledge & Kegan Paul, 1972), pp. 217-221.

98. Lab 2 981/10, 26 March 1923.

99. Roger Davidson and Rodney Lowe, "Bureaucracy and Innovation in British Welfare Policy, 1870-1945," in *The Emergence of the Welfare State in Britain and Germany*, ed. W. J. Mommsen (London: Croom Helm, 1981),. p. 283 and Rodney Lowe, "The Ministry of Labour, 1916-1924," p. 432.

100. Lab 2 229/2, 17 January 1918, p. 13.

101. Rodney Lowe, "The Erosion of State Intervention in Britain, 1917-1924," *Economic History Review* 31, (1978), p. 283.

102. Rodney Lowe, *Adjusting to Democracy*, p. 120.

103. Rodney Lowe, "The Erosion of State Intervention in Britain," pp. 278-281.

104. G. C. Peden, "The Treasury as the Central Department," p. 377.

105. Lab 2 1779/CEB 109/5, 20 October 1919.

106. Lab 2 1779/CEB 109/5, p. 14.

107. Lab 2 1779/CEB 109/5, 20 October 1919.

108. Rodney Lowe, *Adjusting to Democracy*, p. 90 and Roger Davidson and Rodney Lowe, "Bureaucracy and Innovation," p. 282.

109. Peter K. Cline, "Eric Geddes and the 'Experiment' with Businessmen in Government, 1915-22," in *Essays in Labour History: Responses to the Rise of Labour in Britain*, ed. Kenneth D. Brown (London: Macmillan Press, 1974), p. 76.

110. Lab 27 165/GRC CSD), 1922, pp. 66-67.

111. Lab 2 1930/CEB/54, 14 December 1921.

112. T163/14/3, p. 101.

113. Cab 27 167/E Labour 2/221-223, 17 August 1922.

114. Lab 2 1907/CEB 649/1922, 24 November 1922.

115. Lab 2 1907/CEB 649/1922, 9 July 1923.

116. Lab 2 1907/CEB 649/1922, 30 August 1923.

117. Lab 2 1907/CEB 649/1922.

118. Lab 2 1822/CEB 537/2/1921, 1921, p. 225.

119. Rodney Lowe, "The Ministry of Labour: Fact and Fiction." *Bulletin of the Society for the Study of Labour History* 41, (1980), p. 24.

120. V. L. Allen, *Trade Unions and the Government* .

121. Kenneth O. Morgan, *Consensus and Disunity*, p. 77.

122. Jonathan Zeitlin, "Shop Floor Bargaining and the State," pp. 34-36.

123. Such a neo-Marxist view can be found in James Cronin, "Coping with Labour, 1918-1926," in *Social Conflict and the Political Order in Modern Britain*, eds. James E. Cronin and Jonathan Schneer (London: Croom Helm, 1979), pp. 134-135.

124. Peter Cain and A. G. Hopkins, *British Imperialism: Crisis and Deconstruction*, p. 5.

125. Michael Mann, *Sources of Social Power: The Rise of Classes and Nation-States, 1760-1914*, vol. 2 (Cambridge: Cambridge University Press, 1993), p. 88.

# Chapter Five

# Bending German Statism
Pluralist Compromises and Class Interests

On 30 October 1923, the German Labor Ministry promulgated the state arbitration decree, an emergency measure that allowed the Labor Minister and his state arbitrators to enforce arbitration decisions on both employers and trade unions to settle industrial disputes. The Labor Ministry's assertion of power from 1923 to 1930 covered a period that saw the rule of the all-bourgeois governments between 1924 and 1928, the Social Democratic party in power and in opposition, and the break-up of the Grand Coalition in March 1930. On the surface, the resurgence of state *diktat* seems to confirm the cultural argument that national political customs mold policy trajectories and corroborate the statist contention that the history of state structures exercises enduring influence on politics. These two perspectives uphold the view that the German state is the archetype of authoritarian rule.

In reality, German authoritarianism was malleable and context-sensitive. The Labor Ministry veered sharply from its state arbitration policy in crucial junctures. This chapter shows that the state arbitration policy was shot through with pluralist compromises with both employers and trade unions in major industrial disputes, as well as defense of capitalist interests. Several contingencies reoriented industrial relations policy in contradictory ways. Economic crises and crises of industrial relations forced Labor Minister Heinrich Brauns to protect labor. Major industrial conflicts were solved by buying off both sides, rather than through

Notes for this chapter begin on page 134.

arbitration. And crises of political economy compelled the Labor Ministry to side with business interests. The veering and tacking under specific historical conditions enraged both employers and workers, alternately and simultaneously. Labor Minister Brauns took much heat for switching sides. Liberal businessmen derided him as the Minister of the Unemployed ("Arbeitslosenminister") "with a big registry of sins"; the extreme left dubbed him the Employers' Minister ("Arbeitgeberminister") and the Labor Ministry as the "docile instrument of capitalist profit."[1]

## Statism and the Crisis of Industrial Relations and Political Regime in 1923-1930

The statist turn of the Labor Ministry had its origins in the crisis of industrial relations. The postwar Stinnes-Legien agreement between employers and trade unions collapsed during the rampant inflation of 1922-1923. Employers attacked the revolutionary gains of the working class: they rejected collective bargaining, fought the eight-hour day, and curtailed wages with much success.[2] Trade unions lost members to unemployment and lacked the necessary funds to resist employers. Paying only lip service to the Central Cooperative Working Association (ZAG), employers wanted industrial relations to revert to the prewar era.[3] As a result, the ZAG broke down. In addition to the German Iron and Steel Workers Association (Deutsche Metallarbeiterverband, or DMV), which left the ZAG in 1919, the German Association of Wood Workers (Deutsche Holzarbeiterverband) withdrew in 1923 and the socialist Trade Unions, by far the largest trade union, ended its cooperation with employers on 21 March 1924. The institutional void in industrial relations and prospects of escalating conflicts jeopardized the survival of the fledgling Weimar regime. However, economic crisis alone was only a necessary but not a sufficient condition for the German Labor Ministry's intervention in the labor market.

The crisis within the state was the crucial contingency that allowed the Labor Ministry to expand its administrative capacity. Weimar governments came and went due to unstable coalitions. Chancellors held short tenures. Between 1920 and 1928, the period of Brauns's tenure, cabinets were shuffled ten times, and the six chancellors of the period held their post for merely 8.3 months on average. During the entire Weimar period, the chancellorship changed hands sixteen times.[4] Factional politics among ten to sixteen political parties paralyzed the Reichstag (the German Parliament) which passed the Enabling Law on 13 October 1923 to grant the cabinet the power to rule by decree. The crisis of the regime was further compounded by the French and Belgian occupation of the Ruhr and the hunger, unrest, strikes, tension, and end of passive resistance in the occupied region.

Under these socioeconomic and political conditions, the Stresemann government (August-November 1923) gave *carte blanche* to Labor Minister Brauns. Abruptly changing policy course, Brauns promulgated the state conciliation and arbitration decree (Schlichtungsverordnung) on 30 October 1923. The use of compulsory arbitration originated in the wartime patriotic Auxiliary Service Law of December 1916 that allowed an army officer appointed by the War Office to chair a conciliation board consisting of an equal number of employers and workers. Demobilization officers could declare compulsorily binding awards, and their actions were supported by the Labor Ministry.

The state arbitration decree abolished the trade board system and empowered the Labor Minister and his twenty arbitrators to unilaterally declare compulsorily binding awards and forcibly impose collective agreements.[5] These awards, such as increases or decreases of wage rates and working hours, were binding on both parties in a particular dispute and, in some circumstances, binding on an entire industry, extended to portions of the labor force that were not directly involved in the dispute, or applied to those industries outside both the geographical area of the labor dispute and the trade in question.[6] In this respect, the Labor Minister was far more powerful than any army officers in the First World War. The decree took effect on 1 January 1924 and served as "the legal foundation of the German arbitration system until 1933."[7] The state arbitration policy was proclaimed without any parliamentary discussion or approval and perfunctorily announced in the Labor Ministry's official publication.[8] Employers and trade unions protested vehemently against compulsory arbitration, but in vain.[9]

The state arbitration decree turned industrial relations policy upside down.[10] In one stroke, the Labor Minister and his arbitrators gained the power to enforce their decisions and to override the wishes of employers and workers (Table 6). Most significantly, the Labor Minister became the ultimate potentate in determining wages and working hours. He alone declared awards made by arbitrators to be compulsorily binding (decree of 29 December 1923), extended collective agreements to other sections of the labor force, and imposed collective contracts even in the face of resistance from employers and trade unions. Brauns assumed the crucial role of "a traffic policeman who determines and leads the directions of others"[11] in industrial relations and "was more than a mediator between social classes … [he] assumed the functions of arbitrator and leader."[12]

*Table 6:* State Arbitration in Weimar Germany

| Year | Mediation Procedures | | | Rejected Mediation Decisions | | Arbitration | |
|---|---|---|---|---|---|---|---|
| | Total | resolved through arbitration decisions | | Total | | resolved through declaration of awards | through declaration of compulsory binding awards |
| | | | % | | % | | % |
| 1 | 2 | 3 | 4 | 5 | 6 | 7 | 8 |
| 1924 | 18575 | 10562 | 57 | 4968 | 47 | 17 | 4.5 |
| 1925 | 13418 | 8352 | 62 | 4629 | 55 | 15 | 5.3 |
| 1926 | 5043 | 2807 | 56 | 1580 | 56 | 20 | 6.2 |
| 1927 | 8436 | 4910 | 58 | 2723 | 55 | 20 | 6.4 |
| 1928 | 8067 | 4666 | 58 | 2727 | 58 | 16 | 5.4 |
| 1929 | 7109 | 3927 | 55 | 2501 | 63 | 11 | 3.8 |
| 1930 | 4017 | 2104 | 52 | 1381 | 66 | 15 | 5.1 |
| 1931 | 6898 | 3897 | 56 | 2296 | 59 | 28 | 9.5 |
| 1932 | 4791 | 2495 | 52 | 1472 | 59 | 10 | 3.0 |

*Source:* Dietmar Petzina, Werner Abelshauser and Anselm Faust, eds., *Sozialgeschichtliches Arbeitsbuch, Band III: Materialen zur Statistik des Deutschen Reiches 1914-1945*, (Munich: Verlag C. H. Beck, 1978), p. 117.

The German Labor Ministry turned out to be an exemplary case of an interventionist stronghold in a sea of political ineptitude. Brauns single-handedly administered the new interventionist system independently of the political elite, other state agencies, and societal actors. During Brauns's tenure, the Labor Ministry became so powerful that he could assert that it had acquired "practically the meaning of a Department of Interior, and it even surpasses the Department that we nowadays call the Department of Interior."[13] The Labor Ministry under Brauns expanded the social functions of the Wilhelmine Department of Interior and willfully put "strong emphasis on the social."[14]

Heinrich Brauns extended his authority to the front line of arbitration. Though the decree conferred independence on arbitrators in their rulings, arbitrators acted as the "loyal executive organs" (Ausführungsorgane) of the Ministry's labor policy.[15] The labor minister appointed and removed them and chairmen of arbitration boards,[16] and reserved the right to appoint special arbitrators to deal with thorny cases.[17] Brauns selected twenty arbitrators, except for a few such as August Stenzel (leader of the Hamburg Chamber of Professions), Ernst Mehlich, and Rudolf Wissell (socialist trade - union leaders),[18] from his own agency and the Department of Employment (Arbeitsverwaltung). He used meetings with and memoranda to arbitrators to press them into following his policies.[19] Their position was similar to that of the chairman of an arbitration board.[20] State arbitrators intervened at the early stage of labor disputes, according to three-step arbitration policy. Usually, the arbitrator acted as a mediator, helping concerned parties to reach an agreement. If no consensus was reached, arbitrators or arbitration boards would propose a solution that could be accepted or rejected by the parties. If the solution was rejected by one or two parties, then the arbitrator made the decision alone, namely, formulated an award and imposed its terms on employers and workers alike. The Labor Minister would then approve the official declaration of a compulsorily binding award.

Underlying the state arbitration system was Brauns's Catholic solidarist ideology, a kind of precursor to later Christian Democracy.[21] He believed that the interests of employers and trade unions were complementary rather than inherently antagonistic and argued that the socialist and communist principle of class struggle should be used only when all peaceful means had been exhausted.[22] Thus, in his view, the Labor Ministry had the mission to build an industrial community (Arbeitsgemeinschaft), one that would foster industrial cooperation and facilitate what Brauns called the "incorporation of the working class in society."[23] This "sense of national duty"[24] was based on the religious-ethical views of Pope Leo XIII and Mainz Bishop Wilhelm Emmanuel von Ketteler, who promoted the active involvement of the church in workers' lives (Rerum Novarum of 1891). Above all, Brauns argued that the state had to maintain harmony in industrial relations when state interests were at stake: "The state arbitration decree leaves free collective bargaining in the foreground. It will also in fact prevent the economy from exhausting itself in unfruitful conflicts. I consider self-determination in work relations as the first task of economic associations, and where the economic associations cannot carry out this task peacefully, then the Labor Ministry is the last place where conflicts will be prevented."[25] Brauns's dynamic conception of the Labor Ministry was unparalleled in Europe. He considered himself a "Sozialpolitiker von Beruf" – a social policy statesman by vocation – whose goal was to improve labor conditions and industrial relations. A Sozialpolitiker had a vision of social order, and the Labor Ministry had a mission to translate this vision into social policies. This outlook, he asserted, set the German Labor Ministry apart from the labor ministries in other countries, which were mostly led by "lawyers or civil servants."[26] He insisted, in a 1929 volume celebrating the first ten years of existence of the Labor Ministry and published by it, that the Labor Ministry's push for higher wages through its arbitrations contributed to the welfare of the working class and the settlement of numerous industrial disputes.[27]

Brauns considered the official declaration an emergency action to prevent lockouts and strikes from affecting economically vital production and to ward off "direct threats" such as "the atrophy of important economic sectors and the pauperization of certain working classes."[28] State arbitration was a temporary but necessary palliative to ease the economic crisis, to limit and regulate industrial conflicts, and to impose a uniform wage structure.[29] In a speech given at the Reichstag a year before the decree, Brauns underscored the constructive effects of state arbitration:"[T]o promote and secure economic peace in the interests of those immediately concerned as well as in the interests of the common good .... It would be a crime against the German people, if not everything is done to promote economic peace with laws."[30] He further stated:"I have tried, through the arbitration decree, to lead employers and workers to greater cooperation and to the eventual creation of an industrial community. When the associations cannot reach a compromise, when they fight each other and thus hurt production, it is not only the right but also the duty of the government to intervene."[31] Industrial chaos in postwar Germany, he declared, required the government "to dictate from above the working conditions in a bureaucratic fashion in order to promote the spirit of industrial community and to suppress conflicts over contracts."[32]

As a Catholic priest standing in the middle of the political spectrum, Brauns was far from a champion of the working class. Nor did he depend on the support and goodwill of any employers and their political and economic organizations. In this respect, he had the edge over his Social Democratic colleagues. He was insulated from the pressures of both the socialist Trade Unions, which would expect more from Social Democratic labor ministers, and from employers' organizations, which would feel threatened by an SPD politician heading the labor ministry. Brauns's appointment drew less hostile fire than that of his successor Rudolf Wissell of the SPD, who complained to Chancellor Hermann Müller that "the scales had turned against them [trade unions] once the Minister of Labor was a Social Democrat."[33] He was able to stay in office for eight years because of the working alliance between the Social Democrats and the Center party and Christian Trade Unions. This political coalition was instrumental in promoting social policies in favor of workers. Moreover, he was a key figure in several cabinets. He vigorously supported Catholic Center Chancellor Wilhelm Marx, who carried out Brauns's strategy to form a large centrist bloc that made alliances with the right and the left, acted as counsel to Chancellor Gustav Stresemann of the German People's party on social policies and the Ruhr conflict of August-November 1923, and won the confidence of President Ebert and Chancellors Konstantin Fehrenbach, Hans Luther, Wilhelm Marx, and Gustav Stresemann.[34]

*Intervening in Favor of Organized Labor: 1924-1930*

In an inversion of capitalist-worker power relations, the German Labor Ministry used its autonomy to arbitrate in favor of the working class from 1924 to 1930. Brauns and his arbitrators increased wages and reduced working hours, sometimes even in the face of massive opposition, as evidenced, for instance, by a letter of protest against wage hikes from the Economic Association of Central Germany (Wirtschaftsverband Mitteldeutschland) in the region of Sachsen.[35] In 1923, Brauns urged Chancellor Cuno to create public works to fight unemployment:

> The bad situation of the job market and its possible political repercussions are known to you …. *Because of these reasons, it is economically and politically necessary to strengthen the present job opportunities.* In fact, I think that from the standpoint of the Reich's finances, it is highly desirable to create jobs through state commissions [Staatsaufträge], which will have more positive effects on the job market than doing nothing. Withholding public commissions will increase the number of unem-

ployed and *create severe political troubles*. This especially applies to the occupied region [the Ruhr].[36]

Such means were adopted to help trade unions weather inflation and employers' offensives as well as to contain the threat of a communist uprising after the breakdown of collective bargaining in 1923. Prussian Minister of Interior Severing was worried that communist groups were trying to undermine the influence of trade unions. He banned communist cells, known as Proletarischen Hundertschaften, in factories[37] and hoped that employers would raise wages according to the federal index (Reichsindex) and not give a hard time to labor. German government officials agreed that it was, in the words of Severing, in the interests of the state "to strengthen the trade unions as representatives of those supporting order and as a working-class organization loyal to the state, in order to stem the divisive influence of communism."[38] Such worries led him to alert the chancellor about what he perceived as a crisis situation in the capital, Berlin:

> Although the Communist party has been weakened, it still aims at creating a workers' state. It is thus necessary to decrease the number of unemployed, who number 70,000, and there are 200,000 to 300,000 part-timers. In times of civil unrest, these elements are believed to readily follow the Communist party leadership …. I think it is absolutely necessary to create emergency jobs [Notstandsarbeit] in Berlin in order to reduce the number of jobless and part-time workers.[39]

Contrary to the neo-Marxist disorganization thesis, the Labor Ministry spared no effort to organize, rather than disorganize, the beleaguered trade unions, which were regarded as politically moderate and the best bulwarks against destabilizing forces. Brauns declared that the Labor Ministry was the avant-garde in the battles "to maintain and promote the influence of organized labor, and … to discourage all efforts aimed at reducing the prestige of trade unions":[40]

> The profound meaning and the crucial reason for a labor ministry lies in the historical mission of the labor movement of the present, for the people and the state have a common interest in the realization of such movement against all resistance and in the organic inclusion of the labor movement in the community. It is known that before the war the labor movement encountered resistance from industry and commerce despite its increasing importance. The big and heavy industries and Junkers were allied with the state in their struggle against the working class. The labor movement took a revolutionary stance. The Ger-

man Communist movement is the product of a wrong policy. Fortunately, the majority of the working class have rejected Bolshevism.
*The Ministry of Labor contributed to the working class rejection of Commu-
nism because it made the realization of the historical mission of the labor
movement possible.*[41]

The socialist Trade Unions was by far the most important trade
union organization. In membership, it was seven times larger than
the Christian Trade Unions and thirty times larger than the Liberal
Hirsch-Duncker Trade Unions, which represented only one percent of all organized wage earners. In 1920, these three trade
unions had, respectively, 8 million, 1.1 million, and 226,000 members.[42] The socialist Trade Unions (ADGB) was the most powerful
one. It submitted numerous petitions to the state and sent numerous delegations to the Labor Ministry. Overcoming their political
differences, the three trade unions worked together in advancing
workers' demands and protecting labor rights, and also cooper-
ated in bargaining with employers. The labor movement had
access to the cabinet until the June elections of 1920, when the
bourgeois Fehrenbach cabinet replaced the previous coalition.
This bourgeois cabinet entertained "formal, quasi-diplomatic relations with trade unions."[43] Fortunately, the latter still had the ear
of Heinrich Brauns.

Weakened by economic crises and employers' hard-line policies, the three major trade unions had fallen on hard times. They
turned to the state for help. Local state arbitrators were keenly
aware of their predicament. In a lengthy report, the president of
the Arbitration Board described and explained the trade unions'
need for arbitrators:

> The economic crisis has changed the balance of power of 1924 and
> 1925. Employers are getting the upper hand. Trade unions are finan-
> cially so weak that they avoid conflicts with employers, who try to
> decrease wage rates .... In collective bargaining, trade unions look for
> help from state arbitrators in the hope of maintaining wage rates. In
> each case, they call for help from the Arbitration Boards.[44]

Initially opposing state interference, the trade unions gradually
saw the benefits of the state arbitration decree to the labor movement. They could rely on the state machinery to protect wages
and living conditions against aggressive employers. From 1924 to
1929, lockouts were as frequent as strikes, and the number of
working days lost due to the former exceeded those due to the latter.[45] While not formally abandoning free collective bargaining

(Tarifautonomie), the socialist Trade Unions openly argued for strong state intervention in industrial relations and protested against Brauns's instruction to the regional ministries (Länder) of social affairs, dated 30 January 1924, "that the concerned parties should resolve their matters by themselves, that state arbitrators should support collective bargaining, and that the official declaration should be used only when a dispute posed a threat to the common good ...." The ADGB insisted on keeping the official declaration of compulsorily binding awards and on applying it to non-emergency situations as well:

> We think that the official declaration of a compulsory binding award should be used not only when the common good is threatened but also when the situation demands state intervention in the interest of parties and *we think that the Labor Ministry's directive is extremely dangerous because capitalists want to suppress the official declaration. It is not possible to give up the official declaration, given the employers' attitude. We are afraid that further limitations will undermine and practically eliminate the official declaration.*[46]

The ADGB ignored worries from among its own ranks that state arbitration might cause the demise of class struggles. As Clemens Nörpel, a representative of the white-collar workers section of ADGB, declared on 26 October 1925: "This cannot be continued. The eternal access to arbitration committees will kill the class struggle principle among the working class."[47] In addition, the highly class-conscious workers in heavy industry protested against the trade unions giving up their autonomy in favor of state diktat. But this dissenting voice was drowned by the socialist Trade Unions' overwhelming dependence on state intervention. At the 1925 Heidelberg Congress, the SPD adapted to the situation by coining a theory of political wages that called on labor to control the state in order to mold the economic process.

The German Labor Ministry reflected processes too complex to be subsumed exclusively under neo-Marxist theory, on two counts. First, by adjudicating in favor of trade unions and in the face of employers' vehement objections,[48] the Labor Ministry protected the interests of the working class. Thanks to the Labor Ministry's arbitration, organized labor made economic and social gains under Brauns, who was part of the "all-bourgeois" governments from 1924 to 1928, and under the Social Democratic Labor Minister Rudolf Wissell from 1928 to 1930. As a result, the three trade unions became the staunchest advocates of keeping the emergency state arbitration decree. Having been reduced to underdogs since the inflation years, they protested loudly when Brauns tried to address the virulent criticisms of employers and other state officials with a promise to slacken arbitration. Ironically indeed, the decree created a strong labor base identified with the state.[49]

Secondly, the Labor Ministry's pro-labor stance incurred the wrath of employers nationwide. Brauns denied employers the right to exercise any veto power in arbitration. He bluntly asserted that the Labor Minister alone had the right to appoint arbitrators deemed fit by him. Insisting that "the declaration of compulsorily binding awards was a means to protect the general interests of society,"[50] Brauns rebuffed the Federation of German Employers' Associations' (VDA) request that he limit the use of the official declaration.[51] Catholic and Social Democratic Labor Ministers Brauns and Wissell (who continued Brauns's policy until he stepped down in 1930) shook and lost business confidence, especially that of employers in heavy industry. State arbitrators denied employers freedom in setting wage rates and working conditions and frustrated their longing for a return to the prewar domination of labor. The introduction of state arbitration changed a major rule of play in the field of industrial relations. This new rule threatened the employers' long-term interests once the state decided to protect trade unions.

Heavy industry was the most strategic sector in Germany's drive to rebuild and improve economic competitiveness, but it became the Labor Ministry's archenemy. Representing all industry, the National Association of German Industry (Reichsverband der Deutschen Industrie, or RDI) was an imposing presence in Germany. Its first president, Kurt Sorge, the director of the Krupp company, also headed the Federation of German Employers' Associations.[52] The RDI drew its strength from its 78,000 member firms in 61 affiliated associations and emerged as an employers' stronghold after the reorganization of employers' associations on 12 April 1919. This peak organization had enormous weight on the postwar industrial scene, since it represented 70 to 80 percent of all German firms and was an amalgam of the most important heavy and manufacturing industries. Heavy industry, which consisted of mining, metal industry, and machine industry, was the pillar of the German economy and the core of employers' opposition to the socioeconomic policies of the state. These three sectors accounted for 70 percent of working days lost due to conflicts in

1924. Coal mining alone accounted for 89.5 percent of lockouts, or 17 out of 19, and 73 percent of strikes, or 27 out of 37.[53]

Heavy industry employers became "a veto group against 'state socialism' and democracy,"[54] capable of mobilizing members and conducting offensive actions. The attacks were loud, stinging, and persistent. Delegations of industrialists regularly visited Brauns in Berlin and made their complaints known to him and the Economy Ministry. Employers in various industries sent irate letters of protest to the Labor Ministry.[55] As soon as the state arbitration decree had gone into effect, the president and the Wages Committee of the big and strong VDA took a strong stand against wage determination by the state (Tarifzwang) and against any state intrusion into the economy.[56] The VDA, representing all employers' organizations, cried out, by means of letters, conferences, and mass media,[57] for the elimination or at least reform of the state arbitration decree and the practice of compulsorily binding awards. One major employers' newspaper attacked the arbitration system in a full front page.[58] The "economic dictatorship" of the Labor Ministry made headlines throughout the period[59] with sensational titles such as "The Fiasco of the State Arbitration System."[60] Outspoken in its criticisms, the VDA declared that it was not "the business of the state to interfere in the economy."[61]

Though lacking employers' unanimous support, the RDI moved in on the state arbitration system from 1920 onwards. Paul Silverberg, a representative of the largest brown coal company (Rheinische Aktiengesellschaft für Braunkohlenbergbau und Brikettfabrikation, or RAG), gave a speech on 4 September 1926 at an RDI meeting in Dresden, in which he declared that the state should not intervene in industrial relations.[62] In addition to verbal opposition, heavy industry also took action, mobilizing defense associations such as Kampfgemeinschaften (Combat Associations) and Gefahrgemeinschaften (Danger Associations).[63] In 1927, heavy industry refused to abide by the official declaration of compulsory binding awards in Arbeit-Nordwest. Its refusal culminated in a confrontation with the Marx III and Müller II cabinets in 1927, forced the state to back down, and among other things, eventually led to the fall of the Weimar Republic.[64] At the RDI meeting in September-October 1929, the leaders of heavy industry announced an offensive against labor and demanded that priority be given to economic policies (Wirtschaftspolitik) rather than Sozialpolitik.[65] German employers were intransigent toward labor grievances and legislations in favor of labor:

The modernization of employers' attitudes probably was moving
more slowly than that of the workers and their organizations. They
were against the principle of economic democracy; instead, they promoted Werksgemeinschaft [work community] ideology against trade
unions and collective bargaining, and they were against social legislation and social systems in the mid-1920s.[66]

Left furiously knocking at the door of the arbitration system,
industrialists *perceived* that their long-term, fundamental interests
were jeopardized by state arbitration. The Labor Ministry's quasi-
dictatorial intrusion in the private economic sphere deprived
employers of their independence and ability to fix and negotiate
wages and to regulate working hours. "Political" wages were
anathema to employers. An industrialist emphatically stated that
"it is expected that, as long as Brauns is the Minister of Labor, the
business community cannot expect anything from him. Moreover,
the industry should once and for all draw the necessary consequences from the behavior of the present Minister of Labor."[67]
That conclusion was unanimous among employers. The powerful
Federation of German Employers' Associations went on a
counter-offensive against the declaration of compulsorily binding
awards.[68] They branded arbitrators as "strangers" to the economy[69] and as "instruments of the working class."[70] Castigating the
arbitration system for having weakened Germany's competitive
edge in international trade, the leader of the Association of Metal
Employers in the region of Zwickau issued a ferocious but typical
denunciation of state corporatism: "I cannot think of any bigger
nonsense and a bigger stupidity than this arbitration system."[71]
The massive business opposition during the period of 1924-1930
attests to the extent to which the Labor Ministry furthered its goals
at the expense of employers' long-term interests. Heavy industry
employers were incensed that, in their assertion, "in 95 percent of
cases workers demand that officials declare awards compulsorily
binding and that trade unions use the system to reach their
goal."[72] The VDA, the RDI, and the heavy industry in general con-
demned state arbitration as "schematic plans"[73] that stood in the
way of economic recovery, and accused state arbitrators of mas-
terminding a "planned conspiracy."[74] The Ruhr industrialists
grew so disillusioned with the Labor Ministry's arbitration policy
that they withdrew their support for the Weimar state.

The German Labor Ministry under Brauns approximates the
state-centered view that state managers tend to become autonomous of dominant classes in wars, economic crises, and periods of

rapid political change – not to speak of more contentious evidence on potential autonomy in quieter times. The pursuit of state interests prevailed in industrial relations policy between 1924 and 1930. The German Labor Ministry ventured far beyond the constraints of the system and, significantly, failed to accommodate the economic interests of heavy industry. The crises in the government and economy allowed the Labor Ministry to show a statist disposition toward "diktat" (unilateral settlement from above), and a proto-Christian-Democratic disposition toward cross-class accommodation.

## Relative Autonomy and Crises of Political Economy: 1922-1924 and 1930-1933

Upon closer scrutiny, the German Labor Ministry's autonomy cannot be exaggerated. The autonomous processes flourished under specific historical conditions, but, as I try to argue, the Labor Ministry's state arbitration policy was remade in the light of changing contexts. While taking much heat for its independent state arbitration system, the German Labor Ministry veered to the side of employers in 1922-1924 and 1930-1933 when it perceived that the capitalist economy on which the political order rested was in crisis.

The German economy was in shambles in the aftermath of a disastrous war. The bill for war reparations to the Allied forces amounted to 132 billion marks.[75] To accelerate reparations, the French and Belgian military occupied the Ruhr industrial region in 1923. In order to pay reparations and foreign debt, the Weimar government made exports a national priority. These political calculations coincided with the interests of industrialists. In this context, Brauns met employers' demands: substituting the eight-hour working day with the ten-hour working day and cutting wages. Industrialist Fritz Thyssen pounded home to the government that "it is necessary to work more in Germany."[76] His relative August Thyssen offered a barrage of technical constraints against the introduction of the eight-hour day in foundries.[77] Moreover, employers pressed for the cancellation of the demobilization ordinance and of the constitutional protection of trade-union rights.

Turning a deaf ear to protests from organized labor, Brauns adopted measures to help mine owners and to increase production of coal, a major source of export revenues and a major war reparation commodity. He instructed state arbitrators to increase working hours in the three rounds of mediation and arbitration during the coal conflict in the Ruhr of 1923-1924. In November 1923, following the failure of both parties to reach an agreement, the Labor Ministry unilaterally increased the working day from seven to eight hours, effective on 28 April 1924. Arbitrator Ernst Mehlich's official award increased working hours and, at the same time, cut miners' wages by 25 percent.[78] Trade unions fought back with a demand for a 30 percent wage increase in order to compensate for longer working hours. To appease the miners, Mehlich made another official award, conceding a 15 percent wage increase while keeping the new working hours. The Ministry then imposed the Working Hours decree, which increased working hours to ten, on 21 December 1923. Furthermore, Brauns used the state arbitration decree to lengthen working hours to 54-56 hours a week[79] and to set wage rates twenty percent below the prewar level. He also revived the two-shift system, even in some industries where it had been abandoned before the war. Brauns went so far as to tell certain bankers at a cabinet meeting that "he is always for the lengthening of working hours."[80] By acting in favor of industrialists, Brauns alienated trade unions, including his own constituency, the Christian Trade Unions, and wiped out the legacies of the 1918-1919 revolution.

The Depression of 1929-1933 was another contingency that radically reoriented the industrial relations policy in favor of employers. After six years of pro-labor arbitration rulings, the Weimar state, led by conservative presidential cabinets, used the economic crisis to scrap the state arbitration system. The Brüning cabinet, which called itself a "bourgeois united front," used emergency decrees in 1931 to cut wages and render wage agreements meaningless.[81] The Catholic Center Labor Minister, Adam Stegerwald (1930-1932), was unable to prevent Heinrich Brüning from pressing for a balanced budget and cutting wages. To support his austerity measures, Brüning revived, on 9 March 1931, the Einmann-Schiedspruch, the arbitrator's power to single-handedly make an award, disregarding the January 1929 court ruling that banished such practices.[82] Brüning used the arbitration power to break up the Sozialstaat as well as to reduce prices and wages at the same time. He also formed an Economic Advisory Council to formulate the 8 December 1931 fourth emergency decree to carry out his measures. The presidential emergency decree "marked a decisive step away from the arbitration award and contract system of Weimar wage bargaining."[83]

Circumventing Parliament altogether, the successive presidential cabinets stripped the labor minister of his arbitration power. They used the arbitration decree to impose increased working hours and lower real wages. Chancellor Franz von Papen dismissed Social Democrat Rudolf Wissell, the chief government arbiter. In his stead, he appointed a former Krupp executive, Hugo Schäffer, as Labor Minister, removed the Social Democrat ministers in Prussia, and used the emergency decree of 14 June 1932 to dismantle the welfare system.[84] Kurt von Schleicher continued the policy of cutting wages in favor of employers.

Having helplessly watched its long-term interests – profit and capital accumulation – challenged and trampled upon by the Labor Ministry for eight long years, employers were finally able to break the state arbitration system when conservatives took control of the state and helped precipitate the fall of the Weimar Republic. Business power hinged on the capacity of conservative politicians to dominate the polity and turn a severe economic crisis to their advantage.[85]

Structuralist neo-Marxists can argue that their theory explains the policy shifts of the entire interwar period, rather than of specific time segments. From this viewpoint, the capitalist state had a wide range of options as long as it remained within the confines of capitalism.[86] The shifts to the self-determination policy in 1918-1919 and then to the state arbitration decree in 1923 were possible because they contributed to the stability of the capitalist mode of production. The 1918 Stinnes-Legien agreement, which included the adoption of free collective bargaining, reinforced the smooth running of the capitalist economy and the labor market. Far from losing their leverage, employers gained from the agreement. The pact gave them breathing space to adapt to the new environment dominated by organized labor and the SPD, and, in fact, strengthened their position in the interwar economy since the three trade unions pledged to respect private property and free collective bargaining. The pact was an important cornerstone that contributed to the restoration of the bourgeois order. Neo-Marxists would argue that the relatively autonomous state shifted its policies according to fluctuations in the balance of power, but these shifts helped maintain the long-term intrests of capitalists.[87]

Neo-Marxist Fred Block's concept of tipping points can be used to account for the German Labor Ministry's abrupt imposition of state arbitration in 1923. Tipping points are processes that go so far that the state takes over the economy and subjugates capitalist forces.[88] Faced with the collapse of collective bargaining, a rise in industrial conflicts, and employers' aggressive attacks on unions, the Labor Ministry intervened in order to protect the long-term political and economic interests of dominant classes. The short-term interests of employers, namely, the destruction of unions and return to the prewar business domination, threatened the long-term accumulation of capital. Since it was a period of relative economic prosperity, the Labor Ministry went beyond its relative autonomy to arbitrate in favor of the working class, to protect the labor market, and to stem the rising tide of communism. This theory offers a hierarchy of determinants. War, reconstruction, and political objectives led the Labor Ministry to act relatively autonomously, but threats to capitalism elicited pro-capitalist actions. This is consistent with Poulantzas's theory, which moves from the most general abstract determinants of states to the middle-range determinants of day-by-day policy shifts.[89]

Overall, as in Britain, the German Labor Ministry, whether led by the Catholic Center Heinrich Brauns or conservative chancellors, fits structuralist neo-Marxist theory when the capitalist economy and related public order were at stake. The postwar reconstruction of 1923 and the Depression of 1929-1933 are two contingencies that added complexity to the behavior of the Labor Ministry.

However, the multiple context-bound variations of state autonomy during the Weimar era throws into question the claim that structuralist neo-Marxist theory alone can account for the wide range of policy shifts in this era.


## Pluralistic Settlements and Major Industrial Conflicts

While formulating policy in a statist spirit and imposing it on societal groups, the German Ministry ran into serious obstacles. Other state actors and societal groups nibbled at the policy in the implementation stage and skewed its outcomes. Eventually, the German Labor Ministry saw itself transformed by them. When faced with fierce onslaughts from employers, who had to deal with both international competition and considerable labor militancy, the Labor Ministry backed down, responding to pressures from dominant classes and from state actors outside the Labor Ministry.

The German Labor Ministry's autonomy was, even at its full strength, constrained in many respects. Opposition to state arbitration emerged within and outside the state. The Finance and Economy Ministries' attacks held the Labor Ministry in check. Economy Minister Julius Curtius (1926-1929) accused state arbitrators of abusing their enormous power to declare compulsorily binding awards, blaming them for higher prices and soaring unemployment rates. Finance Minister Peter Reinhold denounced state arbitration as being "asocial and economically damaging"[90] and Brauns for compromising his twenty state arbitrators' impartiality by personally appointing them and holding them accountable to himself alone: "[T]he arbitrator is not supposed to receive orders and has the right to make his own decision regardless of his superior's order."[91] Both ministers fumed over being excluded from the arbitration system and having to get Brauns's prior approval before negotiating with trade unions. Besieged by criticisms, Brauns urged his arbitrators to restrict the use of compulsorily binding awards to major industrial disputes;[92] its indiscriminate use, he said, would jeopardize "the significance of arbitration committees and arbitrators themselves." State compulsion should be used only "when one party refuses the official award and when public interests dictate state intervention."[93]

After Brauns left office in June 1928, the once compact state arbitration apparatus was shattered and replaced by a far more diffuse and complex array of forces. Curtius convinced the cabinet to rescind Social Democratic Labor Minister Rudolf Wissell's "absolute and exclusive" authority over the arbitration system and to raise the possibility that "the labor minister should, under certain circumstances, let the cabinet exercise influence on his decisions … when these decisions are related to the policy of the chancellor or the domain of another minister such as the economy minister and to the latter's economic policies."[94]

Though beholden to state objectives and capitalist interests, the German Labor Ministry switched to pluralistic compromises when confronted with major industrial strikes. There are gaping holes in an interpretation of the German Ministry that is based solely on the statist model. Statists acknowledge the fact that state autonomy is historically specific and vulnerable to group mobilization and penetration,[95] but their concept of potential autonomy fails to take account of the existence of multiple processes eating away at state power. A conception of the state as a combination of processes carries more explanatory power than a definition that merely posits the state as a site for autonomous managers. Bending over backwards is paradoxical from a statist perspective stressing essential autonomy, but it is clearly understandable in the framework of processes and contingencies. Such shifts were necessary to re-establish social peace in industrial relations and to ensure political stability. Heinrich Brauns, the architect of the state arbitration decree, bent over backwards in the coal conflict in the Ruhr of May 1924. His successor, Rudolf Wissell, had to relinquish his arbitration power and let the cabinet buy off both sides in the Ruhr iron and steel conflict of October 1928. In both cases, the threat of major industrial disputes to the viability of the Weimar regime pushed the state to change its position.

## *The Coal Conflict in the Ruhr of May 1924*

Brauns and his arbitrators initially favored mine owners in the 1924 Ruhr coal conflict, a major crisis in the Weimar history. Because of the Ruhr conflict, 1924 is known as the "Kampfjahr," or the year of struggles, with a record number of lost working days.[96] In 1923 and 1924, yearning for a return to prewar wage rates and working conditions, mine owners opposed shorter working hours and wage increases and pushed for the eight-and-a-half-hour shift, the cancellation of postwar gains such as vacations and higher wages, and the total abolition of collective bargaining.[97] Having won concessions inconceivable before the war, trade unions were not ready to give in to employers' demands and to sacrifice the long sought-after Sozialpolitik during economic crises.

A standoff prevailed after a series of unfruitful collective bargainings in 1923 and 1924. The socialist, Christian, and Liberal Trade Unions pressed for higher wages. Mine owners were as determined as ever to see their demands satisfied since the Labor Ministry supported longer hours in order to catch up on production. They locked out 380,000 coal miners, or 90 percent of all mining personnel in the Ruhr.[98] Though Brauns had declared Mehlich's award compulsorily binding on 1 May 1924, miners struck and defied the Labor Ministry's ruling. The trade unions declared the compulsorily binding awards void and refused to budge on the issue of the seven-hour shift. In a new round of mediation and arbitration, Brauns asked Dr. Hausmann to arbitrate. But Hausmann's official award on 16 May 1924, which distinguished normal work from overtime, did not resolve the dispute.

After the failure of the second round of arbitration, Brauns appointed Friedrich Syrup, the president of the Federal Employment Department, to assume the functions of a special arbitrator.

In an effort to please both sides, Syrup not only made a distinction between normal hours and overtime,[99] but also granted miners a 15 percent and then an additional 10 percent wage increase, while maintaining the new working hours. Satisfied with the wage increase, the trade unions accepted the deal, and miners resumed work in early June 1924.

Faced with intransigence on both sides, the government and the Labor Ministry had feverishly sought a solution to the crisis. Chancellor Marx and Labor Minister Brauns were concerned about "communist agitators" capitalizing on the issue of an eight-hour day and establishing an independent Ruhr nation.[100] Marx expressed his deep concern about the potentially disastrous effects of this industrial struggle on the nation as a whole. At the cabinet meeting convened on 14 May 1924 in the presence of both employers and workers' representatives, he stated that "the grave international danger of a continuation of the present work stoppages would entail a cessation of coal shipment by [French and Belgian] occupation troops and invite more retaliations against the region of the Ruhr so as to endanger the realization of proposals put forward by the expert panel. In terms of internal security, communism would gain the upper hand in the region where the conflict is taking place."[101] The conflict would, he stressed, jeopardize the government effort to stabilize the German currency and to revamp the economy. Marx entreated both parties to negotiate between themselves and with Labor Minister Brauns. He hoped that reminding both sides of the external military threat and Germany's financial hardship would somehow induce them to move toward breaking the stalemate.

The strategic importance of the coal industry in energy production and war reparations[102] left Brauns with no choice but to buy off both sides with material concessions in the third round of arbitration. Workers were awarded higher wage rates, and the Weimar government agreed to grant generous government credit and financial compensation to coal companies. The end of the one-month industrial dispute was bought at an exorbitant price.[103] Despite the state arbitration decree and a strong organization, the Labor Ministry discovered the limits of its power.

## The Ruhr Iron and Steel Conflict of October 1928

Employers turned a wage dispute into an offensive against the labor movement and the Labor Ministry's arbitration power in the

Ruhr iron and steel conflict of October 1928, the major industrial and political confrontation during the interwar years and by far "the worst labor conflict in the history of the Republic,"[104] which culminated in the Great Lockout of 250,000 workers in the Ruhr. To settle the dispute, the government had to resort to compromises once again.

On 30 October 1928, the iron and steel workers' unions of the three labor federations demanded a wage hike of 15 pfennig per hour.[105] Arbeit-Nordwest, the Employers Association of the Region of the Northwest Group of German Iron and Steel Industrialists, the strongest opponent of collective bargaining before and during the First World War, rejected the demand and made a counter-offer. Meanwhile, it applied to the Labor Ministry and the Economy Ministry for a price increase. The trade unions rejected the counter-offer. To resolve the stalemate, state arbitrator Dr. Joetten intervened in the dispute and awarded 6 pfennig per hour for several categories of workers in the name of public interest.[106] Reluctantly accepting the award, the trade unions nevertheless requested that it be made compulsorily binding. In response, Labor Minister Wissell declared it so on 31 October.

The employers hit the roof. They rejected the Labor Ministry's ruling, questioned the legality of the official award, and contended that the industry could not afford such a wage increase. In a bold move, Arbeit-Nordwest locked out more than 250,000 iron and steel workers on 1 November 1928. At the same time, employers appealed to labor courts. Having lost the appeal at the Land level, they obtained a victory at the Reich Labor Court in January 1929. The Court declared that "the award encroached on the existing collective agreement." This decision came as a severe setback to the unions and the Labor Ministry.[107]

The heavy industry group of Rhine-Westphalia seized upon the crisis to attack the state arbitration system put in place by Brauns and maintained by Wissell, with a view to removing the much-hated state diktat and changing their underdog status vis-à-vis a regime unsympathetic to employers' needs. Although the immediate issues were wage increase and the deterioration of German industry's international competitiveness, the underlying issue was the Labor Ministry's power to declare official awards compulsorily binding.[108] Employers had long fulminated against "political wages" determined by state arbitrators, against the eight-hour day, and against the return to the two-shift system ordered by the government. Arbeit-Nordwest, a conglomerate that consisted of 30 companies with 93,272 workers,[109] controlling 80.5 percent in 1926 and 78 percent in 1928 of German iron and steel production,[110] possessed the necessary resources to wage the fight. Arbeit-Nordwest received the support of the VDA and the RDI on 23 November 1928, whereas the federal state and the Prussian Welfare Ministry supported the locked-out workers by giving them financial assistance.

Heavy industry employers finally were able to force the political elite to curtail the Labor Minister's power in industrial relations. The cabinet, led by Social Democratic Chancellor Herman Müller, pressed Labor Minister Wissell to reconsider the use of compulsorily binding awards. Though Wissell argued that it was "neither necessary nor appropriate" to drop the arbitration decree, which he called a useful measure to avoid "unnecessary industrial conflicts" and to "promote collective agreement,"[111] the cabinet went on to transfer arbitration power to the Minister of Interior, who ended up making concessions to both sides.

Social Democratic Labor Minister Wissell sided with the workers all along. On 5 December 1927, he warned that he would appoint Dr. Joetten as special arbitrator if the employers and trade unions should fail to reach an agreement.[112] Wissell declared Joetten's official award compulsorily binding on 31 October 1928, forcing the employers to accept a 6 pfennig per hour wage increase.[113] He decided, on 20 November 1928, to provide financial assistance to the locked-out workers in this conflict.[114] He emphatically asserted that his was the last word and that the cabinet could not impose a decision on him.[115] Reflecting on the 1928 event later on, Wissell insisted that he would have handled the conflict the same way if given another chance, and that his decisions were protected by laws and the constitution. He wrote that "[f]inally the arbitration system remained intact in essence, despite the landmines laid down by employers."[116]

However, the 1928 Ruhr conflict sent tremors through political circles. The cabinet was concerned with employers' massive opposition to the state arbitration system and was eager to settle the dispute with dispatch lest the economy worsen. "The economic struggle was very costly," declared the finance minister to the cabinet, estimating the loss of 100 million marks per week to the German economy. A swift intervention of the state is needed to keep afloat the finances of the country."[117] The industry was vital to the region of Rhine-Westphalia and to the entire German economy. The lockout had paralyzed the German economy for a month.

Economy Minister Julius Curtius gave his support to Arbeit-Nordwest.[118] He clashed with Wissell in cabinet meetings and challenged the Labor Ministry's arbitration authority. Curtius, a member of the pro-employer German People's party (Deutsche Volkspartei) and a man with family ties to heavy industry, blamed the state arbitration system for inflating wages. He thoroughly disapproved of the Labor Ministry's policy orientation:

> The bureaucracy on Scharnhorststraße [the street where the German Labor Ministry was located] *neglected economic considerations in favor of sociopolitical ones and surrendered to threats from trade unions.* We went ahead with compulsorily binding arbitration and did not think about rejecting it. I was successful in forcing the Labor Minister as the Supreme Arbitrator [Oberster Schlichter] to be accountable to the cabinet. Yet, I failed to stop the wages from growing out of proportion.[119]

Wissell sat tight. He fought back by declaring that "according to the existing regulation the ultimate decision [about the wage dispute in the Northwest iron and steel dispute] lies exclusively in the hands of the labor minister rather than in the cabinet. According to the law, the labor minister is the last instance in arbitration proceedings;"[120] "he is absolutely independent from the cabinet and is the sole, responsible, and ultimate decision-maker in arbitration."[121] These struggles, along with the issue of raising unemployment insurance premiums, led to the intervention of the chancellor and, in conjunction with other events, ultimately to the downfall of the Müller cabinet on 27 March 1930, the last parliamentary government of the Weimar Republic.[122]

The cabinet gave in to political and economic pressures and bypassed Labor Minister Wissell by appointing Interior Minister Severing as a special arbitrator. Severing accepted the appointment, although he knew his acceptance amounted to a repudiation of the authority of his "friend and cabinet colleague" Wissell in industrial relations.[123] The cabinet decision to ask Severing to arbitrate drastically curtailed the independence of the Labor Ministry and discredited the authority of the state arbitration system. Severing was not chosen by the labor minister, nor was he an official of the arbitration apparatus. Moreover, it was Economy Minister Curtius who had suggested Severing be the special arbitrator and who had declared that "the choice should not be viewed as an action of distrust against his colleague Wissell. It is nonetheless true that the labor minister is now seen as an interested party by the employers."[124]

Severing hammered out an agreement calling for the end of Arbeit-Nordwest's lockout on 3 December 1928 and requiring both parties to accept Severing's ruling. The showdown ended in an unsatisfactory compromise to all sides concerned. Employers obtained a partial victory when the courts denied the Labor Ministry the power to declare arbitration awards compulsorily binding without the consent of both capital and labor. However, they did not succeed in their attempt to have the state arbitration system removed altogether and free collective bargaining restored. Deprived of support from other industries and criticized even by the right-liberal German People's party (DVP), heavy industry leaders Gustav Krupp, Albert Vögler, Ernst Poensgen (president of the Employers' Association of the Northwest Group), and Peter Klöckner were ready to negotiate in order to resolve the deadlock. They reopened the plants on 3 December 1928 and were resigned to accepting Severing's special arbitration. Looking for an honorable way out, Vögler and Krupp assured the government that heavy industry did not aim to overthrow the Weimar regime, that they pursued strictly economic goals, and that they "had no grudge against any individual Minister, including the labor minister."[125] Having failed to obtain a clear and complete victory over the state and the workers, president of the Arbeit-Nordwest Paul Reusch resigned on 10 December 1928.[126] Nor could the trade unions claim success. In addition to Joetten's official awards which remained effective until 31 December 1928, Severing gave the workers a wage boost of 1 to 6 pfennig in his 21 December official award. This award fell far short of the 15 pfennig initially demanded. All they accomplished was a token wage increase and a castrated declaration of binding award.

The crux of the matter is that as a result of the dispute, the Labor Ministry lost its capacity to use sanctions and the declaration of official awards. The cabinet questioned the labor minister's arbitration power and considered taking arbitration authority into its own hands.[127] The Ministry came out of the conflict a loser, weakened by the court rulings of 22 January 1929 that forbade state arbitrators to single-handedly make an award (one-man declaration of award, or Einmann-Schiedsspruch).[128] Under the pressure of the Finance and Economy Ministries, Wissell had to advise his arbitrators not to decide on their own.

Overall, autonomous processes did not guarantee state autonomy. Far from serving as a statist site, the Labor Ministry succumbed to societal pressures in crucial conjunctures. It became, even during Brauns's tenure, a constant target of attacks from other state actors and from employers as well. The Labor Ministry underwent several shifts; increasing intervention under Brauns, retreating under his successors, and adopting pluralistic solutions to industrial struggles. The Labor Ministry, whether led by the Catholic Center Heinrich Brauns or the conservative chancellors, worked for capitalism when the interests of the state and employers were at stake in the economic reconstruction of 1923 and the Depression of 1929-1933. The conception of the state as a "potentially autonomous site" turns out to be a fragile one that cannot consistently represent the multiple contextual variations of state autonomy during the Weimar era.

## Notes

1. Quoted in Hubert Mockenhaupt, *Weg und Wirken des Geistlichen Sozialpolitikers Heinrich Brauns* (München: Schoeningh, 1977), pp. 223-224.

2. Gerald D. Feldman, "German Business Between War and Revolution: The Origins of the Stinnes-Legien Agreement" in *Entstehung und Wandel der modernen Gesellschaft: Festschrift für Hans Rosenberg zum 65. Geburtstag*, eds. Gerhard A. Ritter and Hans Rosenberg (Berlin: De Gruyter, 1970), p. 313. Michael Schneider, "Höhen, Krisen und Tiefen: Die Gewerkschaften in der Weimarer Republik, 1918 bis 1933," in *Geschichte der deutschen Gewerkschaften von den Anfängen bis 1945*, ed. Ulrich Borsdorf (Köln: Bund-Verlag, 1987), pp. 333-334.

3. Gerald D. Feldman, *Industrie und Gewerkschaften, 1918-24* (Stuttgart: Deutsche Verlags-Anstalt, 1985), p. 7.

4. The Weimar regime consisted of various coalition governments with different labels: the Weimar coalition (Sozialdemokratische Partei Deutschlands, Deutsche Demokratische Partei, and Zentrum), the bourgeois coalition (Deutsche Demokratische Partei, Zentrum, and Deutsche Volkspartei), the right coalition (Zentrum, Deutsche Volkspartei, and Deutschnationale Volkspartei), and the grand coalition (Sozialdemokratische Partei Deutschlands, Deutsche Demokratische Partei, Zentrum, and Deutsche Volkspartei). For an overview of these political parties, see Georges Castellan, *L'Allemagne de Weimar, 1918-1933* (Paris: Librairie Armand Colin, 1969), pp. 86-128.

5. Nathan Reich, *Labour Relations in Republican Germany* (New York: Oxford University Press, 1938), pp. 72 and 75.

6. Frieda Wunderlich, *Labor under German Democracy: Arbitration, 1918-1933* (New York: New School for Social Research, 1940), pp. 12 and 18. See also Gerald D. Feldman, *Army, Industry, and Labour in Germany, 1914-1918* (Princeton: Princeton University Press, 1966).

7.   Frieda Wunderlich, *Labor under German Democracy*, p. 8.

8.   Ibid., p. 65.

9.   RAM 3146, 1924.

10.  Johannes Walter Bähr, *Staatliche Schlichtung in der Weimarer Republik: Tarifpolitik, Korporatismus und industrieller Konflikt zwischen Inflation und Deflation, 1919-1932* (Berlin: Colloquium Verlag, 1989), pp. 72-92.

11.  Hans-Hermann Hartwich, *Arbeitsmarkt, Verbände und Staat, 1918-1933* (Berlin: Walter de Gruyter and Co., 1967), p. 253.

12.  Ludwig Preller, *Sozialpolitik in der Weimarer Republik* (Stuttgart: Franz Mittelbach Verlag, 1949), p. 509.

13.  Heinrich Brauns, "Zum Kampf um die Sozialpolitik," 5 August 1930, quoted in Ernst Deuerlin, "Heinrich Brauns – Schattenriß eines Sozialpolitikers," in *Staat, Wirtschaft und Politik in der Weimarer Republik. Festschrift für Heinrich Brüning*, eds. Ferdinand A. Hermens and Theodor Schieder, (Berlin: Duncker & Humbolt, 1967), p. 92.

14.  Heinrich Brauns, "Neue Wege der Sozialpolitik," in *Heinrich Brauns, Katholische Sozialpolitik im 20. Jahrhundert: Ausgewählte Aufsätze und Reden von Heinrich Brauns*, ed. Hubert Mockenhaupt (Mainz: Matthias-Grünewald-Verlag, 1976), p. 147.

15.  Hans-Hermann Hartwich, *Arbeitsmarkt*, p. 374.

16.  Ibid., p. 37 and Frieda Wunderlich, *Labor under German Democracy*, p. 13.

17.  Johannes W. Bähr, *Staatliche Schlichtung*, p. 84 and Hans-Hermann Hartwich, *Arbeitsmarkt*, p. 374.

18.  Johannes W. Bähr, *Staatliche Schlichtung*, p. 85.

19.  Hans-Hermann Hartwich, *Arbeitsmarkt*, p. 226.

20.  Johannes W. Bähr, *Staatliche Schlichtung*, p. 84.

21.  Most studies stress the fact that social Catholicism was a major force in German politics. See William L. Patch, *Christian Trade Unions in the Weimar Republic, 1918-1933* (New Haven: Yale University Press, 1985); Alex Hicks, Joya Misra, and Tang Nah Ng, "The Programmatic Emergence of the Social Security State," *American Sociological Review* 60, (1994), pp. 329-349; and Kees Kersbergen, *Social Capitalism: A Study of Christian Democracy and the Post-War Settlement of the Welfare State* (London: Routledge, 1995).

22.  Uwe Oltmann, *Reichsarbeitsminister Heinrich Brauns in der Staats- und Währungskrise von 1923/24: Die Bedeutung der Sozialpolitik für die Inflation, den Ruhrkampf und die Stabilisierung*, Diss. (Kiel, 1968), p. 40. Heinrich Brauns, "Unternehmer und Arbeiter," in *Heinrich Brauns, Katholische Sozialpolitik*, p. 157.

23.  Quoted in Hubert Mockenhaupt, *Weg und Wirken*, p. 176. This quotation is taken from a speech at the fourth party conference of the Catholic Center Party.

24.  Ibid., p. 441.

25.  Ibid., p. 189.

26.  Heinrich Brauns, "Zum Kampf um die Sozialpolitik," 5 August 1930, quoted in Ernst Deuerlin, "Heinrich Brauns," p. 92. More of Brauns's personal documents would be extant had nuns not burned them after his death.

27.  Reichsarbeitsministerium, *Deutsche Sozialpolitik, 1918-1945: Erinnerungsschrift des Reichsarbeitsministeriums* (Berlin: Mittler & Sohn, 1929), pp. 105-109.

28.  RAM 4146, February 1924, p. 111.

29.  Ludwig Preller, *Sozialpolitik*, p. 260.

30.  Heinrich Brauns, "Das Schlichtungswesen," 16 June 1922, in *Heinrich Brauns, Katholische Sozialpolitik,* p. 95.

31.  Hubert Mockenhaupt, *Weg und Wirken,* p. 189.

32.  RAM 3146, 1924, p. 85.

33.  Harold James, *The German Slump: Politics and Economics, 1924-1936* (Oxford: Clarendon Press, 1986), p. 212.

34.  Hubert Mockenhaupt, *Weg und Wirken,* pp. 235-236.

35.  R43I/2055, 30 November 1925, p. 152.

36.  R43I /2028, Nr. 2-8, 15 June 1923, pp. 127-128, italics mine.

37.  R43I/2730, F5, p. 144.

38.  Dokument 101, 4 October 1923, *Quellen zur Geschichte der deutschen Gewerkschaftsbewegung im 20. Jahrhundert,* vol. 2 (Köln: Bund-Verlag, 1985), p. 948 and p. 950, f3.

39.  R43I/2028, 2 August 1923, p. 196.

40.  R43I/2023, B/300, 25 October 1923.

41.  Heinrich Brauns, "Abbau des Reichsarbeitsministeriums," 1933, in *Heinrich Brauns, Katholische Sozialpolitik,* italics mine, p. 183.

42.  Heinrich Winkler, *Von Revolution bis zur Stabilisierung* (Berlin: Verlag J.H.W. Dietz Nachf., 1984) p. 429.

43.  Ibid., p. 412.

44.  RAM 3149, 25 June 1926, pp. 180-184.

45.  Johannes W. Bähr, *Staatliche Schlichtung,* p. 106.

46.  RAM 3146, 8 February 1924, pp. 108-110, italics mine.

47.  Quoted in Johannes Bähr, *Staatliche Schlichtung,* p. 184.

48.  RAM 3149, 25 June 1926, pp. 180-184.

49.  Michael Schneider, "Höhen, Krisen und Tiefen, pp. 279-346.

50.  RAM 3146, February 1924, p. 106.

51.  RAM 3146, 17 April 1924, p. 119.

52.  Gerard Braunthal, *Socialist Labor and Politics in Weimar Germany: The General Federation of German Trade Union* (Conn.: H. Amden, 1978), p. 147.

53.  Johannes W. Bähr, *Staatliche Schlichtung,* p. 105.

54.  Bernd Weisbrod, *Schwerindustrie in der Weimarer Republik: Interessenpolitik zwischen Stabilisierung und Krise* (Wuppertal: Peter Hammer Verlag, 1978), p. 27.

55.  RAM 3146, 19 April 1924, p. 128. Mine owners sent letters of protest. RAM 3147, 1 May 1924, pp. 4-7; newspaper publishers associations sent a seven-page letter of protest against the compulsorily binding awards made by the arbitrator Wissell on 28 January 1924.

56.  RAM 3146, 19 January 1929, p. 33.

57.  RAM 3144, 13 December 1925, p. 14 and R43 I /2359, 8 January 1926, p. 179.

58.  RAM 3148, 12 May 1925, p. 1.

59.  RAM 3147, 20 March 1925, p. 236.

60.  RAM 3149, 26 September 1926, p. 156.

61.  RAM 3155, 1 November 1928.

62.  Reinhard Neebe, "Unternehmerverbände und Gewerkschaften in den Jahren der Großen Krise, 1929-1933," *Geschichte und Gesellschaft* 9, 3, (1983), pp. 304-305.

63.  Frieda Wunderlich, *Labor,* p. 32.

64.  The role of heavy industry in the fall of the Weimar Republic and the rise of Hitler is a hotly debated issue and need not be discussed here.

65. For a history of management-labor relations, see Heinrich August Winkler, *Von der Revolution*, pp. 373-468.

66. Gerald D. Feldman, "The Weimar Republic: A Problem of Modernization?" *Archiv für Sozialgeschichte*, Band XXVI, (1986), p. 19.

67. Rundschreiben des Verbands der Metallindustriellen Krefelds vom 28. 8. 1927, Potsdam, 39.01, 3150, p. 138.

68. RAM 3155, 1 November 1928.

69. RAM 3151, 12 March 1928, pp. 108-109.

70. RAM 3151, 17 April 1928, p. 156.

71. RAM 3147, 26 March 1925, p. 234.

72. RAM 3148, *Die Deutsche Arbeitgeber-Zeitung*, 17 May 1925, p. 1.

73. RAM 2417, 3 November 1928, p. 154.

74. RAM 3159, 30 June 1929, p. 12.

75. For a concise overview of reparations, the Dawes plan, and the Young plan, see Georges Castellan, *L' Allemagne de Weimar 1918-1933* (Paris: Librairie Armand Colin, 1969), pp. 158-162.

76. Nr. 210, "Besprechung mit Vertretern der Ruhrindustrie," 28 May 1924, *Die Kabinette Marx I und II, Akten der Reichskanzlei*, 1 November 1923-June 1924, vol. 1 (Boppard am Rhein: Harald Boldt Verlag, 1973), p. 668.

77. Nr. 358, "August Thyssen-Hütte an den Reichskanzler," 20 November 1924, *Die Kabinette Marx I und II*, 2 June 1924- January 1925, vol. 2, pp. 1185-1188.

78. Johannes Walter Bähr, *Staatliche Schlichtung*, p. 109.

79. William L. Patch, *Christian Trade Unions in the Weimar Republic, 1918-1933* (New Haven: Yale University Press, 1985), p. 88.

80. Nr. 29, "Besprechung des Kabinetts mit Interessenten der Rheinisch-West-fälischen Goldnotenbank," 30. November 1923-3. Juni 1924, 3. Juni 1924-15. Januar 1925, *Die Kabinette Marx I und II, Akten der Reichskanzlei*, 17 December 1923, p. 122.

81. Heinrich Potthoff, *Gewerkschaften und Politik zwischen Revolution und Inflation* (Düsseldorf: Beiträge zur Geschichte des Parlamentarismus und der Politischen Parteien, Bd. 66., 1979), p. 191.

82. Harold James, *The German Slump*, pp. 210-211.

83. Ibid., p. 237.

84. Charles Maier, *Recasting Bourgeois Europe: Stabilization in France, Germany, and Italy in the Decade after WWI* (Princeton: Princeton University Press, 1975). p. 515.

85. John L. Boies, "Money, Business, and the State: Material Interests, *Fortune* 500 Corporations, and the Size of Political Action Committees," *American Sociological Review* 54, (1989), pp. 821-833; Michael Patrick Allen, "Capitalist Response to State Intervention: Theories of the State and Political Finance in the New Deal," *American Sociological Review* 56, (1991), pp. 679-689; Patrick J. Akard, "Corporate Mobilization and Political Power: The Transformation of U. S. Economic Policy in the 1970s," *American Sociological Review* 57, (1992), pp. 597-615.

86. See George Steinmetz, *Regulating the Social: The Welfare State and Local Politics in Imperial Germany* (Princeton: Princeton University Press, 1993), p. 50. He argues that "the 19th century state rarely obstructed the interests of the industrial bourgeoisie." See "The Myth and Reality of an Autonomous State: Industrialists, Junkers, and Social Policy in Imperial Germany," in *Society, Culture,*

*and the State in Germany*, ed. Geoff Eley (Ann Arbor: The University of Michigan Press, 1996), p. 304.

87. David Abraham, *The Collapse of the Weimar Republic: Political Economy and Crisis* (New York: Holmes and Meier, 1986).

88. Fred Block, "Beyond Relative Autonomy: State Managers as Historical Subjects," in Ralph Miliband and John Saville, eds., *The Socialist Register* (London: Merlin Press, 1980), p. 234.

89. See Bob Jessop, *State Theory: Putting the Capitalist State in its Place* (Pennsylvania: The Pennsylvania State University Press, 1990).

90. RAM 3149, 28 January 1926, p. 102.

91. R43I/2055, 28 January 1926, p. 162.

92. RAM 3147, 27 May 1924, p. 72.

93. RAM 3147, 27 May 1924, p. 72. See also RAM 3148, 21 July 1925, p. 28 and RAM 3152, 14 November 1925, p. 9.

94. RAM 3165, 22 December 1928, p. 39.

95. Alfred Stepan, *The State and Society: Peru in Comparative Perspective* (Princeton Princeton University Press, 1978); Dietrich Rueschemeyer and Peter Evans,"The State and Economic Transformation: Toward an Analysis of the Conditions Underlying Effective Intervention," in *Bringing the State Back In*, eds. Peter B. Evans, Dietrich Rueschemeyer, and Theda Skocpol (Cambridge: Cambridge University Press, 1985), pp. 44-77; Peter Katzenstein, *Small States in World Markets* (Ithaca: Cornell University Press, 1985); and Theda Skocpol, *Protecting Soldiers and Mothers: The Political Origins of Social Policy in the United States* (Cambridge: Belknap Press of Harvard University, 1992).

96. Gerald D. Feldman and Irmgard Steinisch, "Die Weimarer Republik zwischen Sozial- und Wirtschaftsstaat: Die Entscheidung gegen den Achtstundentag," *Archiv für Sozialgeschichte* Band 18, (1978), p. 412.

97. Ibid., p. 413. For the description of the event, I relied heavily on the works by Feldman and Steinisch and Bähr.

98. Johannes Walter Bähr, *Staatliche Schlichtung*, p. 109.

99. Gerald D. Feldman and Irmgard Steinisch, "Die Weimarer Republik," pp. 433-434.

100. Nr. 197, "Kabinettssitzung," 8 May 1924, *Die Kabinette Marx I und II*, 1 November 1923-June 1924, vol. 1, p. 627.

101. Nr. 198, Besprechung mit Arbeitgeber- und Arbeitnehmern des Ruhrbergbaues, 14 May 1924, *Die Kabinette Marx I und II, Akten der Reichskanzlei*, vol. 1, p. 630.

102. Johannes Walter Bähr, *Staatliche Schlichtung*, p. 114.

103. Gerald D. Feldman and Irmgard Steinisch, "Die Weimarer Republik," p. 434.

104. Gerald D. Feldman, *Iron and Steel in the German Inflation, 1916-1923* (Princeton: Princeton University Press, 1977), p. 467.

105. Gerard Braunthal, *Socialist Labor and Politics*, p. 151.

106. RAM 2415, p. 171.

107. Gerard Braunthal, *Socialist Labor and Politics*, p. 151.

108. Heinrich August Winkler, *Der Schein der Normalität: Arbeiter und Arbeiterbewegung in der Weimarer Republik 1924 bis 1930* (Berlin: Verlag J. H. W. Dietz Nachf., 1985), pp. 557-558.

109. RAM 3159, 1929, p. 12.

110. Hans-Hermann Hartwich, *Arbeitsmarkt*, p. 196.

111. Rudolf Wissell, "Reform des Schlichtungswesens?" *Magazin der Wirtschaft* 5 Jahrgang, (1929), p. 72.
112. RAM 2415, p. 67.
113. RAM 3160, 31 October 1928, p. 4.
114. RAM 3160, p. 171.
115. Bernd Weisbrod, *Schwerindustrie in der Weimarer Republik*, p. 419.
116. Rudolf Wissell, "Einundzwanzig Monate Reichsarbeitsminister," *Die Arbeit* 4, Jahrgang, H. 4, (1930), p. 220.
117. Nr. 73, 28 November 1928, *Das Kabinett Müller II, Akten der Reichskanzlei*, vol. 1 (Boppard am Rhein: Harald Boldt Verlag, 1973), pp. 255-256.
118. It is difficult to classify Julius Curtius as a die-hard pro-capitalist. There were moments in his career when he stood for class compromise and arbitration rights. When the Arbeit-Nordwest workers were locked out, he called the lockout "repellent." See William G. Ratliff, *Faithful to the Fatherland: Julius Curtius and Weimar Foreign Policy* (New York: Peter Lang, 1990), p. 34. On this occasion, Curtius sided with Social Democrats who urged the government to send relief to workers and their families. As Harold James points out, "the officials of the Reich Economy Ministry occasionally took the side of labour too." See *The German Slump* , p. 213.
119. Julius Curtius, *Sechs Jahre Minister der Deutscher Republik* (Heidelberg: Carl Winter Universitätsverlag, 1948), p. 57.
120. Nr. 181, "Ministerbesprechung," 31 October 1928, *Das Kabinett Müller II*, vol. 1 , p. 181.
121. Ibid., p. 183.
122. Johannes Bähr, *Staatliche Schlichtung*, p. 256.
123. Carl Severing, *Mein Lebensweg*, Vol. 2 (Köln: Greven Verlag, 1950), p. 173.
124. Nr. 73, "Kabinettssitzung mit anschließender Ministerbesprechung," 28 November 1928, *Das Kabinett Müller II*, Vol. 1, p. 257.
125. Nr. 76, "Besprechung mit den Arbeitgebern des Bezirks Nordwest," 30 November 1928, *ibid.*, pp. 268-269.
126. Bernd Weisbrod, *Schwerindustrie*, p. 443.
127. Nr. 85, "Ministerbesprechung," 14 December 1928, *Das Kabinet Müller II, Akten der Reichskanzlei*, vol. 1, p. 303.
128. Johannes Bähr, *Staatliche Schlichtung*, p. 267.

# Chapter Six

# Conclusion
Predicting Policy Shifts

This book grapples with complex realities and argues that the contingency theory of state intervention is the best framework in which to understand the various policy shifts undergone by the British and German Labor Ministries. This alternative approach transcends the static, single-minded conception of a single-group-based unitary actor that, in general, works for either interest groups, or dominant capitalist classes, or state managers. From this point of view, the British and German Labor Ministries were more than pluralist mirrors, labor strongholds, class agents, corporatist brokers, or statist sites. They went beyond the unnecessary a priori assumptions of any theories tested here.

The industrial relations policies of the British and German Labor Ministries were not consistently and exclusively implemented in favor of certain groups and at the expense of others. In the long run, the same policies shifted according to contingencies and turned out to have contradictory effects on state managers, employers, and organized labor. British industrial relations policy met the demands of organized labor and employers for long stretches, but was punctuated by periods dominated by dominant classes and national objectives. Organized labor played a major role in shaping German industrial relations policy after the First World War. However, the policy expressed the will of the state for eight interwar years, and was permeated by dominant classes and pluralistic forces. Policy shifts occurred because the two labor

Notes for this chapter begin on page 150.

agencies had to attend to the plurality of interests, the requirements of capitalism, and the political and economic order of the nation as a whole.

Table 7 provides a detailed summary of the historical contingencies and shifts among inclusionary, exclusionary, and autonomous processes in policy formulation and implementation.

To arrive at this conclusion, I have put competing theories of the state to test. In the final analysis, neither of the British and German cases fits squarely with any of the existing theories of the state. None of the powerful-group theories, with their emphasis on actors' strengths, are able to account for the origins of the British and German Labor Ministries. These two state agencies were not created in response to working-class strength and the influence of socialist political parties. Though organized labor demanded participation in the management of labor affairs in the state, working-class pressure was ineffective in creating labor departments before the war. The prewar British and German states geared their industrial relations policy toward the protection of capitalist interests and rejected any appeals to open up the policy to a plurality of interests. Nor did state managers create the Labor Ministries on their own initiative. On the contrary, they used whatever power they had to delay the emergence of centralized, cabinet-ranking labor ministries specialized in representing the working class. It was the First World War that changed the balance of power in favor of the working class, forcing the wartime British and German governments to use the Labor Ministries as bargaining chips to gain labor support for war and postwar transition.

The national political culture explanation captures the overall policy course of the two Labor Ministries, but falls short of explaining the various shifts. Concepts such as "traditions, "legacies," "ideologies," and "cultures" cannot capture the twists and turns in policy formulation, implementation, and outcome. Indeed, the cultural divide between the two countries is great. The cultural legacy built over centuries of distinctive state-building is a major reason for the British and German Labor Ministries to adopt radically different policies of state intervention in industrial relations during the interwar period. Liberalism assured the dominance of self-determination by employers and organized labor in Britain. The British Ministry under each government (including the two socialist governments of 1924 and of 1929) followed the principle of neutrality and "home rule" in industrial relations. Both employers and organized labor unfailingly advocated home rule and strongly opposed any intro-

***Table 7:*** Contingencies, Sites of Institutional Crises, Processes, and Outcomes in Britain and Germany

| Contingency Situations | Sites of Institutional Crises | | | | Processes | Outcomes |
|---|---|---|---|---|---|---|
| | Industrial Relations | Domestic Political Regime | International Political Regime | Capatalist Property Relations | | |
| **Postwar Institutional Reconstruction** Britain The First World War and economic reconstruction | + | | (+) | | **Inclusionary** The BLM formulated and implemented free collective bargaining policy, allowing unions and employers to settle industrial disputes on their own. | Minimal state intervention prevailed in rhetoric and most industrial conflicts during the interwar period and supported by all political parties. |
| Germany The First World War and military defeat Collapse of Wilhelmine monarchy Treaty of Versailles of 1919 Transition to the Weimar Republic Threats from workers' and soldiers' councils and factory occupations | + | + | + | + | **Inclusionary** The Social Democratic Government and the GLM adopted the pact of self-determination signed by employers and organized labor in 1918. | Free collective bargaining implemented between 1919 and 1923. Organized labor gained recognition and concessions. |
| **Postwar International Leadership Crisis** Decline of British world supremacy Pursuit of internal peace | | + | + | | **Autonomous** Prime Ministers and Treasury's austerity measures weakened the BLM's capacity to maintain its already weak presence in industrial relations. | Force used against strikers. The BLM scratched the Whitley councils, the conciliation bodies that were the centerpiece of self-determination policy. Financial capital strengthened. |
| **Interwar Crisis of Industrial Relations** Threat to political order Major industrial conflicts: the 1924 coal conflict in the Ruhr and the 1928 iron and steel conflict | + | + | | | **Inclusionary** The GLM met employers' and organized labor's demands by buying off both sides in 1924 and 1928. | State arbitration weakened. Cabinet transferred Labor Minister Wissell's arbitration power to minister of interior in 1928. |

| | | | | | | |
|---|---|---|---|---|---|---|
| **Interwar Crisis of Industrial Relations and Political Regime**<br>Inflation of 1922-1923<br>Breakdown of collective bargaining and explosion of industrial disputes<br>Crisis in the state: unstable coalition governments and Parliament ridden with faction politics. | + | + | | | **Autonomous**<br>The GLM issued the state arbitration decree on 30 October 1923 and arbitrated industrial conflicts independently of chancellors, Parliament, and societal groups<br>Brauns imposed Catholic solidarist ideology on industrial relations. | Self-determination abandoned. The state imposed solutions to industrial conflicts not settled by employers and labor. |
| Employers' offensives against labor<br>Threats from Communist and anarchist movements | + | + | | | **Autonomous**<br>The GLM organized labor and arbitrated in its favor between 1924-1930. | Employers unanimous in disavowing state arbitration and the Weimar regime. |
| **Interwar Crisis of Industrial Relations and Economic Institutions**<br>Surge of strikes in postwar years | + | (+) | | | Exclusionary<br>The BLM helped engineering employers organize the NCEO in 1919. | Strengthened employers' position in collective bargaining. |
| Crises threatening political and economic order: the 1921 coal miners' strike and the 1926 General Strike | + | + | (+) | | Exclusionary<br>The BLM helped suppress strikes. | Self-determination suspended to bring order back.<br>Employers cut wages and increased working hours.<br>Punitive legislation in 1927. |
| **Interwar Crisis of Political Economy**<br>Postwar reconstruction of 1922-1924 and competition in the world market<br>War reparations to the Allies | + | + | (+) | | Exclusionary<br>The GLM arbitrated in favor of employers. | Labor gains (wages and working hours) during and after war frozen.<br>Unions against arbitration. |
| Grave crisis threatening political and economic order: Depression of 1929-1933 | + | + | (+) | + | Exclusionary<br>Presidential cabinets stripped the GLM of its arbitration power in 1930-1933. | Cuts in wages and increase in working hours. Conservative policy favoring employers. |

BLM = British Labor Ministry; GLM = German Labor Ministry

duction of compulsion or any greater level of state intervention in the industrial relations system. In contrast, the prewar authoritarian political culture in Weimar Germany reinforced the prevalence of statist rule and provided the context in which the German Labor Ministry under Heinrich Brauns issued the "forced" state arbitration (Zwangsschlichtung) decree in 1923 and solved major social conflicts in a heavy-handed way. The Prussian cultural baggage of state diktat greatly facilitated Brauns in putting into practice his Catholic solidarist idea. The particular political traditions and ideologies that politicians, bureaucrats, employers, and trade unions adhered to profoundly influenced industrial relations policies and the ministerial capacity to intervene in industrial disputes. The contrasting cultural traditions in the two countries made a tremendous difference in how the Labor Ministries were built and how they interacted with employers and trade unions.

Yet, I show that only the contingency theory of state intervention, rather than national-culture interpretation alone, can grasp the causal regularity behind the veering and tacking of the British and German Labor Ministries among inclusionary, exclusionary, and autonomous processes. In spite of cultural differences, state managers in both countries perceived and reacted to their environment in a similar way. To put it simply, a national-culture explanation becomes invalid when confronted with policy shifts at the formulation and implementation levels. British and German state managers, employers, and organized labor gained or lost leverage in industrial relations not as a result of some cultural preconditions, but as a result of specific contingencies that changed the existing balance of power.

Though limited by the small number of cases, this study points to four general conclusions that bear on the predictions of the connections between historical contingencies and the orientations of state policies. These four propositions not only help increase our understanding of the two cases at hand, but also can be used to inch toward a general theory of the state and its interventions in political economy.

## Inclusionary Processes

I argue that labor departments become pluralist mirrors in times of war and economic reconstruction. This thesis goes against the statists' arguments that the state and state agencies become autonomous from societal pressures in those circumstances. My study

shows that organized labor acquired leverage and shaped industrial relations policies only when the First World War and postwar
reconstruction stimulated inclusionary processes in Britain and
Germany. These two contingencies increased the dependence of
the state on workers' support for the war and the postwar transition, considerably strengthened the bargaining power of the labor
movement, and increased trade unions' membership and their
ability to conduct strikes against employers. Under those conditions, the labor movement rose to prominence in national politics
and gained enough weight to shape interwar industrial relations
policies. British trade unions repelled the state's attempt to con-
tinue its wartime practices of compulsory arbitration and firmly set
the course in favor of self-determination. The German socialist
Trade Unions became the driving political force after the collapse
of the old regime, excluding the state from industrial relations and
saving the democratic regime from military coups.

In addition, regime instability and major industrial conflicts
made the German Labor Ministry vulnerable to inclusionary
processes. Strong as it was, the Labor Ministry was unable to
resolve crises of industrial relations through its state arbitration
decree. The labor minister and his arbitrators had no choice but to
forge compromises between workers' grievances and employers'
demands. In the 1924 dispute, Labor Minister Brauns made up for
his failures in mediation and arbitration by buying off both sides
with financial concessions. In the 1928 iron and steel conflict in the
Ruhr, the Labor Ministry was deeply shaken by the disputes – with
employers on the offensive and workers on the defensive – over
the state arbitration system. The cabinet undermined the labor
minister's authority by designating an official outside the Labor
Ministry to make a definitive official award that was designed to
buy off both sides. These two most important industrial conflicts
during the interwar period dealt a heavy blow to the state arbitration decree and forced the Labor Ministry to back down.


## Exclusionary Processes

Both the British and German Labor Ministries became agents of
class cohesion only when state managers perceived that the institutions of the capitalist economy and their reliance on capital accumulation were seriously threatened. The neo-Marxist perspective
stands up to comparative inquiry only in these circumstances.

The British Labor Ministry insisted on neutrality in times of industrial peace, but sided with business in times of major industrial conflicts. Force was, ironically, a logical consequence of self-determination policy. In principle, self-determination rests on the self-regulated market mechanism. Employers and trade unions would solve their disputes through collective bargaining and mediation bodies. In reality, self-determination was ineffective when both sides came to a deadlock. Then, the government had to intervene. The Labor Ministry helped establish independent mediation bodies, but self-determination meant that trade unions, weakened by economic downturns, were left alone and helpless when they clashed against employers. When employers and trade unions could neither resolve their differences by themselves nor turn to state arbitration, then the state could not but fall back on forcible measures to stop workers' unrest. Gaining leverage throughout the interwar years, employers became uncompromising and could complacently rely on the state to send police, troops, and strike-breaking organizations against striking workers. The state invariably reverted to violence to resolve the dispute, thus making organized labor the big loser in every major showdown.

Of the two historical cases, the British Labor Ministry comes closer to a structuralist neo-Marxist model. It organized capitalists, helped defeat major strikes, and shared long-term interests with employers. British prime ministers never intended to let the Labor Ministry become a flagship of the working class within the government. The Labor Ministry's claim of neutrality is, as neo-Marxists can cogently argue, but a facade hiding its *relative* autonomy and pent-up hostility to the labor movement. It is therefore small wonder that Labor Ministry officials worked closely with, and faithfully for, the Conservative political leadership and the two equally order-minded socialist minority governments. Labor ministers, as part of the executive branch, were privy and partial to the hardline policy of repression espoused by the cabinet, and never opposed or resisted the use of troops and strike-breaking organizations. The British Ministry's pro-capitalist behavior complemented its interwar inclusionary practices. However, it must be emphasized that the Labor Ministry was both inclusionary and capitalist, albeit more one or the other at particular times, and subject to conflicting forces such as working-class syndicalism, protection of the capitalist economy, and state officials' pursuit of sterling supremacy. What the British Ministry did in times of peace and in times of industrial conflicts mattered equally.

The German Labor Ministry supported employers whenever its intervention was needed to maintain the capitalist economy and to serve employers' general interests. In 1922-1924, faced with rampant inflation and sagging production, Brauns wiped out the revolutionary gains of the working class when employers demanded longer working hours and lower wages to help them resuscitate the economy and become competitive again in the world market. Despite protests from trade unions, Brauns agreed with employers that the eight-hour day could not be sustained and had to be lengthened and that workers should carry part of the burden of war reparations. The Depression of 1929-1933 set in motion exclusionary processes. The conservative presidential cabinets led by Heinrich Brüning, Franz von Papen, and Kurt von Schleicher seized the occasion to dismantle the state arbitration system of the German Labor Ministry.

## Autonomous Processes

Politicians' concerns with order and international objectives changed the course of industrial relations policies in Britain and Germany. In Britain, the decline of British dominance in the world after the war and the attempt to maintain British world supremacy led state managers to weaken the Labor Ministry's administrative capacity. The Treasury slashed the Labor Ministry's budget, personnel, and programs in an effort to restore sterling supremacy abroad and the return to the gold standard in 1925. To prevent the Labor Ministry from straying from the official course, all the inter-war prime ministers, regardless of their political affiliations, rode roughshod over their labor minister on many occasions. During major industrial confrontations, Liberal Lloyd George, Conservative Stanley Baldwin, and socialist Ramsay MacDonald did not hesitate to snatch the limelight from their labor ministers. The Labor Ministry's marginality had tremendous consequences for the outcomes of major industrial struggles. The absence of strong intervention of the British Labor Ministry – weak conciliation capacity plus virtual absence of arbitration – meant that struggles had to be resolved at the level of the prime minister and the cabinet at the expense of workers' interests, and with the help of repressive and strike-breaking forces.

The major contingencies, such as the 1922-1923 hyper-inflation, the increase in industrial conflicts, and the crisis of the state,

allowed the German Labor Ministry to dominate industrial relations. The policy of state arbitration was the quintessence of state
will, formulated and implemented to consolidate maximum
intervention in industial relations and to further the interests of
the Weimar state, that is, to prevent and settle major industrial
struggles, to preserve collective bargaining, and to implement
wage policy. The Ministry launched sweeping changes in industrial relations – such as the creation of state arbitrators, official
awards, the declaration of compulsorily binding awards, and
political wages – casting itself as an important arbiter between
employers and workers when conflicts remained unresolved by
direct negotiations between the two parties or through other
mediation mechanism.

The German Labor Ministry has all the attributes of a Skocpo-
lian conception of a potentially autonomous state organization
claiming full authority over labor affairs. Instead of organizing
employers and disorganizing labor, Labor Ministers Brauns and
Wissell came to the rescue of the trade unions and the impover-
ished strikers and their families. They protected the embattled
trade unions from employers who craved for the prewar authoritarian order in industrial relations. Employers were furious that
the Labor Ministry and the Weimar regime stood in their way.
They increasingly attacked the Labor Ministry as the employers'
arch-enemy, and vilified it constantly in the press, meetings, and
speeches. But state officials persevered in their autonomous
actions, even at the cost of losing the confidence of employers and,
more specifically, the captains of heavy industry.

Contradictory as it may seem theoretically, the powerful German Labor Ministry does not live up to the expectations of the statist model. Statists have argued that potential autonomy can "come
and go." I would hasten to add that when it comes, potential
autonomy is severely limited by actors both within and without
the state. The state cannot act at will completely, even when exer-
cising its potential autonomy. Although state officials formulate
policies according to their interests, those policies that are uncon-
genial to employers' and labor interests are difficult to implement.
No matter how strong it was, the German Ministry could neither
undermine the employers' position in industrial relations nor jeopardize their existence. Brauns himself was regularly visited by
industrialists and received complaints from the Economy Ministry.
He knew quite well that he had to watch his steps. The German
Labor Ministry could bend some rules, but could not change the

game altogether. It could damage business confidence, but, at the same time, was dependent on the capitalist economy.

## The Global Cultural Context

The uniform responses of the British and German Labor Ministries to contingencies suggests that state actions are shaped by the larger cultural environment. The global institutional context and cultural norms legitimize states in liberal democracies to behave in a similar manner when confronted with contingencies. More precisely, the three processes – inclusionary, exclusionary, and autonomous – are three global cultural logics of state action in the modern world. It can be argued, on the basis of evidence presented here, that the threats to state agenda and capitalism are legitimate ways to trump liberal democracies. If this point is valid, then the contingency theory of state intervention can predict shifts in state policies and account for the behavior of other labor departments and various types of state agencies regardless of differences in national political traditions or legacies.

The two historical cases seem to point to different conclusions. They seem to support historicist claims that the state is an ongoing construction definable only in specific situations; its autonomy is historically specific. This is not the direction I have taken in this book. On the contrary, I provide a historicized version of the contingency theory of state intervention and the groundwork to build a general theory of the state.

The two cases offer clues as to how the contingency theory of state intervention can make potential contributions to a general theory of the state. To be credible, a theory of the state should pay attention to the complex nature of state agencies and shifting policies. The starting point of any analysis of the state and its policies is to examine how and why policies vary over time. State agencies are made and remade by contingencies and the ensuing changes in the balance of power. To argue that the state is multifaceted and needs to be examined from different angles does not mean that this work is anti-theoretical. On the contrary, it transcends the self-righteousness trumpeted by each side and the theoretical overkills of the competing models.

This study provides evidence that certain contingencies, which are the intersections of state structures with historical processes, produce specific outcomes. In Britain and Germany, war led to inclusionary rather than autonomous processes. The Depression in Germany paved the way for the ascendance of exclusionary processes, rather than autonomous ones. Postwar reconstruction led to the ascendance of inclusionary processes. Exclusionary processes were dominant only in extreme situations. I conjecture that these four propositions can be applied to states in capitalist democracies if they share a similar pattern of class configuration and significant presence of organized labor[1] and have gone through advanced industrialization, urbanization, and economic growth. However, much work is needed to theorize the connections among contingencies, the transnational context, processes, and outcomes. Indeed, one should consider some counter-cases of policy shifts. For example, it is possible that in other countries and periods, war gave rise to class-based or statist policies due to different state structures and various combinations of factors. An extensive examination of additional cases will determine whether my contingency theory can be used to inch toward a general theory of the state and its intervention in the political economy.

## Notes

1.   For an overview of labor strength and industrial conflicts, see Charles Tilly, "Introduction [Section IV, The Effects of Short-Term Variations]," in *Strikes, Wars, and Revolutions in an International Perspective: Strike Waves in the Late Nineteenth and Early Twentieth Centuries*, Leopold Haimson and Charles Tilly, eds. (Cambridge: Cambridge University Press, 1989), pp. 433-448.

# Bibliography


## I. Primary Sources

Bundesarchiv, Koblenz: BA, R43I.
Geheimes Staatsarchiv, Berlin: Rep.
House of Lords Record Office, London: F.
Public Record Office, Richmond: Lab2, Lab10, Cab7.
Zentrales Staatsarchiv, Potsdam: RAM.

## II. Secondary and Published Sources

Abraham, David. 1986. *The Collapse of the Weimar Republic: Political Economy and Crisis*, New York: Holmes and Meier.

Abelshauser, Werner. 1987. "Freiheitlicher Korporastimus im Kaiserreich und in der Weimarer Republik," in *Die Weimarer Republik als Wohlfahrtstaat: Zum Verhältnis von Wirtschafts- und Sozialpolitik in der Industriegesellschaft*, ed. Werner Abelshauser. Stuttgart: Franz Steiner Verlag.

Adams, W. S. 1953. "Lloyd George and the Labour Movement." *Past and Present* 3, pp. 55-64.

Akard, Patrick J. 1992. "Corporate Mobilization and Political Power: The Transformation of U.S. Economic Policy in the 1970s." *American Sociological Review* 57, pp. 597-615.

Alford, Robert R. and Roger Friedland. 1985. *Powers of Theory: Capitalism, the State, and Democracy*. Cambridge: Cambridge University Press.

Allen, Michael Patrick. 1991. "Capitalist Response to State Intervention: Theories of the State and Political Finance in the New Deal." *American Sociological Review* 56, pp. 679-689.

Allen, V. L. 1960. *Trade Unions and the Government*, London: Butler & Tanner.

Allison, Graham. 1971. *Essence of Decision: Explaining the Cuban Missile Crisis*. Boston: Little, Brown.

Amenta, Edwin. 1993. "The State of the Art in the Welfare State: Research on Social Spending Efforts in Capitalist Democracies since 1960." *American Journal of Sociology* 99, pp. 750-763.

Amenta, Edwin and Bruce G. Carruthers. 1988. "The Formative Years of U.S. Social Spending Policies: Theories of the Welfare State and the American States during the Great Depression." *American Sociological Review* 53, pp. 661-678.

Askwith, Lord George. 1920. *Industrial Problems and Disputes.* London: J. Murray.

Bagwell, P. S. 1971. "The Triple Industrial Alliance." in *Essays in Labour History*, eds. A. Briggs and J. Saville. New York: Macmillan.

Bähr, Johannes Walter. 1989. *Staatliche Schlichtung in der Weimarer Republik: Tarifpolitik, Korporatismus und industrieller Konflikt zwischen Inflation und Deflation, 1919-1932.* Berlin: Colloquium Verlag.

Baldwin, Peter. 1990. *The Politics of Social Solidarity: Class Bases of the European Welfare State 1875-1975.* Cambridge: Cambridge University Press.

Barnes, Trevor. 1979. "Special Branch and the First Labour Government." *Historical Journal* 22, 4, pp. 941-951.

Beloff, Max. 1975. "The Whitehall Factor: The Role of the Higher Civil Service, 1918-1939," in *The Politics of Reappraisal*, eds. G. Peele and C. Cook, London: Macmillan.

Bendix, Reinhard. 1956. *Work and Authority in Industry: Ideology of Management in the Course of Industrialization.* Berkeley: University of California Press.

Bessel, Richard. 1993. *Germany After the First World War.* Oxford: Clarendon Press.

Biernacki, Richard. 1995. *The Fabrication of Labor: Germany and Britain, 1640-1914.* Berkeley: University of California Press.

Blank, Stephen. 1973. *Industry and Government in Britain: Tthe Federation of British Industries in Politics, 1945-65.* Mass.: Lexington Books.

Block, Fred. 1977. "The Ruling Class Does Not Rule: Notes on the Marxist Theories of the State." *Socialist Revolution* 33, vol. 7, 3, pp. 16-24.

__________. 1980. "Beyond Relative Autonomy: State Managers as Historical Subjects." *The Socialist Register*, eds. Ralph Miliband and John Saville. London: Merlin Press.

__________. 1987. *Revising State Theory: Essays in Politics and Postindustrialism.* Philadelphia: Temple University Press.

Boies, John L. 1989. "Money, Business, and the State: Material Interests, *Fortune* 500 Corporations, and the Size of Political Action Committees." *American Sociological Review* 54, pp. 821-833.

Bonnell, Victoria E. 1980. "The Uses of Theory, Concepts and Comparison in Historical Sociology." *Comparative Studies in Society and History* 22, 2, pp. 156-173.

__________. 1983. *Roots of Rebellion: Workers' Politics and Organizations in St. Petersburg and Moscow, 1900-1914.* Berkeley: University of California Press.

Brauns, Heinrich. 1933 (1976). "Abbau des Reichsarbeitsministeriums," in *Katholische Sozialpolitik im 20. Jahrhundert. Ausgewählte Aufsätze und Reden*, ed. Hubert Mockenhaupt. Mainz: Matthias Grünewald-Verlag.

Brauns, Heinrich. 1933 (1976). *Katholische Sozialpolitik im 20. Jahrhundert. Ausgewählte Aufsätze und Reden*. ed. Hubert Mockenhaupt. Mainz: Matthias Grünewald-Verlag.

Braunthal, Gerard. 1978. *Socialist Labor and Politics in Weimar Germany: The General Federation of German Trade Unions.* Conn.: H. Amden.

British Labour Statistics. 1971. *Historical Abstract 1886-1968.* London: H. M.'s Stationary Office.

Brown, Kenneth D., ed. 1974. *Essays in Anti-Labour History: Responses to the Rise of Labour in Britain.* London: Macmillan.

Bullock, Alan. 1960. *The Life and Times of Ernest Bevin.* Vol.1. London: Heinemann.

Burke, Kathleen, ed. 1982. *War and the State: The Transformation of British Government, 1914-1919.* London: Allen & Unwin.

Butler, Harold. 1950. *The Confident Morning.* London: Faber & Faber.

Cain, Peter and A. G. Hopkins. 1993. *British Imperialism: Innovation and Expansion 1688-1914.* London: Longman.

__________. 1993. *British Imperialism: Crisis and Deconstruction 1914-1990.* London: Longman.

Caldwell, J. A. M. 1959. "The Genesis of the Ministry of Labour." *Public Administration* 37, IV, pp. 267-389.

Carroll, Glenn R. and Michael T. Hannan, eds., *Organizations in Industry. Strategy, Structure, and Selection.* New York: Oxford Univeristy Press, 1995.

Castellan, Georges. 1969. *L' Allemagne de Weimar 1918-1933.* Paris: Librairie Armand Colin.

Citrine, Lord Walter . 1964. *Men and Work.* London: Hutchinson.

Cline, Peter K. 1974. "Eric Geddes and the 'Experiment' with Businessmen in Government, 1915-22," in *Essays in Labour History: Responses to the Rise of Labour in Britain*, ed. Kenneth D. Brown. London: Macmillan Press.

Cronin, James E. 1980. "Labour Insurgency and Class Formation: Comparative Perspectives on the Crisis of 1917-1920 in Europe." *Social Science History* 4, pp. 125-152.

__________. 1982. "Coping with Labour, 1918-1926," in *Social Conflict and the Political Order in Modern Britain*, eds. James E. Cronin and Jonathan Schneer. New Brunswick: Rutgers Universty Press.

__________. 1991. *The Politics of State Expansion: War, State, and Society in Twentieth-Century Britain.* New York: Routledge.

Crouch, Colin. 1993. *Industrial Relations and European State Traditions.*
     Oxford: Clarendon Press.
Curtius, Julius. 1948. *Sechs Jahre Minister der deutschen Republik.*
     Heidelberg: Carl Winter-Universitätsverlag.
Dahl, Robert A. 1961. *Who Governs? Democracy and Power in an American
     City.* New Haven: Yale University Press.
Davidson, Roger. 1972. "Llewellyn Smith, the Labour Department and
     Government Growth, 1886-1909," in *Studies in the Growth of
     Nineteenth Century Government,* ed. G. Sutherland. London:
     Routledge & K. Paul.
__________. 1978. "The Board of Trade and Industrial Relations." *The
     Historical Journal* 21, pp. 571-591.
__________. 1979. "Social Conflict and Social Administration: The
     Conciliation Act in British Industrial Relations," in *The Search for
     Wealth and Stability,* ed. T. C. Smout. London: Macmillan.
__________. 1980. "The Ideology of Labour Administration, 1886-1914."
     *Bulletin of the Society for the Study of Labour History* 40, pp. 29-31.
Davidson, Rogerand Robert Lowe. 1981. "Bureaucracy and Innovation
     in British Welfare Policy, 1870-1945," in *The Emergence of the Welfare
     State in Britain and Germany,* ed. W. J. Mommsen. London: Croom
     Helm.
Dennis, P. 1981. "The Territorial Army in Aid of the Civil Power in
     Britain, 1919-1926." *Journal of Contemporary History* 16, 4 (October),
     pp. 706-719.
Department of Employment and Productivity. 1971. *British Labour
     Statistics: Historical Abstract, 1886-1968.* London: H. M.'s Stationary
     Office.
Desmarais, R. H. 1971. "The British Government's Strike-Breaking
     Organization and Black Friday." *Journal of Contemporary History,* pp.
     112-127.
__________. 1973. "Strike-Breaking and the Labour Government of
     1924." *Journal of Contemporary History* 8, pp. 165-175.
Deuerlin, Ernst. 1967. "Heinrich Brauns – Schattenriß eines
     Sozialpolitikers," in *Staat, Wirtschaft und Politik in der Weimarer
     Republik. Festschrift für Heinrich Brüning,* eds. Ferdinand A. Hermens
     and Theodor Schieder. Berlin: Duncker & Humbolt.
DiMaggio, Paul and Walter W. Powell. 1991. *The New Institutionalism in
     Organizational Analysis.* Chicago: University of Chicago Press.
DiTomaso, Nancy. 1980. "Class Politics and Public Bureaucracy: The
     U.S. Department of Labor," in *Classes, Class Conflict, and the State,* ed.
     Maurice Zeitlin. Mass: Winthrop.
Dobbin, Frank. 1994. *Forging Industrial Policy: The U.S., Britain, and
     France in the Railway Age.* Cambridge: Cambridge University Press.

Domhoff, G. William. 1987. "The Wagner Act and Theories of the State: A New Analysis Based on Class-Segment Theory," in *Political Power and Social Theory*, ed. M. Zeitlin. New York: JAI Press.

Donaldson, Lex. 1995. *American Anti-Management Theories of Organization: A Critique of Paradigm Proliferation*. Cambridge: Cambridge University Press.

Driessen, Martha. 1932. *Die Entwicklung der Reichsarbeitsbehörden, 1919-1924*. Köln.

Eley, Geoff, ed. 1996. *Society, Culture, and the State in Germany, 1870-1930*. Ann Arbor: The University of Michigan Press.

Erdmann, Karl Dietrich, and Martin Vogt, ed. 1978. *Die Kabinette Stresemann I. und II., 13. August 1923 bis 23. November 1923. Akten der Reichskanzlei*. Boppard am Rhein, 2 vols.

Esping-Andersen, Gøsta. 1990. *The Three Worlds of Welfare Capitalism*. Princeton: Princeton University Press.

Esping-Andersen, Gøsta, Roger Friedland, and Erik Olin Wright. 1976. "Modes of Class Struggle and the Capitalist State." *Kapitalstate* 4-5, pp. 186-220.

Evans, Peter B., Dietrich Rueschemeyer, and Theda Skocpol, eds. 1985. *Bringing the State Back In*. Cambridge: Cambridge University Press.

Feldman, Gerald D. 1966. *Army, Industry, and Labour in German, 1914-1918*. Princeton: Princeton University Press.

__________. 1970. "German Business Between War and Revolution: The Origins of the Stinnes-Legien Agreement," in *Entstehung und Wandel der modernen Gesellschaft: Festschrift für Hans Rosenberg zum 65. Geburtstag*, eds. Gerhard A. Ritter and Hans Rosenberg. Berlin: De Gruyter.

__________. 1975. "Economic and Social Problems of the German Demobilization, 1918-1919." *Journal of Modern History* XLCII, pp. 1-47.

__________. 1975. "Die Freien Gewerkschaften und die Zentralarbeitsgemeinschaft," in *Vom Sozialistengesetz zur Mitbestimmung*, ed. Heinz O. Vetter. Köln: Bund-Verlag.

__________. 1977. *Iron and Steel in the German Inflation, 1916-1923*. Princeton: Princeton University Press.

__________. 1985. *Industrie und Gewerkschaften*, 1918-1924. Stuttgart: Deutsche Verlags-Anstalt.

__________. 1986. "The Weimar Republic: A Problem of Modernization?" *Archiv für Sozialgeschichte*, Band XXVI, pp. 1-26.

__________. 1993. *The Great Disorder: Politics, Economics, and Society in the German Inflation, 1914-1924*. New York: Oxford University Press.

Feldman, Gerald D. and Imgard Steinisch. 1978. "Die Weimarer Republik zwischen Sozial-und Wirtschaftstaat: Die Entscheidung gegen den Achtstudentag." *Archiv für Sozialgeschichte* Band 18, pp. 353-439.

______. 1980. "Notwendigkeit und Grenzen sozialstaatlicher Intervention: Eine vergleichende Fallstudie des Ruhreisenstreits in Deutschland und des Generalstreits in Großbritannien." *Archiv für Sozialgeschichte* 20. B., pp. 57-117.

Fligstein, Neil. 1990. *The Transformation of Corporate Control*. Cambridge: Harvard University Press.

Flora, P. and A. J. Heidenheimer, eds. 1981.*The Development of Welfare States in Europe and America*. New Brunswick: Transaction.

Fox, Alan. 1985. *History and Heritage: The Social Origins of the British Industrial Relations System*. London: Allen & Unwin.

Franzosi, Roberto. 1995. *The Puzzle of Strikes: Class and State Strategies in Postwar Italy*. Cambridge: Cambridge University Press.

Fritz, Stephen G. 1984. "The Search for Volksgemeinshaft: Gustav Stresemann and the Baden DVP, 1920-1930." *German Studies Review* 7, pp. 249-280.

Gilbert, Bentley B. 1970. *British Social Policy, 1914-1939*. Ithaca: Cornell University Press.

Gilbert, Jess and Carolyn Howe. 1991. "Beyond 'State vs. Society': Theories of the State and New Deal Agricultural Policies." *American Sociological Review* 56, pp. 204-220.

Goldfield, Michael. 1989. "Worker Insurgency, Radical Organization, and New Deal Labor Legislation." *American Political Science Review* 83, pp. 1257-1282.

Gospel, H. F. 1979. "Employers' Labour Policy: A Study of the Mond-Turner Talks, 1927-1933." *Business History* 21, pp. 180-197.

Haimson, Leopold and Charles Tilly, eds. 1989. *Strikes, Wars, and Revolutions in an International Perspective: Strike Waves in the Late Nineteenth and Early Twentieth Centuries*. Cambridge: Cambridge University Press.

Hall, Peter. 1993. "Policy Paradigms, Social Learning, and the State: The Case of Economic Policymaking in Britain," *Comparative Politics* 25, (April), pp. 275-296.

Hartwich, Hans-Hermann. 1967. *Arbeitsmarkt, Verbände und Staat, 1918-1933*. Berlin: Walter de Gruyter and Co.

Haydu, Jeffrey. 1997. *Making American Industry Safe for Democracy: Comparative Perspectives on the State and Employee Representation in the Era of World War I*. Illinois: Illinois State University Press.

Heclo, Hugh. 1974. *Modern Social Politics in Britain and Sweden. From Relief to Income Maintenance*. New Haven: Yale University Press.

Hicks, Alex and Joya Misra. 1993. "Political Resources and the Growth of Welfare in Affluent Capitalist Democracies, 1960-1982." *American Journal of Sociology* 99, pp. 668-710.

Hicks, Alex, Joya Misra, and Tang Nah Ng. 1994. "The Programmatic Emergence of the Social Security State." *American Sociological Review* 60, pp. 329-349.

Hobsbawm, Eric J. 1990. *Industry and Empire: From 1750 to the Present Day*, London: Penguin Books.

Hooks, Gregory. 1990. "From an Autonomous to a Captured State Agency: The Decline of the New Deal in Agriculture." *American Sociological Review* 55, pp. 29-43.

______. 1991. "The Variable Autonomy of the State: A Comment on 'State and Autonomy'." *American Sociological Review* 56, pp. 690-693.

______. 1993. "The Weakness of Strong Theories: The U.S. State's Dominance of the World War II Investment Process." *American Sociological Review* 58, pp. 37-53.

Hubatsch, Walter, ed. 1983. *Grundriß zur deutschen Verwaltungsgeschichte, 1815-1945*, Band 22. Marburg/Lahn: Johann-Gottfried-Herder-Institut.

Immergut, Ellen. 1992. "The Rules of the Game: The Logic of Health Policy-Making in France, Switzerland, and Sweden," in *Structuring Politics: Historical Institutionalism in Comparative Perspective*, eds. Sven Steinmo, Kathleen Thelen, and Frank Longstreth. Cambridge: Cambridge University Press.

Ingham, Geoffrey. 1984. *Capitalism Divided? The City and Industry in British Social Development*. London: Macmillan.

Jacques, Martin. 1976. "Consequences of the General Strike," in *The General Strike 1926*, ed. Jeffrey Skelley. London: Laurence and Wishart.

James, Harold. 1986. *The German Slump: Politics and Economics, 1924-1936*. Oxford: Clarendon Press.

Jefferey, Keith. 1981. "The British Army and Internal Security, 1919-1939." *Historical Journal* 24, 2, pp. 377-399.

Jefferey, Keith, and Peter Hennessy. 1983. *States of Emergency: British Governments and Strikebreaking since 1919*. Boston: Routledge & K. Paul.

Jenkins, J. Craig and Barbara G. Brents. 1989. "Social Protest, Hegemonic Competition, and Social Reform: A Political Struggle Interpretation of the Origins of the American Welfare State." *American Sociological Review* 54, pp. 891-909.

Jessop, Bob. 1990. *State Theory: Putting the Capitalist State in its Place*. Pennsylvania: The Pennsylvania State University Press.

Jones, Thomas. 1969. *Whitehall Diary, 1916-1925*, ed. Keith Middlemas. 2 vols. London: Oxford University Press.

Kahn, Freund Otto. 1981. *Labor Law and Politics in the Weimar Republic*. Oxford: Blackwell.

Katzenstein, Peter J. 1985. *Small States in World Markets*. Ithaca: Cornell University Press.

______ ed. 1996. *The Culture of National Security: Norms and Identity in World Politics*. New York: Columbia University Press.

Keohane, Robert O. 1984. *After Hegemony: Cooperation and Discord in the World Political Economy*. Princeton: Princeton University Press.

Kersbergen, Kees. 1995. *Social Capitalism: A Study of Christian Democracy and the Post-War Settlement of the Welfare State.* London: Routledge.

Knowles, K. G. J. C. 1954. *Strikes – A Study of Industrial Conflict, with Special Reference to British Experience between 1911 and 1947.* Oxford: Basil Blackwell.

Kocka, Jürgen. 1978. *Klassengesellschaft im Krieg: Deutsche Sozialgeschichte, 1914-1918.* Göttinghen: Vanderehoeck & Ruprecht.

______. 1984. *Facing Total War: German Society, 1914-1918.* Leamington Spa: Berg.

Korpi, Walter. 1983. *The Democratic Class Struggle.* London: Routledge and Kegan Paul.

Krasner, Stephen D. 1978. *Defending the National Interests: Raw Materials Investments and US Foreign Policy.* Princeton: Princeton University Press.

__________. 1983. "Structural Causes and Regime Consequences: Regimes as Intervening Variables." Pp. 1-22 in *International Regimes,* ed. Stephen D. Krasner. Ithaca: Cornell University Press.

Kuisel, Richard F. 1981. *Capitalism and the State in Modern France.* Cambridge: Cambridge University Press.

Laumann, Edward O. and David Knoke. 1987. *The Organizational State: Social Choice in National Policy Domains.* Madison: The University of Wisconsin Press.

Lawrence, Paul R. and Jay W. Lorsch. 1967. *Organization and Environment.* Cambridge: Harvard University Press.

Leggett, Frederick. 1952. "The Settlement of Labour Disputes in Great Britain." Pp. 56-76 in *Meeting of Minds: A Way to Peace through Mediation,* ed. Elmore Jackson. New York: McGraw-Hill.

Lindblom, Charles E. 1977. *Politics and Markets: The World's Political-Economic Systems.* New York: Basic Books.

__________. 1982. "Another State of Mind." *American Political Science Review* 76, pp. 9-21.

Liu, Tien-Lung. 1988. "States and Urban Revolutions: Explaining the Revolutionary Outcomes in Iran and Poland." *Theory and Society* 17, pp. 179-209.

__________. 1997. "On Whose Side is the State? The German Labor Ministry, 1918-1933." *Journal of Historical Sociology* 10, pp. 361-388.

__________. 1998. "Policy Shifts and State Agencies: Britain and Germany, 1918-1933." *Theory and Society* 27, pp. 43-82.

Lowe, Rodney. 1974. "The Ministry of Labour, 1916-1924: A Graveyard of Social Reform?" *Public Administration* 52, pp. 415-438.

__________. 1978a. "The Failure of Consensus in Britain: The National Industrial Conference, 1919-1921." *Historical Journal* 21, 3, pp. 649-675.

__________. 1978b. "The Erosion of State Intervention in Britain, 1917-1924." *Economic History Review* 31, pp. 278-281.

__________. 1980. "The Ministry of Labour: Fact and Fiction." *Bulletin of the Society for the Study of Labour History* 41, pp. 23-27.

__________. 1982. "The Ministry of Labour, 1916-19: A Still, Small Voice?" in *War and the State: The Transformation of British Government, 1914-1919*, ed. Kathleen Burke. London: Allen & Unwin.

__________. 1986. *Adjusting to Democracy: The Role of the Ministry of Labour in British Politics, 1916-1939*. Oxford: Clarendon Press.

Lowi, Theodore J. 1969. *The End of Liberalism: Ideology, Policy, and the Crisis of Public Authority*. New York: W. W. Norton.

Lukes, Steven. 1974. *Power: A Radical View*. London: The Anchor Press.

Luther, Hans. 1960. *Politiker ohne Partei: Erinnerungen*. Stuttgart: Deutsche Verlags-Anstalt.

Lyman, R. W. 1957. *The First Labour Government, 1924*. London: Chapman & Hall.

Maier, Charles. 1975. *Recasting Bourgeois Europe: Stabilization in France, Germany, and Italy in the Decade after WWI*. Princeton: Princeton University Press.

Manley, John F. 1983. "Neo-Pluralism: A Class Analysis of Pluralism I and Pluralism II." *American Political Science Review* 77, pp. 368-383.

Mann, Michael. 1993. *Sources of Social Power: The Rise of Classes and Nation-States, 1760-1914*. Vol. 2. Cambridge: Cambridge University Press.

March, James G., and Johan P. Olsen. 1984. "The New Institutionalism: Organizational Factors in Political Life." *American Political Science Review* 78, pp. 734-749.

Marshall, G. 1979. "The Armed Forces in Industrial Disputes in the United Kingdom." *Armed Forces and Society* 5, 2, (February), pp. 270-279.

Mathews, William Carl. 1986. "The Continuity of Social Democratic Economic Policy from 1919 to 1920: The Bauer-Schmidt Policy" in *Die Anpassung an die Inflation*, eds. Gerald D. Feldman, Carl-Ludwig Holtfrerich, Gerhard A. Ritter, and Peter-Christian Witt. Berlin: Walter de Gruyter.

Matthias, Erich, and Rudolf Morsey. 1962. *Die Regierung des Prinzen Max von Baden. Quellen zur Geschichte des Parlamentarismus und der politischen Parteien*. Düsseldorf: Droste.

Matthias, Eric, ed. 1985. *Quellen zur Geschichte der Deutschen Gewerkschaftsbewegung im 20. Jahrhundert*. Vols. 1-4. Köln: Bund-Verlag.

McDonald, G. W. and Howard F. Gospel. 1973. "The Mond-Turner Talks, 1927-1933: A Study in Industrial CO-Operation," *The Historical Journal* XVI, 4, pp. 807-829.

McIvor, Arthur J. 1984. "Employers' Organisation and Strikebreaking in Britain." *International Review of Social History* 29, Part 1, 3-4, pp. 1-33.

Meyer, John, John Boli, George M. Thomas, and Francisco Ramirez. 1997. "World Society and the Nation-State," *American Journal of Sociology* 103, pp. 144-181.

Meyer, John W. and Richard Scott. 1983. *Organizational Environments: Ritual and Reality.* Newbury Park: Sage Publications.

______. and Brian Rowan. 1978. "Institutionalized Organizations: Formal Structure as Myth and Ceremony." *American Journal of Sociology* 83, pp. 340-363.

______, John Boli, and George M. Thomas. 1987. "Ontology and Rationalization in the Western Cultural Account," in *Institutional Structure: Constituting State, Society, and the Individual*, eds. George M. Thomas, John W. Meyer, Francisco O. Ramirez, and John Boli. New York: Sage Publications.

Middlemas, Robert Keith. 1979. *Politics in Industrial Society: The Experience of the British System since 1911.* London: A. Deutsch.

Middlemas, Robert Keith and John Barnes. 1969. *Baldwin: A Biography.* London: Weidenfeld & Nicolson.

Miliband, Ralph. 1969. *The State in Capitalist Society.* New York: Basic Books.

__________. 1970. "The Capitalist State: Reply to Nicos Poulantzas." *New Left Review* 59, pp. 53-60.

__________. 1973. "Poulantzas and the Capitalist State." *New Left Review* 82, pp. 84-92.

Mills, C. Wright. 1956. *The Power Elite.* New York: Oxford University Press.

Mitchell, B. 1980. *European Historical Statistics.* New York: Columbia University Press.

Mizruchi, Mark and Thomas Koenig. 1986. "Economic Sources of Corporate Political Consenses: An Examination of Interindustry Relations." *American Sociological Review* 51, pp. 482-491.

Mockenhaupt, Hubert. 1977. *Weg und Wirken des Geistlichen Sozialpolitikers Heinrich Brauns.* München: Schoeningh.

Mommsen, Hans. 1978. *Klassenbewegung oder Mitbestimmung zum Problem der Kontrolle wirtschaftlicher Macht in der Weimarer Republik.* Köln: Europeische Verlagsanstalt.

______. 1990. *The Rise and Fall of Weimar Democracy.* Chapel Hill: University of North Carolina Press.

Montgomery, B. G. de. 1922. *British Continental Labour Policy.* London: Kegan Paul.

Morgan, Jane. 1987. *Conflict and Order: The Police and Labour Disputes in England and Wales, 1900-1939.* Oxford: Clarendon Press.

Morgan, Kenneth O. 1979. *Consensus and Disunity: The Lloyd George Coalition Government, 1918-1922.* Oxford: Oxford University Press.

Morsey, Rudolf. 1966. *Die Deutsche Zentrumspartei 1918-1923.* Düsseldorf.

Neebe, Reinhard. 1983. "Unternehmerverbände und Gewerkschaften in den Jahren der Großen Krise, 1919-1933." *Geschichte und Gesellschaft* 9, 3, pp. 302-330.

Oltmann, Uwe. 1968. "Reichsarbeitsminister Heinrich Brauns in der Staats- und Währungskrise von 1923/24: Die Bedeutung der Sozialpolitik für die Inflation, den Ruhrkampf und die Stabilisierung," Dissertation. Kiel.

Orloff, Ann. 1992. *The Politics of Pensions: A Comparative Analysis of Britain, Canada, and the United States, 1880-1940.* Madison: University of Wisconsin Press.

Orloff, Ann and Theda Skocpol. 1984. "Why not Equal Protection? Explaining the Politics of Public Social Spending in Britain, 1900-1911, and the United States, 1880s-1920." *American Sociological Review* 49, pp. 726-750.

Orlow, Dietrich. 1987. *A History of Modern Germany: 1871 to Present.* New Jersey: Prentice Hall.

Patch, William L. 1985. *Christian Trade Unions in the Weimar Republic, 1918-1933.* New Haven: Yale University Press.

Peden, G. C. 1983. "The Treasury as the Central Department of Government, 1919-1939." *Public Administration* 61, pp. 371-385.

Perrow, Charles. 1967. "A Framework for Comparative Organizational Analysis." *American Sociological Review* 32, pp. 194-208.

Petzina, Dietmar, Werner Abelshauser, and Anselm Faust, eds. 1978. *Sozialgeschichtliches Arbeitsbuch, Band III. Materialien zur Statistik des Deutschen Reiches 1914-1945.* Munich: Verlag C. H. Beck.

Peyronnet, Albert. 1924. *Le Ministère du Travail (1906-1923).* Paris: Berger-Levrault.

Pfeffer, Jeffrey and Gerald Salancick. 1978. *The External Control of Organizations: A Resource Dependence Perspective.* New York: Harper and Row.

Phillips, G. A. 1971. "The Triple Industrial Alliance in 1914." *Economic History Review* 24, 1, (February), pp. 55-67.

__________. 1976. *The General Strike: The Politics of Industrial Conflict.* London: Weidenfeld & Nicolson.

Pollard, Sidney. 1974. "The Trade Union and the Depression of 1929-1933," in *Industrielles System und politische Entwicklung in der Weimarer Republik*, eds. Hans Mommsen, Dietmar Petzina, and Bernd Weisbrod. Düsseldorf: Droste Verlag.

Porter, Bruce D. 1994. *War and the Rise of the State: The Military Foundations of Modern Politics.* New York: Free Press.

Potthoff, Heinrich. 1979. *Gewerkschaften und Politik zwischen Revolution und Inflation.* Düsseldorf: Beiträge zur Geschichte des Parlamentarismus und der Politischen Parteien, Bd. 66.

Potthoff, Heinrich. 1987. *Freie Gewerkschaften, 1918-1933: Der Allgemeine Deutsche Gewerkschaftsbund in der Weimarer Republik.* Düsseldorf: Droste.

Poulantzas, Nicos. 1968. *Pouvoir politique et classes sociales.* Paris: Librairie François Maspero.

__________. 1969. "The Problem of the Capitalist State," *New Left Review* 58, pp. 67-78.

__________. 1976. "The Capitalist State: A Reply to Miliband and Laclau," *New Left Review* 95, pp. 63-83.

__________. 1980. *State, Power, Socialism.* London: New Left Books.

Prechel, Harland. 1990. "Steel and the State: Industry Politics and Business Policy Formation, 1940-1989." *American Sociological Review* 55, pp. 648-668.

__________. 1991. "Conflict and Historical Variation in Steel Capital-State Relations: The Emergence of State Structures and a More Prominent, Less Autonomous State." *American Sociological Review* 56, pp. 693-698.

Preller, Ludwig. 1949. *Sozialpolitik in der Weimarer Republik.* Stuttgart: Franz Mittelbach Verlag.

Przeworski, Adam, and Henry Teune. 1970. *The Logic of Comparative Social Inquiry.* New York: Wiley.

Quadagno, Jill. 1984. "Welfare Capitalism and the Social Security Act of 1935." *American Sociological Review* 49, pp. 632-647.

__________. 1985. "Two Models of Welfare State Development: Reply to Skocpol and Amenta." *American Sociological Review* 50: 575-578.

__________. 1992. "Social Movements and State Transformation: Labor Unions and Racial Conflict in the War on Poverty." *American Sociological Review* 57, pp. 616-634.

Radice, Lisanne. 1984. *Beatrice and Sidney Webb: Fabian Socialists.* London: Macmillan.

Ragin, Charles. 1987. *The Comparative Method: Moving Beyond Qualitative and Quantitative Strategies.* Berkeley: University of California Press.

Ratliff, William G. *Faithful to the Fatherland: Julius Curtius and Weimar Foreign Policy.* New York: Peter Lang, 1990.

Reich, Nathan. 1938. *Labour Relations in Republican Germany.* New York: Oxford University Press.

Reichsarbeitsministerium. 1929. *Deutsche Sozialpolitik, 1918-1945: Erinnerungsschrift des Reichsarbeitsministeriums.* Berlin: Mittler & Sohn.

Rimlinger, Gaston. 1971. *Welfare Policy and Industrialization in Europe, America, and Russia.* New York: Wiley.

Rueschemeyer, Dietrich and Peter B. Evans. 1985. "The State and Economic Transformation: Toward an Analysis of the Conditions Underlying Effective Intervention," in *Bringing the State Back In,* eds. Peter B. Evans, Dietrich Rueschemeyer, and Theda Skocpol. Cambridge: Cambridge University Press.

Ruggie, John Gerard. 1983. "International Regimes, Transactions, and Change: Embedded Liberalism in the Postwar Economic Order," in *International Regimes,* ed. Stephen D. Krasner. Ithaca: Cornell University Press.

Saul, Klaus. 1985. "Repression or Integration? The State, Trade Unions and Industrial Disputes in Imperial Germany," in *The Development of Trade Unionism in Great Britain and Germany, 1880-1914,* eds. Wolfgang J. Mommsen and Hans-Gerhard Husung. London: George Allen & Unwin.

Saville, John. 1985. "The British State, the Business Community and the Trade Unions," in *The Development of Trade Unionism in Great Britain and Germany, 1880-1914,* eds. Wolfgang J. Mommsen and Hans-Gerhard Husung. London: George Allen and Unwin.

Schmitter, Philippe C. 1974. "Still the Century of Corporatism?"*Review of Politics* January.

Schneider, Michael. 1987. "Höhen, Krisen und Tiefen: Die Gewerkschaften in der Weimarer Republik, 1918 bis 1933," in *Geschichte der deutschen Gewerkschaften von den Anfängen bis 1945,* ed. Ulrich Borsdorf. Köln: Bund-Verlag.

Severing, Carl. 1950. *Mein Lebensweg.* 2 vols. Köln: Greven Verlag.

Shefftz, M. C. 1967. "The Trade Union and Trade Disputes Act, 1927." *Review of Politics* 29, pp. 387-406.

Skocpol, Theda. 1980. "Political Response to Capitalist Crisis: Neo-Marxist Theories of the State and the Case of the New Deal." *Politics and Society* 10, pp. 155-201.

______ 1984. "Emerging Agendas and Recurrent Strategies in Historical Sociology," in *Vision and Method in Historical Sociology,* ed. Theda Skocpol Cambridge: Cambridge University Press.

______1992. *Protecting Soldiers and Mothers: The Political Origins of Social Policy in the United States.* Cambridge: Belknap Press of Harvard University.

______ and Kenneth Finegold. 1982. "State Capacity and Economic Intervention in the Early New Deal." *Political Science Quarterly* 97, pp. 255-278.

______ and Edwin Amenta. 1985. "Did Capitalists Shape Social Security?" *American Sociological Review* 50, pp. 572-575.

______ and Edwin Amenta. 1986. "States and Social Policies." *Annual Review of Sociological Research* 12, pp. 139-143.

Steinmetz, George. 1990. "The Myth and the Reality of an Autonomous State: Industrialists, Junkers and Social Policy in Imperial Germany." *Comparative Social Research* 12, pp. 239-293.

______. 1993. *Regulating the Social: The Welfare State and Local Politics in Imperial Germany.* Princeton: Princeton University Press.

______. 1996. The Myth of an Autonomous State: Industrialists, Junkers, and Social Policy in Imperial Germany," Pp. 257-318 in *Society,*

*Culture, and the State in Germany,* ed. Geoff Eley. Ann Arbor: The University of Michigan Press.

Stepan, Alfred. 1978. *The State and Society: Peru in Comparative Perspective.* Princeton: Princeton University Press.

Stephens, John D. 1980. *The Transition from Capitalism to Socialism.* New Jersey: Humanities Press.

Stråth, Bo. 1996. *The Organisation of Labour Markets: Modernity, Culture and Governance in Germany, Sweden, Britain and Japan.* London: Routledge.

Sutherland, Gillian, ed. 1972. *Studies in the Growth of Nineteenth Century Government.* London: Routledge & K. Paul.

Tawney, R. H. 1943. "The Abolition of Economic Controls, 1918-1921." *Economic History Review* 23, pp. 1-30.

Terrell, John Upton. 1968. *The U.S. Department of Labor: A Story of Workers, Unions, and the Economy.* New York: Meredith Press.

Therborn, Göran. 1977. *What Does the Ruling Class Do When It Rules?* London: New Left Books.

Thomas, George M., John W. Meyer, Francisco O. Ramirez, and John Boli, eds. 1987. *Institutional Structure: Constituting State, Society, and the Individual.* New York: Sage Publications.

Thompson, James. 1967. *Organization in Action.* New York: McGraw-Hill.

Tilly, Charles. 1975. "Reflections on the History of European State-Making," in *The Formation of National States in Western Europe,* ed. Charles Tilly. Princeton: Princeton University Press.

______. 1984. *Big Structures, Large Processes, Huge Comparisons.* New York: Russell Sage.

______. 1992. *Coercion, Capital, and European States, AD 990-1992.* Cambridge: Blackwell Publishers.

Tournerie, Jean-André. 1971. *Le Ministère du Travail: origines et premiers développements.* Paris: Editions Cujas.

Trades Union Congress. 1915. *Report of Proceedings at the 47th Annual Trades Union Congress, Associations Hall, Bristol, 6-11 September 1915.* London: Cooperative Printing Society Ltd.

Turner, Henry A. 1963. *Stresemann and the Politics of the Weimar Republic.* Princeton: Princeton University Press.

Truman, David. 1971. *The Government Process: Political Interests and Public Opinion.* New York: Knopf.

Vogt, Martin, ed. 1970. *Das Kabinett Müller II, 28. Juni 1928 bis 27. März 1930. Akten der Reichskanzlei.* Boppard am Rhein.

Wateville, A. de. 1926. "The Employment of Troops under the Emergency Regulations." *Army Quarterly* (July), pp. 283-293.

Weisbrod, Bernd. 1978. *Schwerindustrie in der Weimarer Republik: Interessenpolitik zwischen Stabilisierung und Krise.* Wuppertal: Peter Hammer Verlag.

Wigham, Eric L. 1982. *Strikes and the Government, 1893-1981*. London: Macmillan.

Winkler, Heinrich August. 1984. *Von der Revolution zur Stabilisierung: Arbeiter und Arbeiterbewegung in der Weimarer Republik 1918 bis 1924*. Berlin: Verlag J. H. W. Dietz Nachf.

______. 1985. *Der Schein der Normalität: Arbeiter und Arbeiterbewegung in der Weimarer Republik 1924 bis 1930*. Berlin: Verlag J. H. W. Dietz Nachf.

Wissell, Rudolf. 1929. "Die Reform des Schlichtungswesens?" *Magazin der Wirtschaft* 5 Jahrgand, pp. 71-76.

Wissell, Rudolf. 1930. "Einundzwanzig Monate Reichsarbeitsminister." *Die Arbeit* 4, pp. 217-228.

______. 1983. *Aus Meinen Lebensjahren*. Berlin: Colloquim Verlag.

Wright, Maurice. 1972. "Treasury Control, 1814-1914," in *Studies in the Growth of Nineteenth Century Government*, ed. Gillian Sutherland. London: Routledge & Kegan Paul.

Wrigley, Chris, ed. 1987. *A History of British Industrial Relations. Vol. II. 1914-1939*. London: The Harvester Press.

______. 1990. *Arthur Henderson*. Cardiff: GPC Books.

______ 1990. *The History of British Industrial Relations*. London: Brighton.

Wrigley, David. 1976. *Lloyd George and the British Labour Government*. New York: Barnes & Noble.

Wunderlich, Frieda. 1940. *Labor under German Democracy: Arbitration, 1918-1933*. New York: New School for Social Research.

Zeitlin, Jonathan. 1985. "Shop Floor Bargaining and the State: A Contradictory Relationship." Pp. 1-45 in *Shop Floor and the State: Historical and Comparative Perspectives*, eds. Steven Tolliday and Jonathan Zeitlin. Cambridge: Cambridge University Press.

______. 1987. "From Labour History to the History of Industrial Relations." *Economic History Review* XL, 2, pp. 159-184.

Zelditch, Morris. 1971. "Intelligible Comparisons," in *Comparative Methods in Sociology*, ed. I. Vallier. Berkeley: University of California Press.

Zunkel, Friedrich. 1974. *Industrie und Staatssozialismus: Der Kampf um die Wirtschaftsordnung 1914-1918*. Düsseldorf: Droste.

# Index

# A QUESTION OF PRIORITIES

## *Democratic Reform and Economic Recovery in Postwar Germany*

**Rebecca Boehling**

*"… an impressive array of sources … well written information."*  H-German

*"… a much appreciated contribution to the current discussions about the reunification of Germany and what it can mean for its economy and relationships to the other European powers."*  **Wisconsin Bookwatch**

*"… most welcome as the first detailed analysis of political reconstruction in major postwar German cities available in English"*  **Choice**

*"… unique quality. There is really nothing in English – and relatively little in German – that explores the early days of the occupation of Germany with this degree of detail …"*  **Thomas Schwartz, Vanderbilt University**

**Rebecca Boehling** teaches in the Department of History at the University of Maryland, Baltimore County.

Available  320 pages, 12 photos, 1 map, bibliog., index
ISBN 1-57181-159-1 • paperback • **$24.00/£16.00**

*Still available in hardback*
ISBN 1-57181-035-8 • hardback • **$59.95/£40.00**
LC: 96-24204

Volume 2 of *Monographs in German History*
**History/International Relations**

**Berghahn Books**

55 John Street, 3rd Floor, New York, NY 10038, USA
E-mail: BerghahnUS@juno.com • Tel: (212) 233 1075 • Fax: (212) 791 5246
3, Newtec Place, Magdalen Road, Oxford, OX4 1RE, UK
E-mail: BerghahnUK@aol.com • Tel: (01865) 250 011 • Fax: (01865) 250 056

# FROM RECOVERY TO CATASTROPHE
## *Municipal Stabilization and Political Crisis*

**Ben Lieberman**

Historians of the stabilization phase of Weimar Germany tend to identify German recovery after the First World War with the struggle to revise reparations and control hyperinflation. Focusing primarily on economic aspects is however not sufficient, the author argues; the financial burden of recovery was only one of several major causes of reaction against the republic. Drawing on material from major German cities, he is able to trace the emergence of strong local activism and of comprehensive and functional policies of recovery on the municipal level which enjoyed broad political backing. Ironically, these same programs that created consensus also contained the potential for destabilization: they unleashed intense debate over the needs of the consumers and the purpose and extent of public spending, and with that of government intervention more generally, which accelerated the fragmentation of bourgeois politics, leading to the final destruction of the Weimar Republic.

**Ben Lieberman** teaches in the Department of Social Science at Fitchburg State College, Mass.

Available  192 pages, 13 tables, bibliog., index
ISBN 1-57181-104-4  •  hardback  •  **$35.00/£25.00**
LC: 97-19436
Volume 3 of *Monographs in German History*
**History**

**Berghahn Books**

55 John Street, 3<sup>rd</sup> Floor, New York, NY 10038, USA
E-mail: BerghahnUS@juno.com  •  Tel: (212) 233 1075  •  Fax: (212) 791 5246

3, Newtec Place, Magdalen Road, Oxford, OX4 1RE, UK
E-mail: BerghahnUK@aol.com  •  Tel: (01865) 250 011  •  Fax: (01865) 250 056

# THE LION AND THE EAGLE

## *German-Spanish Relations Over the Centuries: An Interdisciplinary Approach*

Edited by **Conrad Kent, Thomas Wolber,** and **Cameron M.K. Hewitt**

The German and Spanish-speaking worlds have, over the centuries, developed an intrinsic relationship, one which predates the Habsburg dynasty and the Renaissance and baroque periods.  The cross-fertilization and challenges have been both fruitful and complex with novel inventions surfacing in one culture often achieving their greatest prosperity in the other: Martin Luther's Protestant Reformation stimulated a response in Spain that was to define the European Counter Reformation; Spanish Baroque writers were seminal in the development of German Romanticism; Carl Christian Friedrich Krause and other nineteenth-century liberals provided the foundation for Spanish reformist efforts on the one hand, while German liberals provided the foundation for Spanish reformist efforts on the other; the music of Richard Wagner transformed Spanish music and the Spanish stage at the turn of the twentieth century; Pablo Picasso and other artists of the Spanish avant-garde sparked the enthusiasm of the Germans before the Nazi era. Today, German and Spanish intellectuals and writers share a similar commitment to the creation of a European culture in the face of resistance from other members of the European Union.

Viewed from a variety of disciplines this volume explores the relentlessly consistent, albeit often forgotten connections between the two linguistic and cultural groups revealing the myriad of ways in which they have shared and transformed literature, art, culture, politics, and history.

**Conrad Kent** is Professor Spanish and Humanities-Classics, **Thomas Wolber** teaches German Studies in the Department of Modern Foreign Languages, and **Cameron Hewitt** is a recent graduate, all at Ohio Wesleyan University.

June 1999 ca. 400 pages
ISBN 1-57181-131-1 • hardback • ca.$49.95/£35.00
**History/European Studies**

**Berghahn Books**

55 John Street, 3rd Floor, New York, NY 10038, USA
E-mail: BerghahnUS@juno.com • Tel: (212) 233 1075 • Fax: (212) 791 5246

3, Newtec Place, Magdalen Road, Oxford, OX4 1RE, UK
E-mail: BerghahnUK@aol.com • Tel: (01865) 250 011 • Fax: (01865) 250 056

# INDUSTRIAL CULTURE AND BOURGEOIS SOCIETY

## *Business, Labor, and Bureaucracy in Modern Germany 1800-1918*

**Jürgen Kocka**
With an Introduction by **Volker R. Berghahn**

Jürgen Kocka is one of the foremost historians of Germany whose work has been devoted to the integration of different genres of the social and economic history of Europe during the period of industrialization. This collection of essays gives a representative sample of his effort to develop, by reference to Marx and Weber, new and powerful analytical tools for understanding the dynamics of modern industrial societies.

*Contents*: Introduction: The Quest for an Integrative History of Industrial Society – From Manufacture to Factory: Technology and Workplace Relations at Siemens, 1847-1873 – Family and Bureaucracy in German Industrial Management, 1850-1914: Siemens in Comparative Perspective – Siemens and the Preventable Rise of AEG – Entrepreneurship in a Late-Comer Country: the German Case – The Entrepreneur, the Family, and Capitalism – German Industrial Entrepreneurs at the End of the 19th and the Beginning of the 20th Centuries – Big Business and the Rise of Managerial Capitalism in the late 19th and the early 20th Centuries – New Energies in the 19th Century: Toward a Social History of the Electricity Business – Authoritarian State and *Bürgerlichkeit*: Toward a History of the German *Bürgertum* in the 19th Century – The Study of Social Mobility & the Formation of the Working Class in the 19th Century – The Middle Classes in Europe – The First World War and the "Mittelstand": German Artisans and White-Collar Workers – The Difficult Rise of a Civil Society: Societal History of Modern Germany

**Jürgen Kocka** holds the chair for the History of the Industrial World at the Free University Berlin and is a permanent Fellow of the Berlin Institute for Advanced Study. He is a member of the Academia Europaea Cambridge and of the Berlin-Brandenburg Academy of Sciences. In 1992 he received the Leibniz Prize of the Deutsche Forschungsgemeinschaft.

April 1999 ca. 288 pages bibliog., index
ISBN 1-57181-158-3 • hardback • ca. **$59.95/£40.00**
ISBN 1-57181-198-2 • paperback • ca. **$19.95/£13.50**
LC: 98-26015      **History**

**Berghahn Books**

55 John Street, 3rd Floor, New York, NY 10038, USA
E-mail: BerghahnUS@juno.com • Tel: (212) 233 1075 • Fax: (212) 791 5246

3, Newtec Place, Magdalen Road, Oxford, OX4 1RE, UK
E-mail: BerghahnUK@aol.com • Tel: (01865) 250 011 • Fax: (01865) 250 056

# NAZISM IN CENTRAL GERMANY
## *The Brownshirts in 'Red' Saxony*

### Claus-Christian W. Szejnmann

Most studies on the spread of Nazism in German society before and after 1933 concentrate on the country's western parts. As a result, so the author claims, our overall picture of the situation has been distorted since the eastern areas contained a substantial portion of the population. Neglecting them means that all generalizations about the Nazi period require further testing. This first comprehensive study of Saxony therefore fills a large gap, also in light of the fact that Saxony was one of the most industrialized German regions. It deals with problems of continuity and change in German society during three distinct phases: constitutional monarchy, parliamentary democracy, and dictatorship. The author shows convincingly that deep-rooted local traditions are what determined the success or failure of Nazism among the local population.

**Claus-Christian W. Szejnmann** received his Ph.D. from the University of London and now teaches modern European History at Middlesex University.

May 1999 ca. 304 pages 12 tables, 6 figs, bibliog., index
ISBN 1-57181-942-8 • hardback • ca. $59.95/£40.00
Volume 4 of *Monographs in German History*
**History**

**Berghahn Books**

55 John Street, 3rd Floor, New York, NY 10038, USA
E-mail: BerghahnUS@juno.com • Tel: (212) 233 1075 • Fax: (212) 791 5246

3, Newtec Place, Magdalen Road, Oxford, OX4 1RE, UK
E-mail: BerghahnUK@aol.com • Tel: (01865) 250 011 • Fax: (01865) 250 056